BURGHLEY

PROFILES IN POWER
General Editor: Keith Robbins

ELIZABETH I (2nd Edn)
Christopher Haigh

BURGHLEY
Michael A R Graves

JAMES VI AND I
Roger Lockyer

CATHERINE DE'MEDICI
R J Knecht

RICHELIEU
R J Knecht

GUSTAVUS ADOLPHUS (2nd Edn)
Michael Roberts

OLIVER CROMWELL
Barry Coward

PETER THE GREAT (2nd Edn)
M S Anderson

THE ELDER PITT
Marie Peters

JOSEPH II
T C W Blanning

NAPOLEON
Geoffrey Ellis

ALEXANDER I
Janet M Hartley

DISRAELI
Ian Machin

JUÃREZ
Brian Hamnett

CAVOUR
Harry Hearder

NAPOLEON III
James McMillan

FRANCIS JOSEPH
Steven Beller

ATATŨRK
A L Macfie

LLOYD GEORGE
Martin Pugh

PÉTAIN
Nicholas Atkin

HITLER
Ian Kershaw

CHURCHILL
Keith Robbins

ATTLEE
Robert Pearce

NASSER
Peter Woodward

DE GAULLE
Andrew Shennan

FRANCO
Sheelagh Ellwood

MACMILLAN
John Turner

KENNEDY
Hugh Brogan

CASTRO (2nd Edn)
Sebastian Balfour

GORBACHEV
Martin McCauley

BURGHLEY

William Cecil, Lord Burghley

Michael A.R. Graves

LONGMAN
London and New York

Addison Wesley Longman Limited
Edinburgh Gate,
Harlow, Essex CM20 2JE,
United Kingdom
and Associated Companies throughout the world

*Published in the United States of America
by Addison Wesley Longman Inc., New York*

First published 1998

ISBN 0 582 30308 7 PPR
ISBN 0 582 30289 7 CSD
Visit Addison Wesley Longman on the world wide web at http://www.awl-he.com

British Library Cataloguing in Publication Data

A catalogue record for this book is available from the British Library

Library of Congress Cataloging-in-Publication Data

Graves, Michael A.R.
Burghley : William Cecil, Lord Burghley / Michael A.R. Graves.
p. cm. — (Profiles in power)
Includes bibliographical references and index.
ISBN 0–582–30289–7 (csd.). — ISBN 0–582–30308–7 (pbk.)
1. Burghley, William Cecil, Baron, 1520–1598. 2. Great Britain—History—Tudors, 1485–1603—Biography. 3. Great Britain—Politics and government—1558–1603. 4. Statesmen—Great Britain—Biography.
I. Title. II. Series: Profiles in power (London, England)
DA358.B9G7 1998
942.05′5′092—dc21
[B] 98–23155
CIP

Set by 35 in 10.5/12pt Baskerville
Produced by Addison Wesley Longman Singapore (Pte) Ltd.,
Printed in Singapore

CONTENTS

LIST OF MAPS

LIST OF ABBREVIATIONS

APC	Acts of the Privy Council
BIHR	Bulletin of the Institute of Historical Research
BJRL	Bulletin of the John Ryland Library
BL	British Library
CJ	Journals of the House of Commons
EHR	English Historical Review
HJ	Historical Journal
HLQ	Huntington Library Quarterly
HLRO	House of Lords Record Office
HMC	Historical Manuscripts Commission Reports
JBS	Journal of British Studies
LJ	Journals of the House of Lords
PRO	Public Record Office
TRHS	Transactions of the Royal Historical Society

PART ONE

BURGHLEY'S CAREER

Chapter 1

INTRODUCTION

When Elizabeth Tudor succeeded her Catholic half-sister Mary I as queen on 17 November 1558, the English kingdom, over which she was to rule for forty-five years, was in a parlous state. The society was sorely divided by the religious conflicts of the Reformation and, most recently, by the bitterness engendered by the burning of nearly three hundred Protestant 'heretics' in just a few years (1555–58).[1] A war against France, waged by Mary's Spanish consort, proved to be costly and resulted in the humiliating loss of Calais, England's last Continental possession, in January 1558. This was a serious blow to national prestige and morale and the return of Calais was high on Queen Elizabeth's priorities during the peace negotiations in 1559. Meanwhile, north of the border, Scotland was governed by a French Regent, Mary of Guise, supported by a French military presence. So, when Elizabeth became queen, England was experiencing a significant degree of demoralisation, foreign threat and religious division.

There were also serious economic problems, exacerbated by debasements of the coinage in the 1540s. Furthermore, wet summers (1555–56), which caused harvest failures and famine, were followed, in the last two years of the reign, by an epidemic 'responsible for the greatest mortality crisis of the sixteenth century'. In these unpropitious circumstances Elizabeth became queen and promptly appointed the Privy Councillors who would advise her and administer her realm from day to day. Foremost among them was William Cecil, who was and would remain her chief minister and most trusted councillor for forty years. It might be regarded as a one-sided relationship. After all, she was an anointed queen and he was just one of her subjects. On the other hand, he was man and she was woman and there were many men who, if they did not actually question her right to rule, doubted her capacity to do so effectively. John Knox had no doubts about their incapacity, when he condemned the 'monstrous regiment of women'. Nevertheless, and despite Cecil's lamentation and frustration, poured out on paper to friends and colleagues, he and his royal mistress worked together for four decades – not always without difficulties, but always with the same long-term objectives in view.

. . .

HISTORIOGRAPHY

The volume of paper spawned by Cecil during his long and conscientious career in service to the Tudors (and also to himself and his family) has, one suspects, proved a discouragement, even a deterrent, to historians. Not only the amount, but also the variety, can be bewildering, because Tudor ministers were also bureaucrats: they dealt both with high policy and pettifogging detail. And the office of Secretary of State had no clearly defined limits on its duties. The random mixing of official and private papers, so typical of the period, further broadens the range. Papers on religion, defence and foreign affairs coexist in the same collection with materials concerning his estates, household, family and personal finances. The paperwork, an immense collection, consists partly of his own letters, memoranda, routine administrative documents, directives, draft parliamentary bills, responses to plaintive petitioners for his help and white papers. It also includes correspondence, despatches, reports, petitions and suits, advices, proposals and instructions from the queen, fellow councillors, government officials, members of the governing élite and lesser folk. Indeed, it amounts to a formidable challenge for any historian who seeks to understand and to evaluate him.

William Camden, the first true historian of Elizabeth's reign, acknowledged the problem in the introduction to his *Annales.* He described how Burghley, having

> set open unto me first, his owne, and then the Queene's Roles, Memorials, Records & thereout, willed me to compile in an Historicall stile, the first beginnings of the Reigne of Queene Elizabeth . . . I obeyed his will, and not unwillingly . . . [b]ut at my

> very first entrance hereinto, a most intricate difficulty did in a manner discourage me; For I light upon moste thicke piles and heapes of writings and instruments of all sorts . . . in regard of the variety of the Arguments, most confused.[2]

Cecil's surviving record of service is the product of a career unparalleled in its length as a prominent officer of state, first under Edward VI and then, from 1558 to 1598, under Elizabeth I. The Lansdowne Manuscripts, State Papers, Domestic and Salisbury papers constitute only the core collection of material produced during that time of dedicated and sometimes frenetic service. They are also a commentary on the burdens of royal office when it was occupied by a conscientious servant. An anonymous contemporary biographer, who had been in Cecil's service for more than twenty years, records that his work as a judge

> drew upon him such multitudes of suits as was incredible but to us that saw it, for, besides all business in Council or other weighty causes, and such as were answered by word of mouth, there was not a day in a term wherein he received not threescore, fourscore, and an hundred petitions, which he commonly read that night, and gave every man answer himself the next morning . . .

Elsewhere the author noted that Cecil also had 'daily intelligence from many countries, and, besides foreign letters, he received not so few as 20 or 30 other letters in a day'.[3]

A politician of Cecil's stature, prominent in Queen Elizabeth's counsels and, particularly as Lord Treasurer and Master of the Court of Wards, exercising unequalled influence in the management of royal patronage, could have had a significant impact on the fortunes of many. Opinions and assessments, contemporary and posthumous, favourable or otherwise, were sometimes committed to paper. Of course, these need to be handled with caution, because, so often, they were not the considered judgements of detached observers. Some were laudatory pieces penned by those who had received or hoped for advancement, favours or protection.[4] Others were distinctly unfavourable, trenchant, hostile, even malicious. They expressed the dissatisfaction, discontent, envy, frustration, anger, even bitterness, of a wide variety of people – unsuccessful patronage seekers, competitors for royal favour, those who accused him of obstructing their advancement,[5] promoters of policies at variance with his and, at the extremes of the religious spectrum, Roman Catholic and godly Protestant activists who were fundamentally opposed to his moderate but firmly Protestant position.

There were also a number of works written by contemporaries, who were not caught up in the struggles for power and influence in the Court, Privy Council and kingdom. They include, most notably, John Clapham's *Elizabeth of England*, Sir Robert Naunton's *Fragmenta Regalia*, William Camden's *Annales* and the *Anonymous Life of Cecil*. They were not politically motivated studies, insofar as they were not designed to advance causes or personal interests during Cecil's lifetime. Nevertheless, these too were not the products of impartial observers. Clapham was grateful to Cecil 'both for my education and maintenance' and he was in his service during the 1590s.[6] Camden was a client of Cecil, who encouraged him to write a history of the reign and gave him access to state papers for that purpose.[7] The anonymous biographer has been convincingly identified by A.G.R. Smith as Michael Hickes. He entered Cecil's service in 1573, became one of his secretaries seven years later and was increasingly responsible for the management of his patronage during the 1580s and 1590s.[8] Naunton was exceptional because he was not in William Cecil's service. In the 1590s his connection was rather with the Cecils' competitor for power, the earl of Essex, to whom he regularly transmitted political news. Furthermore, Naunton's political career did not flourish until the next reign. When in the 1630s he compiled *Fragmenta Regalia* on Elizabeth's political personalities, his political fortunes were plummeting, he was critical of Charles I's government and looked back nostalgically.

All of these works were compiled at various times after Cecil's death and none of them were published in the lifetime of his son Robert, who was created earl of Salisbury and appointed Lord Treasurer by King James I. Therefore, although they extolled William Cecil's virtues, they were clearly not written as a means to preferment during the Elizabethan–Jacobean era of Cecilian prominence. Nevertheless, their eulogistic and largely uncritical character means that they should be treated with circumspection as evidence of his career and achievements. Naunton's admittedly brief pen-portrait concluded with reference to the 'most exquisite abilities' of 'this great instrument of state'. Clapham's account is that of a loyal servant devoted to the memory of his employer. And the anonymous biography is, at one and the same time, a panegyric apology for and in defence of the late Lord Treasurer's political and personal record. It depicts him as a paragon: a man of piety and of 'a noble disposition . . . the sweetest, kind and most tractable nature . . . the height and perfection of a grave and great councillor . . . greatly famous in all nations in Christendom . . . where they held him as the wisest and gravest councillor of Christendom'. Its author apologised for his inability to do justice to 'his perfection and worthiness which, I assure myself, was far greater than any memory or wit of man can describe or record so exactly in paper'.[9]

These contemporary pen portraits of William Cecil also contain a variety of factual errors.[10] More significant – and serious for the historian engaged in an evaluation of his career and achievements – the longest and most detailed of these studies, the anonymous biography, is guilty of both exaggeration and misrepresentation. As A.G.R. Smith pointed out, it ascribed to Cecil a far more important role in the Elizabethan religious settlement (1559) and the recoinage of 1559–61 than was in fact the case. Similarly, its portrayal of Cecil's dominance in the Privy Council was far from the truth.[11] Its author's claim, that he increased the royal profits from the Court of Wards, has been disproved by J. Hurstfield, and his denial, that Cecil profited greatly from management of wardships, is in sharp contrast to Clapham: 'After Sir Thomas Parry's death, he was made Master of the Wards and Liveries, by means whereof he grew rich, and ofttimes gratified his friends and servants that depended and waited on him.'[12] Furthermore, although he portrays Cecil as hostile to monopolies, 'terming them cankers of the commonwealth', it was during his term of office as Lord Treasurer that patents multiplied and the parliament of 1597 protested against so many harmful grants.[13] However, even if the anonymous biographer tended to minimise Cecil's faults and inflate his virtues and successes, he provides invaluable insights into his character and career. He was, after all, someone who worked with, under, and for Cecil for more than half his term of exalted place and office.

Camden's writings differ from those of Clapham, 'Hickes' and Naunton in several important respects. He wrote a history of Elizabeth and her reign, not a memoir of Burghley. It was based, not on mere personal acquaintance, hearsay and prejudiced opinion but on state papers to which he had access. Certainly it was an encomium of the queen, whom he described as '[t]he All-glorious, all virtuous, incomparable, invict and matchlesse Patterne of Princes, the Glory, Honour and mirror of Woman kind, the Admiration of our age'.[14] The Lord Treasurer too was often the object of fulsome tribute. Having protested his own moderation – 'I will not goe too farre in his praises' – Camden continued: 'yet may I say truly, that hee was in the number of those few, who have lived and died with glory. So great a man, whom others admire, I for my part (as was wont in old time to be in holy things) will with silence reverence.' Yet when he arrived at Lord Treasurer Burghley's death in the course of his history of the reign, he wrote an obituary which, whilst eulogistic, was also judicious:

> Certainly hee was a most excellent man, who (to say nothing of his reverend Presence, and undistempered countenance) was . . . adorned with learning, a singular man for honesty, gravity, temperance, industry, and justice. Hereunto were added a fluent and elegant Speech (and that not affected, but plaine and easie), wisedome strengthened by experience, and seasoned with exceeding moderation and most approved fidelity . . . [T]he Queene was most happy in so great a Councellor, and to his wholsome counsailes, the State of England for ever shall be beholden.[15]

On occasions Camden, like the rest, overstates Burghley's achievements: for example, in increasing 'the publike treasure'. Nevertheless, the *Annales* must be considered apart from the mere reminiscences of Clapham and the rest. Camden was the pioneering historian of Elizabeth and her reign, utilising primary sources and critically evaluating them.[16]

Those who, like Clapham, 'Hickes' and to a lesser extent Camden, took pains to commemorate Cecil were indebted to him and loyal to his memory. They were naturally concerned to perpetuate the image of a pious and virtuous, dedicated and successful statesmanlike figure. During the centuries which followed, however, historians were inclined to assess him less autonomously and more in relation to his royal mistress. During and after the Stuart century of deep divisions, bloody conflict, regicide and revolutions there was a tendency to look back nostalgically to the glories of the last Tudor's reign. At a popular level this was registered by the widespread celebration of 17 November, Queen Elizabeth's Accession Day, a practice which continued into the early eighteenth century.[17] Whilst some modern historians have been more critical in their evaluation of her government and its achievements, the fascination and attraction of the reign continues. And the question which, sooner or later, they all address is whether the queen or her chief minister was primarily responsible for its triumphs and achievements or chiefly culpable for its shortcomings and failures.

In the late nineteenth century, for example, J.A. Froude opted for a hero, not a heroine. 'Vain as [Elizabeth] was of her own sagacity, she never modified a course recommended to her by Burghley without injury both to the realm and to herself . . . The great results of her reign were the fruits of a policy which was not her own, and which she starved and mutilated when energy and completeness were most needed.'[18] He depicts the queen in her last years 'standing as it seemed on the pinnacle of earthly glory, yet in all the loneliness of greatness, and unable to enjoy the honours which Burghley's policy had won for her'.[19] In dramatic contrast, however, were A.F. Pollard (in the early twentieth century) and his successors, Sir John Neale and Joel Hurstfield (1930s–1950s) of London University.[20] As Elizabeth was elevated, glorified, and her personal achievements magnified by them, so Burghley's role and significance diminished. Since then historical 'revisionism' has replaced Neale's adulatory representation of the queen by a more critical appraisal of her.[21] However, for two reasons this has not been to the unalloyed benefit of Burghley's reputation. First, in a system of government by personal monarchy a prominent political figure like Burghley can be evaluated only in relation to the queen. His long tenure of high office, together with the queen's trust in him, was the consequence of their shared political beliefs and priorities. Although they had sharp disagreements, they were short in duration. In the long term, as will be seen in due course, they constituted a harmonious partnership. To criticise one about long-term policy is usually (though not always) by implication to criticise the other. Secondly, research into specific aspects of the regime, such as religious policy and management of the state's finances, reveals mutual shortcomings – both must be held culpable for some of the problems which James I inherited.[22]

There is, however, a distinction to be made between the public level of royal policy and political decision-making and the more prosaic administrative and managerial sub-policy level, at which Burghley operated for much, if not most, of his time. In some respects this undramatic but time-consuming activity simply implemented and reinforced policy priorities which he shared with his royal mistress, especially the pursuit of political stability. Nevertheless, much of his daily activity – as Secretary, Lord Treasurer, Master of the Court of Wards, judge, patron, politician in Court, council and country – was carried on without reference to the queen and even without her knowledge. Sometimes he worked covertly against her – not out of disloyalty but rather out of masculine conviction, that he knew what was best for her and the realm. Biographical studies, which encompass both levels of Burghley's activity, also provide opportunities to explore his administrative, political and confidential practices in greater detail and depth than are possible in regnal histories.

Here, however, historians encounter the common problem of his legacy, the embarrassment of paper riches. These create a seemingly unsurpassable problem: how to mine this paper mountain, in order to discover and present an accurate, thorough, clear, and yet reasonably succinct representation of the man, the queen's trustiest counsellor, the active politician and the long-serving prolific, industrious civil servant. Hurstfield illustrated the problem when he cited the case of Edward Nares, the regius professor of modern history in early nineteenth-century Oxford University. His multi-volume study of Burghley was scathingly reviewed by Lord Macaulay, who discovered that on the scales it weighed sixty pounds.[23] Conyers Read's two-volume life, published in 1955–60, is narrative in structure and treatment, runs to more than one thousand pages of text and is rich in primary source material, often set down verbatim. The result is a scholarly and detached study, but one which offers no clearly defined image or assessment of Burghley. B.W. Beckingsale's biography, however, adopted a twofold approach: a chronologically structured but not merely narrative survey and an evaluative study of some aspects of his political career, personality and family life.[24]

In some ways more rewarding to students of Burghley are the monographs dealing with particular institutions, policies or personalities of the Elizabethan regime: for example, Hurstfield on the Court of Wards, Wallace MacCaffrey on foreign policy, Patrick Collinson on religion, Sir Geoffrey Elton and David

Dean on parliaments and A.G.R. Smith on Burghley's patronage secretary, Michael Hickes.[25] Hurstfield (in 1956) and Smith (in 1991) also produced brief but incisive sketches of his life, career and significance.[26] The former drew attention to another problem for historians: not only the sheer volume of material, but also that '[i]t suited a man of Burghley's temperament and skill to operate in the shadows'.[27] Attempting a rounded, coherent picture of him remains a formidable challenge and historians who embark on the task must do so with some trepidation – this one is no exception.

. . .

ORIGINS, EARLY YEARS AND EARLY CAREER

From the very beginning the Cecils – or, as they were then, the Sitsilts – hitched their fortunes to those of their Welsh compatriots, the Tudors. In 1485 Henry Tudor landed in Wales and marched east to defeat King Richard III at Bosworth. David Cecil, member of a family of minor border gentry, was one of the Welshmen who followed him. Henry's success and David's loyalty transformed both their lives: the former became King Henry VII and the latter one of his personal bodyguard of two hundred men. Until his death in the mid-1530s, David prospered, if undramatically, in the service of the first two Tudors, Henry VII and Henry VIII. He was promoted successively to the position of yeoman of the chamber and serjeant-at-arms. He settled at Stamford, where he became prominent in municipal affairs, served as parliamentary burgess five times and profited from two marriages, which brought him local connections and affluence. Over the years he was appointed to stewardships of a number of royal manors in Lincolnshire, Northamptonshire and Rutland. In 1532 he was also selected sheriff for Northamptonshire. So David laid the foundations of the Cecils as an English country gentry family of some substance.[28]

Two of the keys to his success were Court positions, which placed him close to the king, and the fact that David Philip, his relative and patron (until his death in 1506), was in great favour with Henry VII's mother, Lady Margaret Beaufort. Philip, who helped to manage her estates in eastern England, may have been the contact who procured some of Cecil's positions for him. And the fact that his home was in Stamford gave Cecil entrée and explains why he settled there. The inestimable value of access to the monarch and proximity to him, by virtue of one's office and connections, was a lesson learned and not forgotten, either by David, his son Richard or his grandson William, the future Lord Burghley.[29]

In Richard's case his father was his patron, who secured for him, by 1517, the position of page of the chamber in the royal household of Henry VIII. Although the duties were menial, the place gave him close contact with the king and his entourage. Thereafter his promotions were modest and achieved only after many years – first as groom (by 1528) and then yeoman of the wardrobe (by 1539) – but they did give him continuous access to Henry VIII. This may explain not only his promotions but also leases of crown lands and monastic estates, as well as appointment to the office of sheriff of Rutland and to stewardships of royal estates. His promotion to the Northamptonshire commission of the peace in 1539 confirmed his place among the country gentry. Meanwhile he extended the family estates, seizing opportunities presented by the dissolution of the 'lesser' monasteries in 1536.[30]

So, even if Richard did not achieve prominence or distinction at the centre, he advanced the local fortunes of the Cecils as country gentry. As Burghley's anonymous biographer points out, the monarch's approbation could be the trigger for advancement, not only at Court but also in the country. Richard Cecil was groom of the robes,

> a place though now esteemed but mean, yet, at that time of good account, for then the king did ordinarily make himself ready in the robes, where Mr Cecil being chief . . . was in great favour with the King, who gave him both countenance and living, as appeared by the port Mr Cecil lived in . . . [F]or it was then no small preferment or reputation in the world to have the favourable countenance of so bountiful, magnificent a prince as he was.[31]

Nevertheless, princely favour probably mattered less in economic terms than Richard's judicious marriage to Jane Heckington, a Lincolnshire heiress, who brought with her the lordship of Burghley. In September 1520 or 1521 she gave birth to William Cecil.[32] He had three sisters, Elizabeth, Margaret and Ann, but no brothers.[33] So he was born into a classic sixteenth-century situation. He was the only son in a modestly successful family. Primogeniture guaranteed his economic future, but family expectations imposed the onus of achievement on him. His grandfather (whose death is recorded variously as 1536/37 or 1540) and his father (who survived until William was thirty-three) would have watched anxiously over his progress. Perhaps Richard had him marked out for a career at Court when, in 1529, he obtained William's appointment as one of the pages of the robes. Whatever his hopes, he could have had no cause for complaint because, when his life ended in March 1553, he was still only yeoman of the wardrobe, whereas his heir was Secretary of State.

Richard Cecil laid the groundwork for his son's career when he decided that, after his early education in the grammar schools of Grantham and Stamford, William should proceed to university. David Cecil's connection with David Philip, who had been the servant of Lady Margaret Beaufort, foundress of St John's College, Cambridge, may explain why Richard chose to send William there. Or the choice of Cambridge may lie in the simple logistical fact that it was only half the distance from Stamford to Oxford. It is possible, however, that the explanation lies elsewhere. When William went up to Cambridge in 1535, England was in a state of religious ferment. Henry VIII's 'Reformation Parliament' (1529–36) had just broken with Rome and established a national catholic church. At the same time Protestantism had infiltrated England, especially in the south-east, where Cambridge is located. It was dangerous in Henry VIII's reign for those teachers and students who were influenced by it or converted to it to commit themselves publicly. Nevertheless, in the White Horse Tavern by King's College, Cambridge, Thomas Bilney (martyred in 1531) and others debated Lutheran doctrines. And in 1535 the royal injunctions, which reflected the influence of Cambridge's new chancellor Thomas Cromwell, abolished canon law lectures and degrees, required divinity lectures 'to be "according to the true sense" of the Scriptures . . . [whilst] all students were to be encouraged to read the Scriptures privately'.[34]

Cambridge, in and after the 1520s, was exposed and susceptible to new religious beliefs. If Richard Cecil was aware of this, it may have influenced his choice of university for William. He was a friend of the zealous Protestant and Marian martyr John Hooper and, a few months after his son's admission to Cambridge, he publicly defended a sermon in Stamford church on justification by faith.[35]

Whatever the reason for Richard's choice, William Cecil was admitted to Cambridge University in May 1535. He was then only fifteen years old, not an uncommon age for commencement of a university education. The six years of his residence and study there had significant consequences for his future. Education was being secularised as humanistic classical training replaced preparation for an ecclesiastical career. The royal injunctions of 1535, which included Aristotle and Melancthon in the list of prescribed authors, illustrated the dual influence of the New Learning and the Reformation.[36] Both of these European movements shaped Cecil's thinking and beliefs. Prominent in his studies was Greek, a new and fashionable subject at the university. John Cheke, the outstanding Greek scholar of his time, was a fellow of St John's; another great teacher, Roger Ascham, was also there. They became his friends – in Cheke's case his brother-in-law – and important contacts for the future. They also acquired the responsibility for educating future Protestant monarchs. Cheke was appointed to teach Edward in 1544 and Ascham became Elizabeth's tutor in 1548.[37]

At St John's College Cecil displayed the rigorous work-habits and dedication to study and business which were to characterise the rest of his life. The anonymous biographer records that he was 'so diligent and painful as he hired the bellringer to call him up at four of the clock every morning'. However, this may have been the cause of another – in this case anguishing – lifelong legacy of the years at Cambridge: '[W]ith [such] watching and continual sitting there fell abundance of humours into his legs, then very hardly cured, which was thought one of the original causes of his gout.'[38] This afflicted him increasingly as he grew older, especially in the 1580s and 1590s. There was yet one more way in which Cambridge affected Cecil's future. University was the occasion for a romanticism and waywardness of youth, which are eternal characteristics of university students, but which seem strangely foreign to the virtuous, even strait-laced image of the future Lord Burghley. Cecil began to frequent a wineshop run by John Cheke's mother and in which her daughter Mary worked. He courted her and in August 1541 they were married. It was not, either socially or financially, the marriage which Richard Cecil would have chosen for his son.[39] On the other hand, William's brother-in-law was a scholar and teacher of repute. Cheke was known and respected at the

Court of both Henry VIII and Edward VI, to which he provided access for his kin and friends.

In 1541 William Cecil left Cambridge for the lawyers' school of Gray's Inn. During his years at St John's he had been so 'forward, studious and so early capable' that he had been reader of both the sophistry lecture and later 'so learnedly' the Greek lecture, yet he departed without a degree.[40] That was not unusual. Likewise it was common practice for young gentlemen and heirs to landed estates to acquire some knowledge of the common law. It could always prove useful in the management and protection of their properties. However, it seems that the pleasures of the metropolis competed, sometimes successfully, with study. '[A]s his years and company required he would many times be merry among young gentlemen.' There is evidence of his need to borrow money quickly. He also had an unfortunate introduction to gambling, an experience which the anonymous biographer heard from Cecil himself. A 'mad companion' fleeced the novice of all that he possessed, even his bedding and books. Cecil retaliated with characteristic resource and the application of religion to secular purposes: '[He] made a hole in the wall near his playfellow's bed's head, and in a fearful voice spoke thus, through the [hole], "O mortal man repent, repent of thy horrible sin, play, cozenage, and such lewdness, or else thou art damned and canst not be saved".' Next day his companion, trembling, 'penitent and heavy', begged Cecil's forgiveness and restored all his money and possessions to him.[41]

In the remaining years of Henry VIII's reign there is no intimation of William Cecil's future political prominence. His wife Mary gave birth to a son, Thomas, in May 1542, but the marriage was short-lived, because she died on 22 February 1544. Not long afterwards, on 21 December 1545, Cecil remarried. This was, in contrast to his first marriage, a prudent alliance. Mildred was one of the five learned daughters of Sir Anthony Cooke, who served in the Court of Henry VIII and became governor of Edward VI. Her sisters married substantial gentlemen, among them Nicholas Bacon, who was to be Lord Keeper and Cecil's ally and friend in Elizabeth's reign. By his second marriage, therefore, he was drawn into an influential, Protestant network.[42] The future beckoned when his father interceded with King Henry VIII and obtained for him the reversion of the office of *custos brevium*, the chief clerk of the common law Court of Common Pleas.[43] Also, according to Cecil's later recollection, he sat in the Henrician parliament of 1542, though the constituency is unknown and it certainly was not Stamford.[44] When Henry VIII died, William Cecil's career and future prospects were no more than those of the heir of any comfortably placed gentleman.

. . .

THE MID-TUDOR YEARS, 1547–58

On 28 January 1547 Henry VIII died and the royal minority of his heir, Edward VI, began. William Cecil was then a political unknown. Yet only three and a half years later, on 5 September 1550, he became a Privy Councillor and one of the Secretaries of State. The office of Secretary had been transformed into one of the key positions in the Tudor state by Thomas Cromwell during the 1530s. It gave the occupant access, involvement and oversight in most areas of government activity, domestic and foreign, as well as 'free' access to the monarch.[45]

Why was it that Cecil rose to prominence so rapidly? And, a supplementary question here, why was it that, once he had scaled the heights and achieved political prominence, he managed to survive and even flourish in the unstable, often turbulent, and certainly unforgiving politics of Edward VI's reign? The answer to the first question involves a consideration of one of the fundamental characteristics of the Tudor state. Appointments and promotions to positions in the bureaucracy, the Privy Council, offices of state and the royal Court were not dependent on qualifications, examinations, or loyalty to a party political machine. In a system of government by personal monarchy, the prerequisite for advancement was personal connection: who one knew. If one's friends or patron(s) were powerful social or political figures, who were influential with the monarch, this could provide entrée to the Court, royal service or both. Cecil was no exception.

At Edward VI's accession his uncle Edward, earl of Hertford, and his allies gained possession of the king's person. This enabled them to effect a coup, which elevated Hertford to the office of Protector, promoted him to the dukedom of Somerset, and set in train a Protestant reformation. Cecil benefited, for two reasons. He was of Protestant persuasion. And he had a range of connections in government, Court and the royal household: his brother-in-law Nicholas Bacon, Cheke and Ascham, his friend Thomas Smith, his father-in-law and, of course, his father. In 1547 he entered Somerset's service, followed him north in a military campaign against the Scots and was present at the battle of Pinkie. In September of the following year he became the duke's personal secretary. Personal service to a great man could be – and in Cecil's case was – transmuted into royal service to the crown. This was because the protectorate government of Somerset was characterised by incompetence.[46] His costly and coercive Scottish policy failed, his socio-economic policies were ill-conceived, provoking public disorder and an alienated élite, and his failure to consult the Privy Council isolated him at the centre. As Somerset's incompetence and arrogance magnified, so did opposition to him and support for his rival, John Dudley, earl of Warwick. In October 1549 the Protector was toppled from power. Cecil now learned, from painful experience, that the only condition worse than lack of a patron was to be the loyal client of a failed patron. The slings and arrows of Somerset's misfortune were also visited upon his personal secretary, who spent over two months (November 1549–January 1550) in the Tower.

Thereafter Cecil manœuvred himself successfully through the dangerous waters of Edwardian politics. This was especially important during the continued rivalry between the fallen Protector and Warwick. Cecil now assumed the role of intermediary, attempting to reconcile the two men. If his motives were self-preservation and advancement he certainly succeeded. He appears to have enjoyed the respect, even trust, of both Somerset and Warwick, and he survived, unscathed, the final fall, trial and execution of the ex-Protector in 1551–52. As one of his friends, Sir William Pickering, observed, Cecil had been 'found undefiled with the folly of this unfortunate Duke'.[47] The political *via media*, which he adopted after his release from the Tower, served him well: in September 1550 he was appointed Privy Councillor and third Secretary of State, and just over a year later (on the same day that Warwick was elevated to the dukedom of Northumberland) he was knighted. He also served as personal secretary to both Northumberland and the king. It was significant, because it was a precedent for his Elizabethan position, when he was to be principal Secretary of State and the queen's private secretary.[48]

Northumberland's emergence as master and manager of Edwardian government, between 1549 and 1552, also benefited Cecil. During 1549 and thereafter the earl cultivated him in correspondence and by personal contact too.[49] Meanwhile Cecil's experience accumulated. He sat in the first (four-session) parliament of Edward VI's reign and, in 1548, he was involved in the legal proceedings against the ardent Catholic bishop of Winchester, Stephen Gardiner.[50] But it was as Secretary that he flourished and, at the same time, underwent his political apprenticeship for his long Elizabethan future. In the process he learned much about the arts of management and administration, simply because the Secretary had to be a jack-of-all-trades. Rapidly he displayed those personal qualities which were to characterise his political career: thoroughness, attention to detail, the capacity to handle formidable workloads, caution, discretion and tact, coupled with firmness, in dealings with other royal servants and those who sought benefits from the crown. They were qualities which would benefit royal government and also ensure his long-term tenure of prominent place, thereby enabling him to fulfil his own aspirations. Cecil was involved in both foreign and domestic affairs and the management of royal finances. He corresponded with diplomats, ecclesiastics, local dignitaries and officials and prominent politicians. He also received domestic and foreign news from agents in England and abroad. He was the target of complaints of aggrieved subjects, of petitions from those promoting suits for royal favour and the recipient of grateful letters from those whom he was able to oblige.[51] In addition, he frequently attended Privy Council meetings[52] and served in both Edwardian parliaments (1547–52 and March 1553).[53] Though there is little evidence of Cecil's activity during parliamentary sessions, as a Secretary of State he acquired some responsibility for preparing the official 'book' or legislative programme including, probably, the subsidy bill. In December 1552 he even discussed with Northumberland the most appropriate season in which to summon Edward's second parliament, and devised justificatory arguments for the proposed subsidy.[54]

One of the principal reasons for Cecil's rapid rise to prominence in Edward VI's reign was his relationship with Northumberland. The duke displayed increasing confidence and trust in him. Although he was Lord President of the Privy Council the duke was not a frequent attender and he managed it through Cecil. The Secretary conveyed Northumberland's views, kept the Council's papers and generally handled business with efficiency. However, when the king's signature was required, it was more often obtained by the President's close associates, and 'special friends', Thomas Lord Darcy of Chiche and Sir John Gates, than by Cecil. It was perhaps a lesson not lost on him when he became Queen Elizabeth's personal and private secretary. In Edward's reign his role should not be exaggerated. Darcy and Gates also acted on the President's behalf in the Council. Nevertheless, there is evidence of Northumberland's appreciation of his efforts, on occasions offering friendly advices, thanking him for his services and expressing concern about his ill-health.[55] For his part Cecil, having moved deftly away from Somerset in the years 1549–51, became 'Northumberland's man', as the imperial ambassador described him.[56] During the years of Edward VI's reign he learned the arts of political management and survival and also became experienced in the business and administrative processes of government.

In one other important respect those years were a formative experience. They consolidated and probably reinforced Cecil's attachment to the Protestant faith. Of course his service in government, first in the Protector's household and then as Secretary of State, meant that he was one of those involved and even identified with the Edwardian Protestant Reformation process. In 1548, for example, he actively participated in official efforts to persuade Bishop Gardiner to conform to the religious changes: Gardiner later complained that Cecil 'with his pen, took occasion to prick me more than, I trusted, my Lord's Grace himself would have done'.[57] Three years later Cecil was the chief organiser of debates on the Eucharist, some of which took place at his London home. And in 1552 Archbishop Cranmer passed his completed draft of the forty-five articles of faith to Cecil and his first wife's brother, Sir John Cheke, who handed them on to the Council for consideration.[58] This in itself is a reminder that the Secretary was one of a network of adherents to the new faith who were prominent in Edwardian governing circles: not only Cheke but also Cecil's brother-in-law, Nicholas Bacon, and his father-in-law, Anthony Cooke. The 'Cambridge connection', including Roger Ascham and Sir Thomas Smith, was prominent in this network. Some, amongst them Cecil, Cheke and Smith, were 'Athenians', who rejected the corrupt contemporary pronunciation of Greek.[59]

However, whilst there is no doubt about Cecil's commitment to the new faith, he was and remained a moderate, tending to side with more conservative reformers such as Cranmer, rather than with the radicalism of such activists as John Hooper.

The new church, the careers and even personal security of Cecil and other members of the Edwardian regime were imperilled by the onset of Edward VI's terminal illness in 1553. His legitimate successor, in accordance with the Succession Act of 1544 and Henry VIII's will, was the devout Roman Catholic Mary Tudor. Northumberland's attempt to divert the succession to Lady Jane Grey, who was married to his son, Guildford Dudley, was embodied in a legal instrument approved by the dying king. When the duke required the crown's law officers, councillors and other prominent political figures to sign it, he was, as the law officers attested, implicating them all (Cecil included) in treason. Coercive pressure by duke and king caused them to submit, though Cecil was the last to sign. Northumberland's cause, however, was a lost one. Support rapidly gathered around Mary after Edward's death. Councillors, nobles and others – many, like Cecil, signatories to the instrument – distanced themselves from the duke and covertly acted against him. In the days which led to Northumberland's fall and Mary's triumph the Secretary discreetly shifted allegiance from the former, just as earlier he had from Somerset. The anonymous biographer reflected that 'he carried the matter so temperately as he kept his conscience free, his truth to the Crown, and himself from danger'.[60] These cannot be designated merely cynical political actions. They were natural pragmatic responses in the cause of self-preservation and, in 1553, Cecil's conduct was also motivated by a profound respect for the legitimate succession, as set forth in the Succession Act of 1544. This belief in the loyal subject's duty to obey the law and the monarch's lawful rights also manifested itself in the new reign. Both Somerset and Northumberland had governed in the king's name, but, as they too were only subjects, the pragmatic Cecil's loyalty to them was only conditional. In contrast, Mary Tudor was the legitimate sovereign.

Mary's succession was not the prelude to a widespread revenge campaign. She forgave Cecil along with most others for their unwilling complicity in Northumberland's treason and he was duly pardoned on 6 October 1553.[61] From the beginning and throughout the reign his position was consistent, if not clear. As a loyal subject it was his duty to obey her government and to conform, at least outwardly, to the restored Roman Catholic faith – but no more. According to the anonymous biographer, when some pressure was put upon him to serve in her government he replied that

> as he would ever serve and pray for her in his heart and, with his body and goods, be as ready to serve in her defence as any of her loyal subjects, so she would please to grant him leave to use his conscience to himself and serve her at large as a private man rather than to be her greatest councillor.[62]

So Cecil retreated to his estates and conducted himself as a dutiful subject. John Clapham's explanation of his behaviour however, was less flattering than that of the anonymous author: Although, he wrote, Cecil was suspected of being 'ill affected' to Roman Catholicism, he added that 'he seemed at the first to conform himself thereto in some points, as I have heard it reported, which haply might proceed either from youth and human frailty, unwilling to hazard the hopes of worldly preferment, or else from want of sufficient instruction at that time in matters of religion'.[63] Clapham's rather denigratory description rightly identifies Cecil's characteristic circumspection and strong sense of self-preservation, but it hardly does justice to the man who had been actively involved in Edwardian debates on the Eucharist.[64]

The position which Cecil adopted was a sensible *via media,* which accommodated both his self-interest and his principles. Royal service would inevitably require him to assist in the restoration of the Roman Catholic church. In private life he could avoid political perils and, at the same time, conduct himself as a dutiful and loyal subject. Nevertheless, he was true to his word, that he would 'serve her at large as a private man': he was one of those who escorted the papal legate, Cardinal Pole, from Brussels to Westminster in November 1554; in the following April he was a member of the English delegation which went to France, in an unsuccessful attempt to negotiate a peace between Emperor Charles V and the French king, Henry II; and he served as a Justice of the Peace of the quorum in Lincolnshire.[65]

It was as one of the more prominent country gentry in Lincolnshire that he was returned knight of the shire to Mary's fourth parliament in 1555. He was active in legislative business and a number of bills were committed to him, presumably for amendment, redrafting or as committee convener. These included the measures for increase of arable land and 'for re-edifying of decayed houses', whilst the first fruits and tenths bill was referred to Cecil and others in order to be articled. The anti-enclosure legislation was favoured by the government, whilst Mary was determined that first fruits, which had been transferred by statute to the crown in 1534, should be restored to the papacy. However, Cecil's involvement does not mean, as Beckingsale suggests, that he was acting on the government's behalf, because it was the house of commons which decided to whom bills should be committed for scrutiny and amendment. In any case, Cecil's Edwardian experience of parliaments, government and enclosure problems suffices to explain why the house chose him.[66]

Cecil was also active in speech, particularly during the debate on a government bill which was aimed at Protestants living in unlicensed exile abroad. It would deprive them of revenue from their property if they failed to return by an appointed date. The fact that this was a troublesome parliament was largely due to exiles and first fruits. It has been commonly assumed that the cause of conflict was religious: Protestant parliamentary opposition was resisting the implementation of a Roman Catholic programme. Jennifer Loach has demonstrated, however, that both of these measures were contentious because they infringed property rights. With reference to the exiles bill, she wrote that 'Any member of this parliament [and that includes Cecil] may have disliked [it] on the grounds of an attack on property rights without having any sympathy for the religious sentiments of the exiles'. At some point in this parliament, as Cecil himself records, 'I spoke my mind freely and incurred some ill will', adding rather sententiously that 'it was better to obey God than men'. But what position he took and on what grounds he did so are not clear.[67]

Certainly the anonymous biographer identifies some members opposed to a government bill and links Cecil with them:

> In the Parliament time there was a matter in question for something the Queen would have pass, wherein Sir Anthony Kingston, Sir William Courtney, Sir John Pollard, and many others of value,

> especially western men, were opposite. Sir William Cecil, being their speaker, having that day told a good tale for them, when the House rose they came to him and said they would dine with him that day.

Evidence cited by Read shows that these and other members regularly met at 'Arundel's house' in the City of London. They had made known their intention to resist in parliament those matters which they disliked. They also declared themselves to be good Protestants who were opposed to the queen's Catholic proceedings. There is, however, no evidence that they rehearsed tactics and organised an opposition. Furthermore, the anonymous biographer's reference to Cecil may mean simply that, in stating his own concerns, he was also expressing theirs – not that he was their appointed spokesman.[68]

Nevertheless, the episode landed him in an embarrassing and potentially serious situation. He agreed to dine with them on condition that they did not discuss parliamentary matters. Although they agreed, 'some began to break promise, for which he challenged them'. When the Privy Council learned of the meeting, those present, with the exception of Cecil, were arrested, imprisoned and interrogated. He was summoned before two councillors, William Lord Paget and his old Edwardian co-secretary, Sir William Petre, in order to explain his conduct. Fortunately his account satisfied them and no further action was taken against him.[69] Whilst Cecil's conduct in this parliament seems uncharacteristic, that may be an unjustified assumption that he was always and by nature discreet, circumspect and never a creature of impulse. Perhaps there was in him an impetuous streak, typified in his first imprudent marriage, his pleasant days at Gray's Inn, and again in the 1555 parliament – a streak which only long years of responsibility in Queen Elizabeth's service taught him to control. Even then, did that impetuosity manifest itself again in the precipitate action leading to Mary Stuart's execution in 1587?

After the 1555 parliament, Cecil withdrew to the life of a country gentleman for the rest of Mary's reign. Whatever was the motive for his conduct in that parliament – religion or property rights – there is no questioning his Protestant convictions. Furthermore, he was in touch with Protestants abroad, including his brother-in-law, John Cheke. He received affectionate letters from his father-in-law, Sir Anthony Cooke, who was in Strasbourg, one of the exiles' favourite refuges. Indeed, Cecil's attitude to the exiles' bill may have been influenced by the threat which it posed to Cooke. He also managed the financial affairs of Francis, earl of Bedford, who besought him to 'be good to my wife and children' while he was abroad on military service.[70] The two men were to be closely allied in the politics and religion of Elizabeth's reign. That reign began when the childless Mary died on 17 November 1558. For Cecil it brought promise of re-entry into national political life. However, there was one shadow cast across his future: the painful, sometimes crippling gout, which had already afflicted him in the reigns of Edward and Mary and which would worsen as he grew older.

. . .

NOTES

1. Although the unpopular impact of the 'martyrdoms' may have been exaggerated, the Marian persecution clearly influenced the attitudes of some Elizabethan politicians and religious activists. D.M. Palliser, *The Age of Elizabeth: England under the Later Tudors, 1547–1603* (Harlow, 1983), p. 17.
2. C. Webster (ed.), *Health, Medicine and Mortality in the Sixteenth Century* (Cambridge, 1979), p. 27; W. Camden, *Annales: The True and Royall History of the Famous Empresse Elizabeth, Queene of England* (London, 1625); *Annales: The Historie of the Most Renowned and Victorious Princesse Elizabeth* (London, 1630).
3. A.G.R. Smith (ed.), *The Anonymous Life of William Cecil, Lord Burghley* (Lampeter, 1990), pp. 66, 78.
4. For example, Thomas Norton, imprisoned in the Tower in December 1581 for indiscreet comments about Queen Elizabeth's courtship with a French prince, wrote to his wife, recommending that she and his son and heir offer prayers to his patron, Cecil, whose 'wisdome in knowlege' he extolled, declaiming 'how dere he hath ben to my soule' and adding that he 'can do me most good'. M.A.R. Graves, *Thomas Norton: The Parliament Man* (Oxford, 1994), p. 125.
5. The anonymous biographer commented on slanderous reports that he hindered men from rising, but proceeded to deny it. During the 1590s the earl of Essex, Elizabeth's last favourite, must have reached the same conclusion when his promotion of clients to high office was repeatedly frustrated by the appointment of

Cecilians. A.G.R. Smith, *William Cecil, Lord Burghley: Minister of Elizabeth I* (Bangor, 1991), pp. 25–6; idem, *Servant of the Cecils: The Life of Sir Michael Hickes* (London, 1977), pp. 53–4.

6. E.P. and C. Read (eds), *Elizabeth of England: Certain Observations concerning the Life and Reign of Queen Elizabeth by John Clapham* (Oxford, 1951), pp. 6, 71. (Hereafter *Clapham.*)
7. Camden, *Annales,* fol. B1; C. Haigh (ed.), *The Reign of Elizabeth I* (Basingstoke, 1984), pp. 6–7.
8. Smith (ed.), *Anon. Life,* pp. 9–10; idem, *Servant of the Cecils,* pp. 46, 55–80.
9. J.S. Cerovski (ed.), *Sir Robert Naunton's Fragmenta Regalia or Observations on Queen Elizabeth, Her Times and Favourites* (London, 1985), p. 55 (hereafter *Naunton*), *Clapham,* pp. 22–3; Smith (ed.), *Anon. Life,* pp. 13, 70, 74, 118–19, 146–7.
10. *Clapham,* pp. 23–4; Smith (ed.), *Anon. Life,* pp. 11–12.
11. However, Smith also notes that, later in the text, the anonymous biographer contradicts himself. In order to exonerate Cecil from culpability for the council's mistakes, he argued that he was unable to 'rule' or direct Elizabeth or the council. Smith (ed.), *Anon. Life,* pp. 26–9.
12. Ibid., pp. 24–5; *Clapham,* p. 75.
13. Smith (ed.), *Anon. Life,* p. 108; J. Thirsk, *Economic Policy and Projects* (Oxford, 1978), pp. 33–4, 51–60, 89, 98–9; Smith, *Burghley,* p. 39; see below, pp. 159, 165.
14. Camden, Introduction to *Annales* (1625).
15. Ibid. (1630), pp. 128–9.
16. Ibid. (1630), p. 129.
17. J.E. Neale, 'November 17th', in *The Age of Catherine de Medici and Essays in Elizabethan History* (London, 1971), pp. 100–6.
18. J.A. Froude, *History of England from the Fall of Wolsey to the Defeat of the Spanish Armada,* 12 vols (London, 1881), XII, p. 508.
19. Ibid., p. 503.
20. A.F. Pollard, *The History of England from the Accession of Edward VI to the Death of Elizabeth* (London, 1913); J.E. Neale, *Queen Elizabeth I* (London, 1934); idem, *Elizabeth I and her Parliaments,* 2 vols (London, 1953–57); J. Hurstfield, *Elizabeth and the Unity of England* (London, 1960).
21. See Haigh (ed.), 'Introduction' in *Reign of Elizabeth,* pp. 1–25, for an evaluative survey of the historiography of Elizabeth I.
22. e.g. P. Williams, *The Later Tudors: England, 1547–1603* (Oxford, 1995), pp. 365–6.
23. J. Hurstfield, 'William Cecil, 1520–1598: Minister to Elizabeth I', *History Today,* VI/12 (Dec. 1956), pp. 791–2.
24. C. Read, *Mr Secretary Cecil and Queen Elizabeth* (London, 1955); idem, *Lord Burghley and Queen Elizabeth,* London, 1960; B.W.

Beckingsale, *Burghley: Tudor Statesman 1520–1598* (London, 1967). Both Read and Beckingsale presented favourable assessments.
25. See Bibliographical Essay below for the relevant works by these historians.
26. Hurstfield, 'Minister to Elizabeth I'; Smith, *Burghley*.
27. Hurstfield, 'Minister to Elizabeth I', p. 793.
28. S.T. Bindoff (ed.), *The House of Commons, 1509–1558*, 3 vols (London, 1982), I, p. 602; Beckingsale, *Burghley*, pp. 3–6.
29. M.K. Jones and M.G. Underwood, *The King's Mother: Lady Margaret Beaufort, Countess of Richmond and Derby* (Cambridge, 1992), pp. 126–7, 129, 133, 142, 281; Read, *Secretary Cecil*, p. 18.
30. Ibid., pp. 19–22; Beckingsale, *Burghley*, pp. 6–7, 8–13; Bindoff (ed.), *House of Commons*, I, p. 603.
31. Smith (ed.), *Anon. Life*, pp. 39–40.
32. Cecil himself cited both 1520 and 1521 as the year of his birth, Read, *Secretary Cecil*, p. 22.
33. Smith (ed.), *Anon. Life*, pp. 41–2; Beckingsale, *Burghley*, p. 7.
34. H.C. Porter, *Reformation and Reaction in Tudor Cambridge* (Hamden, Conn., 1972), p. 50.
35. Beckingsale, *Burghley*, p. 12.
36. Porter, *Reformation*, p. 50.
37. Read, *Secretary Cecil*, pp. 27–8; Beckingsale, *Burghley*, pp. 15–17.
38. Smith (ed.), *Anon. Life*, pp. 43–4.
39. Read, *Secretary Cecil*, pp. 27–8; Beckingsale, *Burghley*, pp. 19–20.
40. Smith (ed.), *Anon. Life*, pp. 44–5 and n. 76.
41. Ibid., pp. 46–7; Read, *Secretary Cecil*, pp. 30–3, Beckingsale, *Burghley*, p. 22.
42. Read, *Secretary Cecil*, pp. 29, 34–5; Smith, *Anon. Life*, pp. 49–50.
43. Smith (ed.), *Anon. Life*, p. 48. The office, worth £240 a year, passed to him in 1548. Read, *Secretary Cecil*, p. 32.
44. Bindoff (ed.), *House of Commons*, I, pp. 603–4.
45. The treatises of Robert Beale and Nicholas Faunt (both dated 1592) were written almost half a century after Cecil's first appointment to the office, but they describe accurately enough the functions and responsibilities of Edwardian secretaries. C. Read, *Mr Secretary Walsingham and the Policy of Queen Elizabeth*, 3 vols (Oxford, 1925), I, pp. 423–43; C. Hughes (ed.), 'Nicholas Faunt's Discourse touching the Office of Principal Secretary of Estate, &c, 1592', *E[nglish] H[istorical] R[eview]*, 20 (1905), pp. 499–508.
46. Somerset's inept management is charted in M.L. Bush, *The Government Policy of Protector Somerset* (London, 1975), e.g. pp. 4–6, ch. 2 *passim*, pp. 160–1, and D.E. Hoak, *The King's Council in the Reign of Edward VI* (Cambridge, 1976), esp. pp. 169–72, 178–80, 188–90, 260–2.

47. P.F. Tytler, *England under the Reigns of Edward V and Mary*, 2 vols (London, 1839), II, p. 194.
48. D. Starkey (ed.), *The English Court from the Wars of the Roses to the Civil War* (London, 1987), p. 130.
49. Read, *Secretary Cecil*, pp. 46, 78–81. In 1552 he visited Cecil's home at Burghley. Bindoff (ed.), *House of Commons*, I, p. 604.
50. Read, *Secretary Cecil*, pp. 46–7.
51. e.g. *Historical Manuscripts Commission Reports*, Salisbury MSS, Vol. I, pp. 80–2, 86–8, 90–2, 95–124; B[ritish] L[ibrary], Lansdowne MSS, 2, nos. 53–4, 56–9, 60–1, 63, 65, 67–77, 90–3, 95–8; 3, nos. 1–15, 18, 21–2, 28–34, 38–41.
52. For example, between his appointment in September 1550 and 16 June 1553 he was recorded as present at 471 (or 77%) of the 611 council meetings. J.R. Dasent (ed.), *Acts of the Privy Council of England*, 32 vols (London, 1890–1907), III, pp. 118–511, and IV, pp. 3–289.
53. He sat for Stamford in 1547–52, and probably for Lincolnshire in March 1553. Bindoff (ed.), *House of Commons*, I, pp. 603–5.
54. Ibid., pp. 604–5; P[ublic] R[ecord] O[ffice], S[tate] P[apers], 10/18/6.
55. Hoak, *King's Council*, pp. 137–9, 142–4, 158–9; J. Guy, *Tudor England* (Oxford, 1988), p. 242; S. Haynes (ed.), *A Collection of State Papers relating to Affairs in the Reigns of King Henry VIII, King Edward VI, Queen Mary and Queen Elizabeth, 1542–70* (London, 1740), pp. 136–8; BL, Lansdowne MS, 3, no. 23, 7 May 1553.
56. Hoak, *King's Council*, p. 143; see D. Hoak, 'Rehabilitating the Duke of Northumberland', in J. Loach and R. Tittler (eds), *The Mid-Tudor Polity, c.1540–1560* (London, 1980), p. 40.
57. J.A. Muller (ed.), *The Letters of Stephen Gardiner* (Westport, Conn., 1970), pp. xxxii, 495.
58. Read, *Secretary Cecil*, pp. 84–5; Guy, *Tudor England*, pp. 224–5.
59. Ibid., pp. 224, 253.
60. M. Levine, *Tudor Dynastic Problems, 1460–1571* (London, 1973), pp. 71, 74, 161–4. Read, *Secretary Cecil*, pp. 99–101; Smith (ed.), *Anon. Life*, p. 51.
61. *Calendar of Patent Rolls, Philip and Mary*, 4 vols (London, 1936–39), I, p. 453.
62. Smith (ed.), *Anon. Life*, p. 52.
63. *Clapham*, p. 74.
64. Read is sympathetic to Clapham's analysis. Read, *Secretary Cecil*, pp. 102–3.
65. Ibid., pp. 103–6, 113; Beckingsale, *Burghley*, pp. 61, 64. As Read pointed out, Cecil's first service to Mary – escorting Pole, whose task was to restore papal supremacy in England – was in stark contradiction to his own religious position.

66. Bindoff (ed.), *House of Commons*, I, p. 605; Read, *Secretary Cecil*, pp. 109–10; Beckingsale, *Burghley*, pp. 62–3; T. Vardon and T.E. May (eds), *Journals of the House of Commons* (London, 1852), I, pp. 43–5. (Hereafter *CJ*.)
67. Read, *Secretary Cecil*, p. 110; J. Loach, *Parliament under the Tudors* (Oxford, 1991), pp. 83–4.
68. Smith, *Anon. Life*, p. 54; Read, *Secretary Cecil*, p. 108.
69. Smith, *Anon. Life*, pp. 54–5.
70. Read, *Secretary Cecil*, p. 112; Haynes (ed.), *State Papers*, pp. 203–5; *HMC*, Salisbury MS, I, p. 142.

Chapter 2

THE NEW REGIME, 1558–67

By 17 November 1558 Cecil, building on the foundations laid by his grandfather and father (whom he succeeded in 1553), had established himself as an affluent country gentleman of some prominence. He had also acquired, through his education, marriages, Protestant affiliations and Edwardian royal service an extensive network of connections, which would benefit him in the years ahead. By far the most important political connection which he had established was with the Princess Elizabeth. She was now the new queen, granddaughter of King Henry VII, under whom Cecil's grandfather had launched the family fortunes. Their association dated back to Edward VI's reign. By 1548 she was corresponding with him, either directly or through Thomas Parry, her cofferer, about her property and also on occasions to intervene with Somerset on her behalf. In 1550 she appointed him to be the surveyor (or overseer) of her estates at an annual salary of twenty pounds. He appears to have exercised that office, largely by deputy, until her accession in 1558 and in that capacity he corresponded with both Parry and his mistress.[1] Although Cecil's connection with the future queen was not political, his private service to her, as well as his public reputation acquired in Edwardian governing circles, created that trust and confidence in him which she expressed when she named him Secretary of State in November 1558.

There were other reasons too why Cecil was an appropriate if not natural choice to occupy that key office. He possessed both the necessary skills and the experience acquired in Edwardian government. Indeed, he was one of the few relatively experienced hands in the Privy Council appointed by

Elizabeth in 1558. By then he had amply demonstrated those characteristic qualities of conscientious attention to duties, formidable work capacity, discretion and propriety not ostentation. These were all valuable assets in a minister and councillor. Furthermore, and of special significance, Elizabeth and Cecil had much in common. They had a mutual respect for learning which owed much to Ascham, Cheke, and others of the Cambridge connection. They had a similar experience of political ups and downs in mid-Tudor politics and both had spent time in the Tower. Perhaps, as a consequence of this, they were cautious, conservative and regarded political stability as a top priority, although of course these qualities in Cecil may not have been apparent to the queen in 1558. They also had in common an attachment to Protestantism of a conservative rather than radical kind. In particular, religious practice must conform to the law and it was subordinate to the need for public order and political stability. However, Cecil was to demonstrate a covert sympathy towards moderate reforming godly Protestants which Elizabeth entirely lacked.

Cecil's religious position and conduct during Mary Tudor's reign may have been known to Elizabeth. He outwardly conformed (just as she did) to Roman Catholicism as restored by parliamentary statute. She would have recognised in him two desirable attributes: his legalism and a public acquiescence in the establishment of a church contrary to his own convictions. In other words, he believed in loyalty to the state and, therefore, to its royal head. Elizabeth recognised this when, three days after her accession, she appointed him Secretary of State and Privy Councillor and uttered these words:

> This judgement I have of you that you will not be corrupted by any manner of gift *and* that you *will be faithful to the state*; and that without respect of my private will you will give me that counsel which you think best and if you shall know anything necessary to be declared to me of secrecy you shall show it to myself only.[2]

'Fidelity to the state' was the key clause. Cecil responded immediately by giving her 'that counsel' which he thought best. The new regime was beset with urgent political, religious and economic problems, of which some, but not all, were legacies of the previous reign. Some were interrelated and had serious international implications. Cecil itemised them in one of those memoranda which were to characterise his advisory role during the next forty years: 'To recover Scotland to the former amity with England', to reach an agreement with Mary Stuart, queen of the northern kingdom, and 'To establish in the Church of England an uniform order'. He also acted promptly to restore the currency. It was to Cecil's credit that he moved so speedily to tackle and resolve the initial problems of Elizabeth's regime.[3]

Nevertheless, those problems were serious, threatening and not easily soluble, especially because they were interrelated: Elizabeth inherited the Anglo-Spanish war against France, mounted by Mary Tudor and her consort Philip. It had resulted in the loss of Calais, England's remnant of its medieval Continental empire. Furthermore, the 'auld' Franco-Scottish alliance had been cemented by the marriage of the Scottish queen, Mary Stuart, to the French Dauphin Francis in April 1558. Whilst Mary lived in France, Scotland was governed by Mary of Guise, her mother, supported by a French military presence. A Franco-Scottish invasion of northern England during the hiatus of power, as a new monarch organised her government and before she could re-establish a Protestant church (as was generally anticipated), was widely feared in northern England. Nor was Elizabeth's kingdom strong, united, ready and able to resist such a threat with confidence and success. Her inheritance was a troubled one. All kinds of problems beset the country: social unrest; the crown's poverty; a weak and depressed economy with a serious and continuing imbalance of trade, because it produced little of international value apart from cloth; frequent dearth of foodstuffs; inflation fuelled by debasements of the coinage in the reigns of Henry VIII and Edward VI; and endemic disease including the plague and influenza in 1557–58.

Within this disturbed environment the accession of Elizabeth I on 17 November 1558 heralded two more problems. She was the fourth monarch in little more than a decade and she came to the throne as a childless spinster. This raised a number of urgent considerations. Who would succeed her if she died without heirs of her body? The strongest claimant was Mary Stuart, whose Roman Catholic, Franco-Scottish credentials would divide the country and possibly result in civil war and foreign intervention. It was, of course, assumed that Elizabeth would marry and that her husband would govern. So her choice of husband would naturally draw England into one of Europe's armed camps: pro-Habsburg or pro-French, Catholic or Protestant. It was a daunting challenge for a young, twenty-five-year-old queen who had to rule over a political system monopolised by males. The second problem was not unrelated, because it concerned religion. It was an urgent, 'burning' issue, which divided, in varying degrees, all European countries and England was no exception. Many devout Protestants had fled into exile in Mary Tudor's reign, almost three hundred had been burnt alive for their faith and many more had concealed their beliefs and waited for a better day. That day had now come. There was an atmosphere of uncertainty, fear and animosity. Was religious civil war a possibility? It all depended on which way the new queen would go and how skilfully she moved the kingdom in the direction of her choice. Furthermore, it should be remembered, her domestic religious policy would have a crucial effect on her relations with France, Scotland and Spain, any one of which could threaten national security.

What part did Cecil play in the unravelling of this tangled web in the opening years of the reign? So far as the religious 'settlement' in the 1559 parliament is concerned, his prominence should not be assumed, nor should his role be exaggerated. Relatively little is known about the crucial parliament which re-established a Protestant English church. Furthermore, Norman Jones challenges the common assumption about the centrality of Cecil's role when he writes: 'Elizabeth, with the aid of William Cecil (*or perhaps* Cecil, by the authority of Elizabeth), set about resolving the problems she faced and attaining the end she desired from her first day on the throne.' In other words it was a partnership in which both were active but in which Elizabeth, by virtue of her position and personality, tended to retain the initiative. This was evident in the government's religious policy between her accession on 17 November 1558 and the meeting of her first parliament on 25 January 1559. Among the written advices which she received during the first weeks of her regime, as to the direction which she should take in religion, there is none from Cecil, despite his fondness for memoranda. Not that he was inactive. His notes, that the preacher at St Paul's Cross in London should not stir up religious conflict, were a personal reminder that the hardline Marian Catholic bishop of London, Bonner, whose right it was to appoint such preachers, might provoke such strife. Shortly afterwards, on 27 December 1558, a royal proclamation, for which Cecil was doubtless responsible, forbade preaching either by Catholics or by over-enthusiastic Protestants. Nevertheless, it was the queen, not her minister, who provided the initial momentum for reform, when she introduced liturgical changes in her chapel. These were then incorporated in the proclamation which authorised their use throughout the kingdom. This was not merely a safeguard against civil disorder, which was already occurring. The queen was also signalling to the forthcoming parliament the Protestant direction of her religious policy.[4]

When parliament met on 25 January 1559 it was Cecil's brother-in-law, Lord Keeper Nicholas Bacon, who pointed the way ahead to a church free from Roman Catholic 'idolatry and superstition' and declared the need for uniformity of religion. Accordingly, government bills to establish a royal supremacy and religious uniformity were introduced in the commons. The former was the subject of lengthy debate before the two measures were combined in committee. The new composite bill, which declared the queen to be supreme head, authorised a book of common prayer and imposed penalties for refusal to use it, was passed, after heated discussion, on 23 February and sent to the lords. There it encountered powerful resistance from the archbishop of York, the united bishops and some lay peers. A committee, dominated by religious conservatives, stripped the bill of all provisions which changed the order of worship (apart from allowing the laity at communion to receive both the wine and the bread). As for the title of supreme head, Catholic resistance, combined with male reluctance to authorise a woman to assume the title, left her free to adopt it, but it did not provide her with the statutory authority to do so. In this form the bill passed the lords and was despatched to the lower house. Elizabeth, Cecil and the other councillors were in an acute dilemma. At first the queen contemplated the dissolution of parliament. However, that would have left her without clearly defined legitimate authority over a church which was administered by Roman Catholic bishops and which retained the Catholic order of worship. So she changed her mind and adjourned parliament over Easter. Perhaps she acted on advice from Cecil and other councillors, but, as so often, information on the Secretary's activity and role in these proceedings is lacking. The government's plan of attack was twofold: to hold a public disputation between Protestant and Catholic divines in order to discredit the latter and, at the same time, to draft more acceptable supremacy and uniformity bills. On 31 March and 3 April the refusal of the Catholic disputants to obey the moderator caused him to end the public debate, and soon afterwards two of the participating bishops were sent to the Tower for 'disobedience to common authority'.[5]

Having weakened the Catholic opposition in the lords, the government submitted to parliament the new bills for supremacy and uniformity. They contained important modifications, which were designed to meet criticisms, allay some fears and win votes. In the former, 'supreme head' was replaced by 'supreme governor'. Not only would the Catholics refuse to recognise anyone but the Pope as supreme head; there was also widespread objection to assumption of that title by a woman. Cecil performed a public relations exercise when he informed the commons that the queen's humility prevented her from accepting it. There were two additions to the new uniformity bill. One was an ornaments rubric, which required that the ornaments of the church and clerical vestments in use in 1548–49 should be retained. The other was a merger of the conservative 1549 and more radical 1552 formulae for the administration of the communion. This enabled both Catholics and godly Protestants to extract different interpretations of the communion service from the composite formula. It looks like another vote-catching device intended, partly at least, to soften up the recalcitrant house of lords. The bill for the supremacy rapidly passed the commons and lords after amendments by both houses. However, that for uniformity encountered stiff resistance in the lords, despite the modified nature of the new bill and the absence of two Catholic bishops in the Tower. The house amended it and, at the final vote, it passed by only twenty-one to eighteen. So the new church was established by statutory authority but without the support of any of the lords spiritual or of convocation (the church assembly).[6]

Despite the paucity of evidence, it would be reasonable and natural to assume that official policies and actions in this parliament reflected the queen's religious position and that they resulted from her decisions, taken in consultation with her Privy Councillors. Among those advisers Cecil and Bacon would have been prominent. They were, like Elizabeth, moderate Protestants and their appointment to the key offices of Secretary and Lord Keeper was a signal mark of her particular trust in them. Throughout her reign she allowed no monopoly of confidence and sought advice widely from Privy Councillors, whilst Cecil himself had to work through the Council. But, in 1559, there were, among the other active and prominent councillors, men who were connected with him by kinship, friendship, a shared Cambridge experience and religious persuasion: for example, Francis, earl of Bedford, Sir Nicholas Bacon, Sir Ambrose Cave, Sir John Mason and Sir Thomas Parry. Most of them had served in Edward VI's government and, as Norman Jones observed, Cecil, 'the engine of policy in the government', and his associates 'carried with them the Edwardian tradition, and in many ways Elizabeth's policy at the beginning of her reign echoed that tradition'.[7]

Nevertheless, the record of Cecil's role in the crucial parliament of 1559 is scanty, uninformative, erroneous, even malicious. For example, the hostile count of Feria, the Spanish ambassador, reporting on the supremacy bill debate in the commons, recorded that 'some of the members spoke in favour of reason so strongly that it was necessary for Cecil to get up a wrangle in order to carry out the wicked plan, and the bill then passed'. What the Secretary's nefarious scheme was, and how he accomplished it, remains a mystery. Similarly the anonymous biographer describes how the public disputation between Catholic and Protestant divines was 'so politically handled and . . . wisely, learnedly and temperately governed' by Cecil, whereas in fact the moderator was Bacon. Fragmentary and suspect evidence notwithstanding, it seems that queen and Secretary worked for similar ends and largely achieved what they wanted. Although, after the passage of the uniformity bill through both houses, opponents attempted to persuade Elizabeth to veto it, Cecil was reported as being 'earnest with the book [of common prayer]' which it authorised and she gave her assent to it. Together they had secured the establishment of a *via media* church. It was not an ideal which they strove for but simply what it was possible to achieve in the face of fierce parliamentary resistance.[8] At the same time they also managed to shore up the crown's beleaguered finances, by transferring to it papal first fruits and tenths, suppressing the few religious houses revived by Mary Tudor, and obtaining statutory authority to acquire the lands of bishops in return for advowsons and tithes of equal value.[9]

As the new regime laboured to establish a new religious order, which would avoid civil discords, it had to cope with external problems. These inter-related, not only with each other but also with the challenges of national security and stability within England. The Anglo-Spanish peace negotiations with the French presented Cecil with a problem, because the queen demanded the return of Calais or, in lieu of that, an unrealistically large indemnity. Although he was not directly involved in the discussions, he recognised that the government depended on Spanish support simply to terminate hostilities, because it lacked coercive power to secure anything more. Yet, at the same time, he had to contend with a royal mistress who threatened her negotiators with decapitation if they agreed to peace without the restoration of Calais. On 19 March 1559 a peace treaty left Calais in French hands, but with the face-saving formula that it would be restored after eight years. Of course it never was.[10]

If Cecil was not actively engaged in the peace negotiations with France he was, in contrast, instrumental in resolving the Scottish problem, at least in the short term. Mary Stuart's claim to the English throne was both an affront and a threat to Elizabeth. Furthermore, when Henry II of France was killed in July 1559 Mary became queen-consort of Francis II and the danger of French rule in Scotland increased. By then, however, Scottish Protestant nobles were raising rebellion against Mary of Guise's French-Catholic regency. Cecil saw it as an opportunity to expel the French from Scotland, assert England's lordship over its neighbour and thereby secure its northern border. This was a complex task, which would test his diplomatic and political skills. He persuaded a divided Privy Council to support action, but the conflict of priorities with the queen was more difficult to resolve. Elizabeth had no sympathy with either Scottish Presbyterianism or its inspiration, John Knox. Her innate political conservatism also deplored rebellion against an anointed monarch, even though the monarch in this case was an absentee Catholic, Mary Stuart. Relations between queen and minister were sorely strained and with 'sorrowful heart and watery eyes' he contemplated stepping down. Yet step-by-step he accomplished his aim. Elizabeth provided the Scottish rebels with money, then weapons, naval assistance and finally troops. The operation was typically underfunded and militarily inept. When, however, France agreed to negotiate, it was the Secretary of State who travelled north in May 1560 to conduct the peace negotiations. The Treaty of Edinburgh, which he and Dr Nicholas Wotton signed in July 1560, was a personal triumph for him. The French military presence ended, a Scottish government was installed, some fortresses were to be demolished, and Elizabeth's 'undoubted right to the Crown of England and Ireland is fully confessed and acknowledged'. It illustrates, once again, Cecil's capacity for bold action, even at the risk of royal displeasure. It also demonstrates how the queen was, in Wallace MacCaffrey's words, 'very much a novice in her royal profession'.[11]

Elizabeth's inherited legacies from previous reigns were not only religious, political and international, but economic too. Successive devaluations of the coinage in the reigns of Henry VIII and Edward VI had stimulated inflation and reduced the value of English currency on foreign exchanges. This increased the cost of imports – particularly serious because England imported such a wide variety of commodities for its manufacturing industries and for basic and luxury consumption. The new government was deluged with advice on currency reform, not only from private individuals and financial reformers such as Thomas Gresham, but also from Secretary Cecil (who introduced Gresham to the queen). He argued, we are told, 'that [the] realm cannot be rich whose coin is poor or base, and he would also say . . . that [the] realm must needs be poor that carrieth not out more than it bringeth in'.

He was, however, preaching to the converted. Elizabeth, who had drafted a memorandum on the subject, intended reform from the very beginning of the reign. In 1560–61 a new coinage, with increased silver content, replaced the old debased currency. Although it did not halt inflation, it restored England's position in the international money market. William Camden recorded the revaluation as her greatest achievement and the inscription on her tomb acknowledges it as one of her three great successes, next only to the settlement of religion and a long period of peace. The anonymous biographer typically overstated Cecil's originating role in the process, attributing the recoinage to his 'politic advice'. However, Conyers Read is probably correct when he argues that, at the practical level, the Secretary 'provided the ways and means'.[12]

The government's actions in 1559–61 established the new regime on a firm and stable footing. It was, however, still beset with problems. The statutory settlement of religion in 1559 was followed by the royal injunctions of the same year. Some of these emphasised conservative practices, such as clerical dress, church music, kneeling at communion and the requirement that congregations bow their heads when Jesus was named. The thirty-nine articles of faith, devised by Convocation in 1563, were also an amalgam which did not satisfy the godly Protestants. They regarded the settlement of 1559 as a starting point for further reformation, whereas Elizabeth viewed it rather as the terminus. Where did Cecil take his stand in this division of opinion? He was, as events were to demonstrate, a political Protestant. A politically stable kingdom took clear precedence over a godly community, modelled on Calvin's Geneva. He was at the same time, however (and unlike his queen), a supporter of moderate reform, both in 'matters indifferent' and in measures designed to improve the education and preaching skills of the clergy.

Elizabeth's insistence that ministers wear traditional clerical garb provoked the vestiarian controversy, characterised by widespread resistance and public outbursts in London. So in 1565 she insisted that the bishops devise a set of orders for conformity. The so-called *Advertisements* were drawn up in 1565 and issued, without the queen's public support, in the following year. They contributed to the rise of nonconforming puritanism and its most radical, even revolutionary, expression, Presbyterianism. The position which Cecil assumed in this controversy was characteristic of him. He may have sympathised privately with the nonconformists. Nevertheless, he gave precedence to order and stability and so, in his public capacities as Secretary and as chancellor of the University of Cambridge, he sought obedience and conformity.[13]

Internal religious division was flanked by escalating religious conflict in France and Scotland. Across the English Channel there was a deteriorating political situation, as religious conflict developed between Huguenots (Protestants) and Catholics under Guise leadership, resulting in the outbreak of civil war in 1562. The advantages of English military intervention in France were increasingly canvassed in Elizabethan governing circles and Cecil was no exception. It could benefit the Protestant and English causes because a Guise triumph might draw France and Spain together, threatening both Elizabeth's kingdom and its religion. Furthermore, conquered French territory might be used as a bargaining counter for the restoration of Calais, an argument which particularly appealed to the queen. On the other hand, the cautious, cost-counting and politically calculating Secretary was well aware of the administrative and financial liabilities which such intervention might entail. Doubts and fears were confirmed when the resultant English expeditionary force, despatched to Normandy in 1562–63, proved to be a costly and humiliating failure. The final outcome, the treaty of Troyes, in April 1564 yielded Elizabeth nothing but modest financial compensation, which fell far short of the costs of war. It may also have persuaded Cecil to be cautious about such foreign adventures in the future.[14]

The Guise connection linked together not only Scottish and French political developments but also the English political situation in the 1560s. The Scottish queen, Mary, part-Stuart and part-Guise, claimed the right to the English throne and demanded that Elizabeth recognise this. This would have mattered less if Elizabeth had heirs of her body, but she was unmarried. So long as she remained a spinster, England's future stability remained in doubt and, in consequence, the succession became a controversial and sustained issue. The pretensions of Mary Stuart, who styled herself 'Queen of England', magnified and intensified the issue, which also took on a sense of urgency. Wife of Francis, heir to the French throne, she became queen of France when he succeeded Henry II as king in 1559. However, Francis II died in December 1560 and, in August of the following year, she returned to rule Scotland without relinquishing her claim to the English throne too. It was still generally assumed by the male governing class in England that Elizabeth would marry, mother heirs and leave governance to her consort. In the meantime, however, she was expected to designate an order of succession. Her near-death from smallpox in 1562 emphasised the need for immediate action on this. Elizabeth, who seems to have feared the creation of a reversionary interest if she named a successor, refused to do so. Cecil, however, was anxious that she should settle the matter and guarantee political stability, either by marriage or a designated order of succession.

The only two viable candidates as legitimate heirs, if Elizabeth should die childless, were Mary Stuart and Catherine Grey. Catholic Mary was unacceptable in Protestant governing circles. To Cecil in particular she was abhorrent. Although he was only a moderate Protestant, he was rabidly anti-Catholic, because he regarded Catholicism, whether Spanish, French or domestic, as the prime threat to England's political stability and independence. The other candidate, Catherine Grey, was widely canvassed by Protestants, including John Hales, a minor royal official, who in early 1563 wrote a pamphlet advancing her claims and rejecting those of others. By then, however, Catherine had contracted a clandestine marriage with Edward, earl of Hertford, and, as Cecil wrote to the earl of Sussex on 12 August 1561, she is 'big with child' and committed with her husband to the Tower. A commission of enquiry appointed by the queen invalidated the marriage and from then on Catherine's was a lost cause. So, when Hales' pamphlet appeared in print, Elizabeth launched another enquiry because she suspected that others were involved in its promotion and publication. Although discreet Cecil was not among them, telling Sir Thomas Smith that 'surely I am and always have been circumspect to do nothing to make offence', the queen was not entirely convinced.[15]

There remained the viable alternative of royal matrimony, and Elizabeth was certainly not short of suitors. During the first ten years of her reign they included Philip II of Spain, the earl of Arran (heir to the Scottish throne), King Erik XIV of Sweden, the boy-king Charles IX of France and especially Archduke Charles, younger son of the Habsburg German emperor. The archduke's suit, which was favoured by most Privy Councillors and especially by Cecil, was prolonged but also doomed to failure. Elizabeth would not accede to the Austrian insistence that Charles should be allowed the open practice of his Catholic religion and she was equally insistent that she should meet him first, before making a decision. By the end of the 1560s negotiations had fizzled out and so had Cecil's hopes.[16] Perhaps Elizabeth was simply game-playing. Cecil and his fellow councillors should have heeded her words to the 1559 parliament: that she would be content to live and die a virgin.

There was one important exception to the queen's game-playing, if that indeed is what it was. In January 1559 she appointed Robert Dudley, son of the Edwardian duke of Northumberland, as master of the horse. Her evident infatuation for him and his ambition to marry her provoked scandalous rumour and threatened the stability and integrity of the regime, especially as he already had a neglected and ailing wife, Amy Robsart. When, in September 1560, she was found dead at the foot of the stairs in their home, there was widespread suspicion of murder. Whether or not Elizabeth had wished to marry him, that was now out of the question. In contrast to Mary Stuart, Elizabeth would not risk political scandal and conceivably her throne for a match made possible by highly suspicious circumstances. Nevertheless, in 1559 she had made him a Privy Councillor and five years later she elevated him to the earldom of Leicester. Dudley was not merely a handsome and charming courtier but an active politician who brought with him an influential following. As such he became a challenge and a rival to Cecil in the inner counsels of government. His pretensions to the place of royal consort were slow to wither and die and he was active in attempts to influence royal policy directions.

Cecil did not remain quiescent in the face of such challenges. In 1566 he drafted a memorandum, which weighed up the pros and cons of marriage to Archduke Charles and the earl of Leicester. The former would guarantee the friendship of the Spanish Habsburg King Philip II and provide the means to resist France and Mary Stuart. In contrast, 'Nothing is increased by marriage' to Leicester, who was 'infamed by death of his wife . . . far in debt' and anxious only 'to enhance his own particular friends to wealth, to offices, to lands'. One cannot imagine Cecil presenting this to the queen, but it does clearly identify his policy position on a hoped-for royal marriage.[17] Whilst he would not overtly challenge her apparent inclination towards a Dudley marriage, he was prepared to counter actively her favourite's Catholic Spanish dalliance in foreign affairs. In 1561 Dudley had a hand in an attempt by the Spanish ambassador, Alvarez de Quadra, to persuade Elizabeth to admit a papal nuncio into England. Cecil fortuitously uncovered a Catholic conspiracy and thereby put an end to the scheme. In 1564 he also supported Elizabeth's proposal for the marriage of Dudley (now Leicester) to Mary Stuart, partly because it would remove his chief rival in Court and council and terminate the possibility of a matrimonial alliance with the English queen.

The Anglo-Scottish marriage did not eventuate. Favourite and Secretary remained rivals on the English political scene, especially during the crisis years of 1568–72. They often disagreed on policy directions, especially in foreign affairs. Nevertheless, in Penry Williams' words, 'for the most part their rivalry was friendly and contained'. When the scandal of his wife's death destroyed Dudley's prospects of marriage to Elizabeth, he wrote to Cecil, 'I thank you very much for your being here. And the great friendship you have showed towards me, I shall not forget . . . Forget me not, though you see me not, and I will remember you and fail ye not.' Later, Cecil was to commend Leicester for advising the queen to marry Archduke Charles or the young French king, 'Wherein surely, perceiving his own cause not separable, he doth honourably and wisely'. Often thereafter, for as long as Leicester lived, they would write to or about each other in courteous and friendly fashion. They were not competing faction leaders. Indeed, Cecil wrote to his confidant and friend, Sir Thomas Smith, in 1565, 'I have no affection to be of a party, but for the Queen's Majesty.'[18]

Widespread concern within the English governing élite, that the succession had not been settled, ensured that the subject would be raised when parliament met in 1563. The purpose of its summons was financial assistance towards the cost of the expedition to Normandy to help the French Huguenots. Cecil, returned as senior knight for Northamptonshire, now emerged as the government's front man and parliamentary manager. He had already organised the drafting of the subsidy bill before parliament met. On 20 January he moved for a subsidy, making 'an excellent declaration . . . of the great charges defrayed by the queen's majesty and of the causes of the wars in France . . . concluding to consider for the aid'. Later in the session he was instrumental in seeing through the commons a bill to increase both the strength of the navy and English fishing fleets.

Whilst the Secretary worked dutifully to accomplish the queen's financial objectives in parliament, he knew that a settled succession would be the ultimate political priority of many members. He certainly wanted it and perhaps he even sought it, especially after the queen's near-fatal bout of smallpox. As he told Sir Thomas Smith, 'I think somewhat will be attempted to ascertain the realm of a successor to this crown, but I fear the unwillingness of her Majesty to have such a person known will stay the matter.'[19] It is difficult to believe that he was not aware of the parliamentary pressure which would be placed on her. On 19 January the commons appointed a committee to draw up a petition, requesting Elizabeth to name a successor if marriage was not soon forthcoming. The committee's draft was read to the house by Thomas Norton, a Londoner who was emerging as, and would continue to be for eighteen years, Cecil's most energetic parliamentary aide. This suggests that Cecil was privately in sympathy with the petitioners and even covertly organising pressure on the queen. All of his endeavours, however, came to naught, because Elizabeth rejected pressure either to marry or to order the succession. At the end of the session he grumbled that 'I am so fully occupied to expedite matters in this Parliament that I have no leisure almost to attend any other things'. But he was unable to expedite what mattered most to him – a settled succession.[20]

When, more than three years later, in September 1566, parliament was recalled for money, neither marriage nor succession were any nearer resolution. Continuing and growing concern about future stability and security made it inevitable that these matters would be raised – and, perhaps, with more urgency than they had been in 1563. Furthermore, Privy Council and governing class were both divided over the credentials of the rival candidates to succeed Elizabeth if she died childless: Mary Stuart and Catherine Grey. Historians are not in agreement as to what happened in this session or what the motives and objectives of the major participants were. One thing is clear, however, and that is the queen's insistence that she, not parliament, had the sole right to arrange the succession. However, although the evidence is patchy and the story is punctuated with gaps of ignorance, it is possible to identify Cecil's objectives, and to sketch at least the outlines of his performance in pursuit of them. One can also detect, at least at this stage in his career, his continued willingness and ability to take risks when he believed that the circumstances warranted it.

In this, as so often in future parliaments, Cecil's conduct was dichotomous: he laboured in the royal interest, but this sometimes necessitated lobbying against the queen in order to compel her into action in what he perceived to be her own best interest. In specific terms, in 1566 he sought a subsidy grant and a settled succession. On the one hand, as chief conciliar manager in the commons, he 'made an excellent Declaration of the Queen's charges'. A committee was promptly appointed to consider the tax rates and times of payment, and it was Cecil who assumed control of the committee, recorded those who attended and the agreed rates, and on 19 October reported back to the house on its proposals. It was another peacetime tax, but there were precedents for that and, in any case, it was to be made by instalments over a longer period than usual. Nevertheless, the subsidy bill moved slowly and by 27 November it had had only one reading. Then the queen publicly remitted one-third of the tax, whereupon the commons gratefully gave it a second reading. However, the measure was then committed – unusual for the subsidy – and it did not finally pass the house until 12 December. The delay was caused by 'arguments' over the subsidy preamble, partly over the wording of the tax grant, but also because some members wanted it to include a promise to arrange the succession and to commit herself to marriage. Indeed, it helps to explain the slow passage of the subsidy bill because there was widespread commons' concern and activity 'to the end to have the succession established': for example, a lords' deputation and bicameral preparations for a joint petition, forestalled by the queen's intervention. Cecil was no neutral bystander, as his own jottings indicate, although how actively involved he was in the parliamentary attempts to pressure Elizabeth into action on this occasion is not known. Certainly he was prominent in drafting the subsidy preamble which she so angrily rejected. So the queen obtained some much-needed money without surrendering her freedom of initiative on marriage and succession. Cecil's gloomy memorial, drafted near the end of the session, reflects his disappointment:

> The succession not answered
> The marriage not followed.

Even the one important achievement of the session, the subsidy, yielded less much-needed money, because of the queen's remittance of the third instalment. Cecil's personal parliamentary experience in 1566 was to be repeated in the future: his loyal duty as the queen's servant and councillor at times conflicted with his frustration at her obstinate inaction, his unspoken belief (implicit in the memorial) that she was wrong and his conviction that he knew what was best for her and the realm. At a Privy Council meeting before parliament met, he had discussed tactics for trying to secure the queen's marriage or her naming of a successor to the throne and later Elizabeth actually accused him of stirring up the commons.[21]

Despite continued governing-class concern about the succession (especially Mary Stuart's pretensions to the English crown), growing trade problems with the Low Countries,[22] and the increasing frustration of many English Protestants at the lack of further reformation, a process of political stabilisation occurred during the 1560s. It was, to some extent at least, a consequence of the actions and policies of the queen and her councillors, especially Cecil, not only in domestic affairs but also in international relations. The traditional fundamentals of English foreign policy were, in the words of the experienced politician William Lord Paget, 'natural enmity' with France and the consequent need for amity with the House of Burgundy, which ruled the Low Countries. Unfinished cloth, which was England's chief export and, in the form of export customs duties, the crown's most important source of revenue, was traded in the Low Countries. Therefore it was economic and financial common sense to maintain friendly relations with its ruler, Philip II, the widower of Elizabeth's half-sister, Mary I. As king of Spain, with a Mediterranean and New World empire, Philip was the most powerful prince in Christian Europe. Therefore it was also political common sense to cultivate his friendship as a security against France and its Scottish connection. This is what Elizabeth endeavoured to do throughout the 1560s, at least until 1568. She operated through Cecil, whose task it was to manage international relations in accordance with her policy guidelines. However, the burdens of responsibility and his capacity for hard work took their toll. He suffered from recurrent illnesses, especially gout.[23] Then, in 1568, Mary Stuart's arrival in England began a reverse process of political destabilisation.

Events in Scotland during the 1560s had repercussions in English domestic politics and at times imperilled Cecil's position. Amongst the possible candidates as Elizabeth's successor were Margaret Douglas, Henry VIII's niece and countess of Lennox, and her son Henry Lord Darnley. However, in 1565 Darnley also became a suitor for Mary Stuart's hand in marriage. During the previous two years Elizabeth had proposed that the Scottish queen should take Robert Dudley as her consort and she had created him earl of Leicester in order to enhance his status and acceptability. Leicester, who still sought to be the English queen's consort, opposed the move. Cecil, who was quick to see the personal benefit to be derived from this, was in favour. It was equally understandable that Leicester should approve of Mary's growing attachment to Darnley and that Cecil should fear it. As he recorded, in a memorandum of 2 June 1565 and in his account of a Privy Council meeting two days later, the Mary–Darnley marriage would combine to threaten Elizabeth's throne and strengthen 'the Romish religion'.[24] Shortly afterwards Mary seized the political and diplomatic initiative when, on 29 July 1565, she married Darnley. The future James VI of Scotland and I of England was born on 19 June in the following year. The fact that Mary already had an heir, whilst Elizabeth remained unmarried and childless, must have heightened the succession concerns of Cecil and other members of the two houses when parliament met just over three months later.

The conduct of the dissolute, irresponsible Scottish king-consort, however, triggered a dramatic sequence of events which no one could have predicted. On 9 March 1566 a group of nobles, urged on by the suspicious and jealous Darnley, dragged the queen's secretary, David Riccio, from her presence and murdered him. In February 1567 Darnley too was killed. The earl of Bothwell was the suspected perpetrator and Mary's complicity was widely believed. Popular suspicion seemed to be confirmed when the queen was willingly abducted by Bothwell and bound in marriage to him. There followed, in quick succession, noble rebellion, her military defeat, abdication, imprisonment, escape, yet another defeat in battle, and flight into England in May 1568, in search of Elizabeth's assistance against her rebellious subjects. Scottish developments between Darnley's murder and Mary's flight imposed considerable strain on relations between Elizabeth and Cecil. There was a natural and basic difference in priorities: Cecil saw the possibility of friendly relations with the Protestant regency government which had been established in Scotland when Mary fell. Elizabeth could not contemplate collaboration with rebels, who had deposed an anointed monarch. Her prime objective was the liberation of the Scottish queen. The Secretary was, for a time, under a cloud of royal disfavour. Mary's arrival in England simply added to his problems. Would Elizabeth act to restore her to the Scottish throne? How would her presence on English soil affect international relations? Would she also become a focus for alienated English Catholicism and discontented, marginalised political elements? The 'crisis' years of 1568–72 would provide Cecil with some of the answers.

. . .

NOTES

1. e.g., *HMC*, Salisbury MS, I, nos. 403, 434; Haynes (ed.), *State Papers*, p. 131; Read, *Secretary Cecil*, pp. 63–5, 473 n. 13; Beckingsale, *Burghley*, pp. 66–7. Clapham regarded Cecil as acting deviously with an eye to the future: secretly offering his service to the Lady Elizabeth, 'by little and little [he] insinuated himself into her good opinion'. *Clapham*, p. 74.
2. PRO, SP, 12/1/7; Read, *Secretary Cecil*, p. 119.
3. Hurstfield, 'Minister to Elizabeth I', p. 799.
4. Norman L. Jones, *Faith by Statute: Parliament and the Settlement of Religion 1559* (London, 1982), pp. 17–26, 31, 36–47; idem, *The Birth of the Elizabethan Age: England in the 1560s* (Oxford, 1993), pp. 12–13; P.L. Hughes and J.F. Larkin, *Tudor Royal Proclamations*, 3 vols (London, 1964–69), II, pp. 102–3.
5. Jones, *Faith by Statute*, pp. 84–127; *APC*, VII, p. 78; R. Brown *et al.* (eds), *Calendar of State Papers, Venetian*, 9 vols (London, 1864–98), VII, p. 65.
6. Jones, *Faith by Statute*, pp. 129–150; A. Luders, T.E. Tomlins *et al.* (eds), *Statutes of the Realm*, 11 vols (London, 1810–28), IV, pp. 350–8.
7. Guy, *Tudor England*, pp. 253–4; Jones, *Faith by Statute*, pp. 32–4; P. Williams, *The Tudor Regime* (Oxford, 1979), pp. 425–6, 453.
8. M.A.S. Hume (ed.), *Calendar of State Papers, Spanish, 1558–67* (London, 1892), p. 33; Jones, *Faith by Statute*, p. 151; Smith (ed.), *Anon. Life*, pp. 56–7; P. Collinson, *Elizabethan Essays* (London, 1994), p. 239.
9. Advowsons – the right of appointment to church livings – and tithes were not in practice equitable financial compensation for the loss of estates.
10. Haigh (ed.), *Reign of Elizabeth*, p. 35; Beckingsale, *Burghley*, pp. 70–1, 74, 86; Haynes (ed.), *State Papers*, pp. 342–3; Read, *Secretary Cecil*, pp. 390–1.
11. Beckingsale, *Burghley*, pp. 78–85; Haigh (ed.), *Reign of Elizabeth*, pp. 48–9; W.T. MacCaffrey, *Elizabeth I* (London, 1993), pp. 63–4, 67, 359–60; Haynes (ed.), *State Papers*, pp. 327, 334–5, 346–7, 351–7.
12. Palliser, *Age of Elizabeth*, pp. 137–9; Jones, *Birth of Elizabethan Age*, pp. 230–6; Smith (ed.), *Anon. Life*, pp. 57–8; Read, *Secretary Cecil*, pp. 122, 194–7.

13. P. Collinson, *The Elizabethan Puritan Movement* (London, 1967), pp. 69–70; Jones, *Birth of Elizabethan Age*, pp. 53–65; Read, *Secretary Cecil*, pp. 358–9; see below, p. 177.
14. Read, *Secretary Cecil*, pp. 239–60; Beckingsale, *Burghley*, pp. 95–9, 101–2; T. Wright (ed.), *Queen Elizabeth and her Times*, 2 vols (London, 1838), I, pp. 93–6, 116–23, 130–3.
15. Williams, *Later Tudors*, p. 243; Read, *Secretary Cecil*, pp. 230, 234; Graves, *Norton*, pp. 101–3; Wright (ed.), *Queen Elizabeth*, I, pp. 68–9, 172–3, 179–80.
16. Read, *Secretary Cecil*, pp. 326, 334, 336–7; Wright (ed.), *Queen Elizabeth*, I, pp. 183–4, 211.
17. Haynes (ed.), *State Papers*, p. 444.
18. Williams, *Later Tudors*, p. 242; Haynes (ed.), *State Papers*, pp. 361–2; Wright (ed.), *Queen Elizabeth*, I, p. 209.
19. *CJ*, I, p. 63; P.W. Hasler (ed.), *The House of Commons, 1558–1603*, 3 vols (London, 1981), I, pp. 583–4; Wright (ed.), *Queen Elizabeth*, I, p. 121.
20. *CJ*, I, pp. 63, 72; Neale, *Eliz. I and Parls.*, I, p. 127; Wright (ed.), *Queen Elizabeth*, I, p. 126.
21. See below, p. 96; G.R. Elton, *The Parliament of England, 1559–1581* (Cambridge, 1986), pp. 162–5 and n. 54, 365; PRO, SP, 12/40/88 and 102; *CJ*, I, pp. 74–5, 78–9; Neale, *Eliz. I and Parls.*, I, pp. 162–4; PRO, SP, 12/40/68; ibid., 12/41/36; Beckingsale, *Burghley*, pp. 110–13; M. Levine, *The Early Elizabethan Succession Question, 1558–1568* (Stanford, Calif., 1966), pp. 171–88.
22. Read, *Secretary Cecil*, pp. 289–92, 295–300.
23. Ibid., p. 369; Beckingsale, *Burghley*, pp. 112–13.
24. Read, *Secretary Cecil*, pp. 318–25.

Chapter 3

CRISIS AND THE GROWTH OF CONFLICT, 1568–83

Mary Stuart's arrival in England in May 1568 deeply disturbed Cecil. Two years earlier William Maitland Lord Lethington, Mary's adviser, had written to him asserting that she was 'undoubtedly heir to the crown' and especially rejecting the argument which the Secretary seems to have upheld that, as a foreigner, she was 'incapable of the inheritance of England'. In a memorandum drafted shortly after Mary fled to England, however, Cecil marshalled arguments which reflected his constant hostility to her. He stressed the need for action: to counter her dangerous and unacceptable claim to be queen of England, not after Elizabeth 'but afore her', and to preserve the recent alliance with Scotland. However, he also saw dangers in every alternative course of action, whether she was isolated in England, returned to Scotland or sent to France. The situation was further complicated by Elizabeth's emphasis on legitimacy and her preference for a Marian restoration. Finally, it was decided to hold her in isolation from possible political contacts and to conduct an investigation into her guilt or innocence with respect to her husband's murder.

Sir Francis Knollys, in whose custody Mary was placed when she arrived in England, observed her to be a formidable combatant and told Cecil so:

> [T]his lady and princess is a notable woman . . . She showeth a disposition . . . to be bold . . . a great desire to be avenged of her enemies [and] . . . a readiness to expose herself to all perils in hope of victory . . . The thing that most she thirsteth after is victory, and it seemeth to be indifferent to her to have her enemies diminished, either by the sword of her friends . . . or by division or quarrels raised among themselves.

Knollys also passed on her warning to him that 'if we did detain her as a prisoner, we should have much ado with her'. The implications of what he said agreed with the Secretary's own opinion. He consistently believed that Mary wanted to be queen of two kingdoms and that, in order to achieve her ends, she would attempt to bring in foreign allies and become a focus of Catholic and other discontents in England.[1]

Cecil was not mistaken, because the entry of the deposed Scottish queen into England was a catalyst, which fused together internal and international politico-religious problems. On the one hand she arrived during a diplomatic revolution, in which there was a progressive role-reversal between traditional Anglo-Burgundian amity and Anglo-French enmity. The English government's relations with Spain deteriorated during the 1560s, due to its sympathy (rather than active support) for the Low Countries' rising against Spanish rule from 1566 and, in the following year, Sir John Hawkins' invasion of the Spanish New World trade monopoly. In 1568 both countries recalled their ambassadors and, although Philip II replaced his, the new appointee, Guerau de Spes, was aggressive and hostile to Cecil.[2]

There is no evidence that the Secretary advocated assistance for the Dutch or approved Hawkins' venture. Yet his conduct in 1568 indicates that, nonetheless, he had taken up an anti-Spanish position. Later in that year some Spanish ships, en route to the Low Countries, took shelter in English harbours from storms and French Protestant privateers. They were carrying a consignment of money, loaned to Philip II by Italian bankers in Genoa and destined for the new military regime of the duke of Alva in the Low Countries. At de Spes' request, Elizabeth agreed to provide the vessels with a protective escort to Antwerp, but then changed her mind and borrowed the money herself. She justified her action on the grounds that the money was not Philip's legal property until it was delivered in the Low Countries. The ambassador encouraged Alva to take reprisals and he promptly confiscated English property and arrested English merchants, whereupon the English government retaliated in kind. The result was a serious diplomatic crisis which even threatened war. This was averted because it was not in the interest of either side. Nevertheless, this challenge to Spanish power and a trade embargo, which lasted until 1573, marked a dramatic foreign policy shift for which

Cecil was primarily responsible. An Anglo-Spanish agreement, negotiated in 1572, did not restore cordial relations, but simply poured oil on the troubled waters of the last few years.[3]

At the same time Cecil was prominent in the diplomatic activity leading to an Anglo-French rapprochement. In his lengthy *Short Memorial of the State of the Realm*, drafted in 1569, he argued that both France and Spain wanted to restore Roman Catholicism throughout Christian Europe and that they would use Mary Stuart as 'Instrument' to accomplish their purpose in England.[4] In contrast to the provocative anti-Spanish conduct over the Genoese loan, however, Cecil's attitude to France was cautious, even conciliatory. When religious civil war broke out there again in 1568, military intervention was not advocated as in 1562–63. In 1571–72, after the collapse of the project for a marriage between Elizabeth and the Austrian Archduke Charles, negotiations, supported by Cecil, were in train for her to wed the duc d'Anjou, brother of the French king. When he proved to be obdurate in his demand for the open practice of the Catholic faith, Elizabeth was offered his younger brother, the duc d'Alençon, instead. Though nothing came of either proposal, the two countries negotiated the Treaty of Blois in April 1572. It was essentially what Cecil wanted, a mutual defensive alliance, which would help to secure England and Ireland, but not an alliance of war, for which the English government lacked the resources.

Shortly afterwards, in August, there occurred the Saint Bartholomew's massacre of French Protestants in Paris and the French provinces. It provoked public outrage in the English Court and governing circles, but neither monarch nor minister was prepared to let it damage or negate the new alliance. Firm Protestant that he was, Cecil was appalled, but he was playing for the high stakes of national and dynastic security. In any case, although he was prominent in the queen's counsels, there were clear limits to both his influence and authority in matters of policy. The queen sought advice from other Privy Councillors, some of whom, such as Leicester, were willing to disagree with him.[5]

Mary Stuart's arrival in England in 1568 and England's diplomatic realignments of the following years were inseparable from the internal political crisis of 1568–72. Indeed, in large measure they contributed to it. It was also a time of crisis and eventual triumph for Cecil. The Elizabethan political world was not characterised by faction conflict before the 1590s. Nevertheless, it was a keen and often competitive climate, in which prominent courtier-politicians vied for influence with the queen, her favour and the profits which could accrue from that. Cecil, the bureaucratic, methodical royal workhorse, was a member of the Privy Council, which held its meetings at Court; he needed regular access to the queen; and he was her personal secretary. Although he was not a fashion-conscious peacock like the courtly, good-looking Leicester, who aspired to be her consort, he was no less the courtier-politician. During the 1560s the two men often conflicted as a consequence of their competitive ambitions and their policy differences. They disagreed, for example, over the choice of marriage partners for both the English and Scottish queens, and Leicester's brief advocacy of a pro-Spanish position.[6] Yet rivalry was not synonymous with enmity.[7] This is true of many of the prominent political aristocrats of the 1560s. The duke of Norfolk, as the earl of Sussex lamented to Cecil, stood in 1569 'in worse terms of amity than you in foretimes did', but later he expressed relief at their rapprochement.[8] However, Mary Stuart's arrival in England brought together a number of internal discontents, which focused on the queen's Secretary as villain or possibly as convenient scapegoat. Cecil's personal crisis in 1569 in some ways parallels that of Thomas Cromwell thirty years before. He was, in the eyes of some, the archetypal *nouveau*, displacing the noble counsellors of ancient lineage. Furthermore, he was the Protestant minister, sidelining old reputable Catholic families, such as those of the northern earls of Westmorland and Northumberland and the southern earl of Arundel. Rival and jealous courtiers, such as the earls of Pembroke and Leicester, sought to bring him down, for policy as well as personal reasons.

The catalyst of crisis was the Norfolk–Mary marriage scheme. It was supported by a broad aristocratic network, including nobles of both Protestant and Catholic faith. Its objectives were settlement of the succession and establishment of more amicable relations with Spain. These required in turn the removal of Cecil. He was staunchly anti-Catholic and consistently hostile to Mary. He was also regarded as guilty of creating Spanish hostility, by his provocative action over the Genoese loan in 1568, and of politically marginalising some of the great old noble families. The opposition to Cecil, therefore, was motivated not only by self-interest but also by a concern for national security. There developed a Court conspiracy which sought to remove him and guarantee political stability, through a marital union and revival of noble influence in royal counsels. At this point the queen rather than her Secretary became the motivating political force. As Conyers Read wrote, the conspirators 'had not yet learned Cecil was the pilot but not the captain of the ship of state'. They schemed to arrest him at a council meeting and consign him to the Tower, but, as both Clapham and Camden report, the queen learned of their intentions, personally intervened and in February 1569 'prevented the same before it came to execution'.[9] Then in September Leicester, one of the conspirators, informed Elizabeth of the projected marriage. Norfolk, displaying characteristic indecision and cowardice, fled but soon returned to accommodation in the Tower. The northern earls, Northumberland and Westmorland, then rose in rebellion, but failed to secure mass support or to free Mary Stuart. The uprising collapsed and the earls fled.

So the next phase in the crisis was over, but not the crisis itself. A papal bull, *Regnans in Excelsis,* condemning Elizabeth as heretic excommunicate and usurper and depriving her of the crown, was already in circulation among the northern rebels. In the following year it was publicly released and called upon her subjects to reject her orders and authority, on pain of excommunication. By then Cecil was firmly in control. Events had worked in his favour, the queen had publicly endorsed her trust in him and those who had manœuvred against him were discredited or divided, either by their religion or their personal interests. As for Norfolk, he had learned no lessons from his experience when he was released from the Tower in August 1570. Although he had submitted to the queen and solemnly undertaken not to marry Mary Stuart, he continued his dalliance with her. Worse still, he became embroiled in a conspiracy, masterminded by an Italian financier, Robert Ridolfi, to free Mary Stuart, marry her to Norfolk and restore England to Catholicism. Spain and English Catholics were drawn into the grand scheme. Even before Cecil knew of his complicity in the Ridolfi plot, he had got the measure of England's only duke. As early as January 1569 he had drafted a damning commentary on Norfolk's marital schemes 'without making her Majesty privy thereto'. When Elizabeth's government uncovered the conspiracy and identified the culprits, Norfolk was doomed.

In January 1572 he was convicted of treason and on 2 June he was executed.

So Cecil emerged from the crisis of 1568–72 with his status, prestige and authority enhanced. Throughout those years he had dutifully continued to fulfil his role as counsellor and watchdog in the queen's interest. He investigated disloyalty, promoted the ardently anti-Catholic Francis Walsingham and drafted characteristically wide-ranging and weighty policy memoranda on strategies to be pursued, whilst pursuing those who would threaten her rule. His opponents were in disarray, in flight, tainted with treason or, like the earl of Leicester, seeking ways back into royal favour. Meanwhile, in March 1570 the queen delegated to Cecil the responsibility for stamping her letters – a signal mark of trust in a royal servant.[10] Furthermore, less than a year later, on 25 February 1571 (during a winter in which he was for some time crippled with gout), Cecil was elevated to the peerage. The queen made him Baron of Burghley: partly for his services before and during her reign, but also for his circumspection, wisdom, faithfulness and other qualities recited in the letters patent of creation. His ennoblement, during the extended political crisis since 1568, was a public royal expression of support for him. It was also significant that, during the ceremony, he was escorted by the earl of Leicester. They remained competitors for influence with the queen. However, although Leicester was party to the attempt to unseat Cecil in 1569, that resort to such drastic courses of action was exceptional. As Simon Adams and John Guy have stressed, Elizabethan politics, at least before the 1590s, was marked by collegiality rather than by factionalism.[11]

On 2 April 1571, just five weeks after his ennoblement, Burghley took his seat in the house of lords. It was an emergency Parliament, summoned to deal with the prolonged and deepening crisis of which the catalyst was Mary Stuart. In 1570, prior to his ennoblement, he and Sir Walter Mildmay were sent by Elizabeth to negotiate with Mary the terms of her restoration to the Scottish throne. They duly reported to the queen, but there is no record of the Secretary's opinion of her as a consequence of their personal contact. The only guide is his unremitting pursuit of her destruction in the years which followed.[12] This is because she became central to his conception of a grand Catholic conspiracy against his royal mistress, her government and kingdom. This was a conspiracy which encompassed the Papacy, Spain, the English Catholic community and Mary Stuart. It is highly improbable that any such grand design existed at this time. Nevertheless, it seems to have motivated the Secretary's thinking and actions. He personally penned uninspired, even turgid and thankfully unpublished tracts against the northern rebels and the papal bull. He also began to utilise the services of clients, who, before and after his ennoblement, helped to advance his causes in a variety of ways. The most prominent and active was, as previously mentioned, Thomas Norton, who rushed into print racy, colourful pamphlets against the 'pretended marriage' of Mary Stuart and Norfolk, the northern rebels of 1569 and the papal bull of 1570.[13]

Cecil's need of these men was heightened during the two 'crisis' parliaments of 1571 and 1572. The house of lords, in which he now sat, was capable of influencing the commons and even guiding the opinions of some of its members. Nevertheless, Burghley still needed eyes, ears and managers there for a variety of reasons: radical Protestant manœuvres required to be monitored, even obstructed, and personal projects necessitated prompters and promoters. Above all, when he set out to press the queen into particular courses of action – against disloyal English Catholics, traitors such as the duke of Norfolk, and the ultimate target, Mary queen of Scots – he depended on 'front men' in the lower house to publicly risk what he would not dare. The precise nature of the relationship between Burghley, the parliamentary manager, and those members of the commons who worked on his behalf, cannot always be evidentially confirmed. Sometimes we are driven back to possibilities or probabilities of a circumstantial kind. Nevertheless, there is sufficient evidence of an ongoing utilisation of such men both within and outside parliament. And Norton himself acknowledged that Burghley and other councillors employed him in 'the parliament time'.[14]

The 1571 parliament met in the gathering shadow of Mary Stuart's arrival in England, the northern Catholic earls' rebellion, and the papal bull excommunicating Elizabeth in 1570. Lord Keeper Bacon's opening address to parliament explained the purpose of its meeting in characteristically vague terms: 'for defence of the state'. That uninformative statement was the prelude to the introduction of a conciliar legislative programme. It consisted of a new treason law, a measure against the importation of papal bulls and another to punish the leaders of the northern rebellion. The first of these made it treason to attempt 'any deadly hurt to her Majesty', to maintain that she was not 'lawful queen', or to declare that she was 'an heretic or usurper'. If it was an obvious, immediate response to the bull of excommunication, it also implicitly targeted Mary Stuart, who had laid claim to the English throne. After thirteen years in the service of a 'do-nothing' queen, who clung to the *status quo*, Burghley was intent on manœuvring her with parliamentary pressure to take positive action against her papal-Catholic enemies. He did this by promoting such legislative measures and encouraging parliamentary support for their enactment in order to secure Elizabeth's assent to them. She herself acknowledged the pressure on her in 1571 when she publicly declared that,

> In this parliament it was shewed us of a bill devised of for our safety against treasons, whereof when we had the sight of it liked us not. Nevertheless being persuaded by our council of the necessity thereof, and that it was for our safety, we were contented the same should proceed.[15]

In contrast, Burghley was foiled and frustrated by an obdurate queen when he supported the bill for coming to church, which was designed to combat absenteeism due both to recusancy and to apathy. Bishops and councillors promoted it – indeed, Bishop Grindal of London drafted the original proposal for the bill. It passed the commons and was amended by a lords' committee which included Burghley. After a joint conference of the two houses the upper chamber gave its assent, but then the queen vetoed it. The supreme governor, ultra-sensitive to parliamentary interference in her management of the church, also thwarted attempts to effect further religious reformation, albeit changes only of a moderate kind. Burghley was becoming adept at co-ordinating parliamentary pressure, designed to weaken royal resistance. On this subject, however, he had to walk carefully and act cautiously, because he did not want to jeopardise his position and prospects. This is evident in the case of the so-called 'alphabetical bills', labelled A to F by the commons' speaker or clerk in the parliamentary session of 1566–67, when they appeared too late to be enacted. They were not interlocking pieces of a co-ordinated reform programme. Nor were they a grand design mounted by a godly puritan opposition, as Neale argued. They were simply a medley of disparate specific proposals concerning resident clergy, corrupt presentation to church livings, simony (the buying and selling of livings) and other clerical abuses and shortcomings. The most important was Bill A, which gave statutory authority to the thirty-nine articles of religion, enacted by convocation in 1563. In 1571 the ABC bills reappeared in parliament, along with the *Reformatio Legum Ecclesiasticarum*, a codified reform of the canon law. Bishops and Burghley were deeply involved in the advancement of these projects. It was Burghley's client, Thomas Norton, who presented to the commons both the alphabetical bills and the *Reformatio*. However, when the radical puritan, William Strickland, introduced a measure to revise the book of common prayer, he effectively sabotaged the efforts of the moderate reformers. The queen stepped in and, in John Guy's words, Burghley 'ran for cover'.[16]

Even as the Secretary of State worked to advance the cause of national security in the 1571 parliament he was also unravelling the tangled threads of the Ridolfi conspiracy. It proved to be the greatest threat to Elizabethan security yet: an international alliance, encompassing the Spanish ambassador, the Papacy, Mary Stuart and some English Catholics, and also implicating the duke of Norfolk. Its dual objective was the removal of Elizabeth and her replacement by the deposed Scottish queen. Robert Ridolfi, a North Italian banker from Florence who masterminded the plot, suddenly returned home in 1571, leaving behind him conspiratorial confusion, as Norfolk was tried and condemned to death, Guerau de Spes, the Spanish ambassador, was expelled and the stage was set for the 1572 parliament. This was truly an emergency parliament, summoned to meet in May 1572, when the annual summer plague season threatened. There is little doubt that Elizabeth had been reluctant to call it and that she had done so only as a result of conciliar pressure. Norfolk had been under sentence of death since mid-January and Mary's complicity in the Ridolfi plot had been established. Yet Elizabeth was unwilling either to authorise Norfolk's execution or to proceed against another anointed monarch, albeit a deposed one. These were the all-consuming concerns of this session and Burghley, operating from the lords, was the masterminding managerial politician. Due to lack of evidence, his role in earlier Elizabethan parliaments often cannot be identified with certainty. In contrast, his objectives and activity are unmistakable in the relatively rich surviving documentary sources for this session.

When parliament opened, Lord Keeper Bacon's speech illustrated the unusual and urgent circumstances. No money was requested. Although the time of the year was 'unseasonable' for a parliament, the cause of its calling, 'to devise laws for the safety of the Queen's Majesty . . . was so necessary and so weighty as it could not otherwise be'. Thereafter Burghley's hand and influence can be detected everywhere: in the persistent lobbying for Norfolk's death, in bill drafting and amendment, joint conferences, petitioning, and in orchestration of the commons through the Speaker Robert Bell, Thomas Dannett, Thomas Digges, Thomas Norton and other conciliar clients. The queen succumbed to continuous pressure when Norfolk was executed during the session. So far as Mary was concerned, however, all their efforts were in vain. Elizabeth would not agree to a bill of attainder but only one excluding her from the succession. Even to that measure she refused her assent, after it had passed both houses.[17]

The session could have held no satisfying memories for Burghley. He was afflicted with gout and there was little reward for his pain and labour. He left no recorded comment about the death of Norfolk, at various times his friend, ally, critic and opponent, but who entrusted his children to him before he died. In contrast, he lamented at length to Francis Walsingham, both during and after the session, about the bill against Mary. On 21 May, in mid-session, he wrote that 'there can be found no more soundness than in the Common House, and no lack appearing in the higher house, but in the highest person such slowness in the offers of [security] and such [delay] in resolution as it seemeth God is not pleased that the [security] shall succeed'. The session over and his hopes dashed, Burghley confided: 'All that we laboured for and had with full consent brought to fashion, I mean a law to make the Scottish Queen unable and unworthy to wear the crown, was by her Majesty neither assented to nor rejected, but deferred . . . But what all other wise and good men may think thereof you may guess. Some here have, as it seemeth, abused their favour about her Majesty, to make herself her most enemy.' The earl of Leicester was of the same opinion. Furthermore, Burghley was addressing a receptive audience when he wrote to Walsingham, who was then ambassador to France. His revealing and confidential comment, about the queen and some of those around her, also registered his trust in the recipient of his letters. Walsingham was a devout Protestant, whose major concern was always national security against the ongoing Catholic menace, above all 'that devilish woman' Mary Stuart. Burghley, who had secured his return to the early Elizabethan parliaments, was his chief benefactor, drawing him into royal service. After diplomatic service in France in 1571–73 he was appointed Secretary of State.[18]

Walsingham's appointment was partly a recognition of his ability both in diplomacy and intelligence work. But it was also due to Burghley's promotion in the previous year. In April–June 1572 he was elected and installed as knight of the garter. This was the prelude to his appointment, in July 1572, to the office of Lord Treasurer, which had been vacant since the death of the marquess of Winchester in March. Although Sir Thomas Smith was promptly appointed to succeed Burghley as Secretary, he was aged, in ill-health, unsure of himself and reluctant to take the initiative even on routine matters. In December 1573 Walsingham was also appointed Secretary and assumed effective control of the functions and responsibilities of the secretarial office. However, that control was not exclusive. For the remainder of Burghley's life and career the queen consulted him on matters of 'great moment' and he continued to act, correspond and administer on a wide variety of concerns, which were non-financial and not obviously related to the office of Lord Treasurer.

The queen's trust in him was the key. However, the flexible range of his activities was also the consequence of a lack of strictly defined functional parameters for each of the major royal offices.[19] Thomas Fanshaw's *Practice of the Exchequer Court,* written for the new Lord Treasurer in 1572, precisely identified Burghley's powers and responsibilities. He supervised and administered the finances of royal government and the royal household, and served as presiding judge of the Court of Exchequer.[20] But this did not preclude his involvement and activity in other aspects of government. Nevertheless, Conyers Read regarded his shift to the Treasury as a 'momentous' change. It removed from him the administrative burden of the secretaryship and 'he was primarily hereafter a counsellor'. A.G.R. Smith, however, agrees with MacCaffrey, who regarded Burghley as 'the dynamo' who, between 1572 and the onset of war with Spain thirteen years later, ensured the continued effectiveness of day-to-day government. Gradually the ageing process and recurring gout would diminish his capacity, even at times when urgent business needed prompt resolution. But, despite age and illness, he continued to handle a formidable volume and range of business.[21]

So Burghley's elevation to the treasurership did not cause or encourage him to opt out of the multifarious activities of the secretaryship. Between the appointment of Smith and Walsingham as Secretaries, in July 1572 and December 1573, over 400 letters and papers in the Lansdowne manuscripts, State Papers and Salisbury manuscripts attest to the fact that he remained and was regarded as the linch-pin of government. They range from suits, letters of thanks, information from agents in Scotland and overseas, diplomatic correspondence and ecclesiastical matters (especially concerning puritans and papists) to his orders for the navy, instructions to the new president of the council in the north, and his memoranda on Irish affairs, defence of the realm against possible invasion, and uniformity of order in Anglican church services. They also reveal how Secretary Smith frequently deferred to him, advising him, for example, when he received reports and letters from the north, Scotland and Ireland.[22] Scotland was a particular cause of concern to Burghley, because of the civil war which had divided it since Mary Stuart's flight to England in 1568. The Marians were, however, finally defeated in 1573 when Edinburgh Castle fell after a siege in which English forces participated. The regency of the earl of Morton (1572–80) was grateful for Elizabeth's assistance in ending the civil war and firmly committed to a continued alliance with her. So in 1572–73 her government established harmonious, or at least working relationships with the Scots, France and Spain. For a few years in the 1570s Elizabeth, Burghley and other councillors experienced a period of relative calm before the storm.

At home, however, problems multiplied and magnified. The frustrated aspirations of godly reformers during the 1560s led the younger generation of puritans into more radical, even extreme, courses. In 1572 two London preachers, Thomas Wilcox and John Field, issued the *Admonition to the Parliament*. It condemned the Anglican prayer book and proposed the replacement of episcopal church government by a Presbyterian system. This placed Burghley in a dilemma. He had always favoured further reformation of a kind which would improve the funding and education of the clergy, especially their ability to preach. Indeed, in contrast to the queen's obdurate resistance to change, he had favoured parliamentary measures which sought to further such objectives. However, he could not condone a fundamental attack on the order of worship and government of the church. Already in 1570 Burghley, as chancellor of Cambridge University, had allowed its governing body to expel Thomas Cartwright, the Presbyterian inspiration behind Wilcox and Field, from his university offices. This did not, however, diminish his drive for moderate reform. It probably explains why, when Matthew Parker died in 1575, he actively canvassed and secured Edmund Grindal's promotion from the archbishopric of York to Canterbury. Burghley, who had been his devoted patron since the beginning of the reign, would have been aware that he carried with him to the highest ecclesiastical office under the crown the hopes and expectations of godly reforming activists.

Both the Treasurer and the archbishop sought reformation of the ministry and church courts and both attached importance to preaching, but once again the queen's obdurate conservatism proved to be the obstacle. When in 1576 Grindal refused to obey her order to suppress meetings of clergy and laity, designed to raise spiritual standards, she suspended him from the exercise of his office as archbishop. He remained in limbo until his death in July 1583, whereupon Elizabeth chose the anti-puritan disciplinarian, John Whitgift, as his successor. Burghley did not have a hand in Whitgift's promotion. That is not surprising. Grindal questioned some important features of the new church, including the queen's position as supreme governor. Elizabeth's action in appointing him was a misjudgement, whilst Burghley's advocacy of him was a political miscalculation on his part. From then on Burghley's influence in matters ecclesiastical markedly diminished.[23]

In contrast, his importance in anti-Catholic activities grew. The appointment of Walsingham as Secretary certainly freed Burghley from much routine daily toil. But he remained a key figure in diplomacy and internal security, both of which were concerned with the perceived and growing Catholic menace. Although, at least until the late 1570s, the threat of grand conspiracy, uniting domestic and international Catholicism, had less substance in fact than in the fertile imaginative fears of Burghley, Knollys, Leicester, Mildmay and other councillors, it provided the dynamic for action. Beckingsale underestimated

Burghley's role when he described him, from 1572 onwards, as 'a reserve engine rather than the permanent driving force of the government'. In fact he was no less active than before in matters concerning the security and safety of queen and kingdom, although it should be added that his activity was punctuated with periods of illness, for example in 1573–74, 1575 and 1577. He recognised that, whilst the rebellious Dutch, the internal turbulence of France, the shifting politics of Scotland, conflict in Ireland, and the Spanish juggernaut were all separate political phenomena, they also constituted interrelated challenges and threats. Open military assistance to the Dutch Protestant rebels, for example, would mean war with Spain – a war for which England lacked the money and men, equipment and expertise.

Burghley's reluctance to act boldly stemmed as much from realism as from an inherent caution. Whereas Leicester and Walsingham pressed for overt military intervention throughout the 1570s, Burghley tended to opt for the alternative of secret assistance. There was an apparent inconsistency in his policy towards the Dutch. So in late 1575 he was advocating either covert or open assistance; in 1577–78 and especially in 1584 after the assassination of the rebel leader, William of Orange, he supported Leicester's pressure for military intervention; but a year later, in 1585, he was for a while opposed to such action. There are several reasons for such variations. He loyally acted on instructions from the queen, whose policy swings were frequent. His own policy had security of the realm as its prime objective and the most suitable courses of action to this end varied according to the ever-changing international situation. In contrast, Leicester and Walsingham were consistently in favour of aiding the Dutch, because their objective was defence of Protestantism. And, unlike the Lord Treasurer, they did not have to consider the financial consequences of a possibly protracted war against imperial Spain.[24]

Burghley's French policy was equally flexible but consistently directed towards the same objective of national security. He was especially troubled by the possibility of French intervention in the Low Countries and occupation of 'the maritime parts', for they 'may be too potent neighbours for us'. In 1571 he was doubtful if the recent Anglo-French 'amity', expressed in the Elizabeth–Anjou marriage negotiations, would be long-lasting. And throughout the decade his guiding conviction was that either Spanish or French control of the Low Countries constituted a threat to the safety of the realm. A military pact between the French duke of Anjou and the Dutch in 1578, whereby he became the official 'Defender', and two years later recipient of the hereditary sovereignty of the Low Countries, caused alarm. Until 1574 he had been the duc d'Alençon, when he succeeded to the duchy of Anjou. In the early 1570s he had already engaged in extended and unproductive marriage negotiations with Elizabeth. These were resumed in 1578–81. Was Elizabeth's motive practical and political or was it personal and emotional? No one knew, but her publicly ardent pursuit of Anjou divided the Privy Council. Burghley, backed by considerable conciliar support, advocated the marriage, but his Chancellor of the Exchequer, Sir Walter Mildmay, opposed it. Elizabeth depended on her Lord Treasurer to advocate the marriage match in the Privy Council. But support dwindled as Leicester, Sir Christopher Hatton and other councillors joined Mildmay in opposition to it, and Burghley was left at the head of a rump of proponents. The negotiations were inconclusive and Anjou's death in 1584 ended the possibility of a marriage-based alliance with France.[25]

Elizabeth's relations with Spain and France could not be divorced from the politics of her northern neighbour, Scotland, and her subject kingdom, Ireland. So long as Morton controlled the government, Scotland did not pose a threat to English security and Burghley showed little interest in its affairs. The regent, however, steadily alienated the Presbyterian clergy, Scottish nobles and the young king, and in 1577 discontented factions began to coalesce against him. From then on, as Morton's position deteriorated, English agents north of the border communicated with the Lord Treasurer as well as with Secretary Walsingham. The arrival in Scotland of Esmé Stuart, Seigneur D'Aubigny, from France in 1579 was fatal for Morton and spelt danger for England. D'Aubigny was a protégé of the Guises, who led the Catholic forces against French Protestantism. He was also a cultivated courtier and cousin of James VI, who received him warmly. He rapidly became earl, then duke, of Lennox (1580–81) and a powerful force in Scottish politics. He had a leading hand in the fall of Morton, who was imprisoned on a charge of complicity in the murder of the king's father. The dramatic revival of French influence in Scottish politics led some English politicians to press for military intervention. However, Elizabeth was opposed because it might provoke a hostile French reaction, whilst Burghley was curiously inactive. In 1581 Morton was tried and executed. Scotland was now in a dangerous state of flux and there was a distinct possibility of a Scottish political orientation towards France, with the king's favourite Lennox as the catalyst. The complex politics of the following years, however, led to the expulsion of Lennox in 1583. They culminated, two years later, in an Anglo-Scottish agreement, whereby James VI promised not to assist Elizabeth's enemies and, in return, received an annual pension of £4,000.[26]

The English government's problems in Ireland proved to be less tractable and were indeed exacerbated by changes in its policies during the 1570s. When attempts to establish privately funded English colonies failed in 1571–76, Burghley observed that 'hard it were to reduce any province to conformity without the special charges and countenance of her Majesty'. In the future the 'plantation' of Ireland would be a government operation. Furthermore, the colonising ventures of the 1570s were based on the dispossession, not only of Irish clan chieftains, but also of their native subject populations. The brutality with which English Lords Deputy, colonisers and soldiers attempted to implement these policies and eliminate opposition simply exacerbated resistance among both native Irish and Old English. The result was a generation of rebellions, beginning with James Fitzmaurice Fitzgerald in Munster (1569–73). Although he was defeated, he escaped abroad only to return with a small force in 1579 and raise revolt. He was accompanied by a papal nuncio, Nicholas Sander, and later he was reinforced by a contingent of Italian and Spanish troops, funded by the pope. Burghley had been quick and correct to recognise that Fitzmaurice's return provided an opportunity for Spain to attack England through a postern gate. He drafted the proclamation which condemned the rebels as traitors. He also tried to spur the queen into quick action and adequate funding. Nevertheless, management of Irish affairs was largely in Walsingham's hands.

The Fitzmaurice venture failed and in 1580 the 600 foreign soldiers were massacred when they surrendered. Nevertheless, it was a significant episode, because it associated Irish opposition with the Spanish and papal forces of the Counter-Reformation. It was also an indicator of deteriorating Anglo-Spanish relations.[27] Burghley was usually concerned that provocative actions might drive Spanish hostility beyond the point of negotiation and diplomatic manœuvring to armed conflict, even though he was himself guilty of such provocation, as in the 1568 seizure of the Genoese bankers' loan. As Lord Treasurer he was acutely aware of the crown's limited financial and military resources, especially in comparison with those at Philip II's disposal. Nevertheless, Spanish grievances accumulated, partly due to the queen's shortsighted practice of backing English interlopers, who encroached on Spain's proclaimed monopoly of trade in its Caribbean empire. So, in 1568, she lent royal authority to John Hawkins' third slave-trading voyage to the West Indies (and Burghley too subscribed to some interlopers' expeditions). In 1577, however, Francis Drake embarked on a more ambitious incursion into the Spanish colonial world. He was supported by the queen, Leicester, Walsingham and other courtiers, but not by Burghley, who was excluded from the organisation of the voyage. Nor was he made privy to its objectives. When, after circumnavigating the globe, Drake's expedition returned, laden with plunder to the value of half a million pounds sterling from Spanish possessions, the queen knighted him. She then became an accomplice to his piracy by receiving much of the plunder for her own use. Burghley was disturbed by such publicly provocative action, which could only hinder attempts to mediate with Spain a political settlement in the Low Countries. The prospect of such a settlement, however, receded in the following years. Papal expeditions to Ireland in 1579 and 1580 were, as we have seen, aided by Spain. In 1580 Philip II's acquisition of Portugal and its fleet greatly increased his naval power and encouraged a more aggressive foreign policy.[28]

The Spanish threat was magnified by developments in the Low Countries. A military reconquest of the south began in 1578 and culminated in the capture of Antwerp by the duke of Parma in 1585. In 1579 the southern Catholic provinces withdrew support for rebellion and made peace with Spain. Throughout this period the English government's priority was support to the beleaguered Dutch, but it was divided over the kind of assistance. Burghley was particularly concerned to ensure that the rebels did not turn, in frustration, to France for help, because French control of the Low Countries' coastline and ports would be no less dangerous than Spanish possession of them. Elizabeth, however, was unwilling to provide prompt substantial aid. As we have seen, this realised Burghley's worst fears, when, in 1578, the Dutch signed a military agreement with the French duke of Anjou. That may be why she resumed negotiations for marriage with Anjou at this time: in order to exploit his position and military activity there in the English interest. Although the prospects of such a marriage were effectively dead by 1582, Elizabeth proceeded to lend him considerable sums, amounting eventually to £70,000, to finance his military operations. In this way, as Penry Williams points out, her anti-Spanish military activity remained indirect. Anjou, however, proved to be a political and military failure who abdicated and withdrew to France in 1583. Nevertheless, this meant the end of military assistance to the Dutch rebels, for whom 1584 was a black year: their leader, William of Orange, was assassinated; and the French Holy Catholic League, under Guise leadership, joined in alliance with the Catholic champion, Philip II. By 1585 there existed powerful arguments in favour of English military intervention to aid the Dutch. Despite their mutual caution, preference for peace, reluctance to aid subjects in revolt against their ruler and their search for alternative ways of helping the rebellious provinces, both the queen and Lord Treasurer came to recognise the need for direct action.[29]

In characteristic fashion Burghley penned a detailed analysis of the situation. He drew attention to Spain's hand in hostile activities during and since the crisis years of 1568–72, most recently in Ireland and the Throckmorton conspiracy of 1581.[30] He considered the recent augmentation of Spanish power: the wealth and navy of the Portuguese empire, the Franco-Spanish rapprochement and the presence of a large Spanish army in the Low Countries. Furthermore, any enterprise launched against England would receive support from disaffected English Catholics and supporters of Mary Stuart.[31] Although Burghley was a reluctant interventionist, in 1584/85 he showed, as he had done before, that he could recognise and was prepared to approve, even advocate, bold and positive action when necessity demanded it. The interventionists, led by Leicester and Walsingham, had their way. Although Elizabeth refused the Dutch offer of sovereignty, and her offer of troops to defend Antwerp came too late to save it, by the Treaty of Nonsuch in August 1585 she committed herself to the provision and financing of an English army for the duration of the war. She was to receive three Dutch ports as security for the eventual reimbursement of her expenses.

The threats, real or imagined, to the safety and position of the queen and to the stability and security of her church and realm were not merely external. Ever since the time of the northern rebellion, Norfolk's marriage scheme, the papal bull of excommunication and the Ridolfi plot, Burghley was convinced that Mary Stuart was prepared to conspire, incite rebellion and seek foreign intervention, in order to rule both England and Scotland. For a few years following 1572, however, there was a relative calm as threats diminished: Fitzmaurice's rebellion in Ireland was suppressed; Scottish amity was secure with Morton; Spanish power in the Low Countries collapsed in 1576 when a mutinous unpaid army sacked Antwerp, causing the southern Catholic provinces to join the Dutch Protestant rebellion; the agreement with Alva restored Anglo-Spanish trade; and the Treaty of Blois ensured stable relations with France, which was, in any case, embroiled in its own politico-religious troubles. Within England the Catholic community preferred the quiet life. Political activity in favour of Mary Stuart was not evident.

It was during this hiatus that parliament was recalled for financial assistance in 1576. As Burghley was now in the lords, it fell to Sir Walter Mildmay, Chancellor of the Exchequer, to make the official request for money in the commons. He acknowledged 'that wee bee in quietnes at home and safe inough from trowbles abroad', but he warned that 'wee ought in tyme to make provision to prevent any storme that may arrise either here or abroad'. Burghley was not prominent in a generally harmonious session, although he must have been embarrassed by proceedings against his ex-ward, Arthur Hall, for his abuse of the members' privilege of freedom from arrest for debt. In only one episode, the intercameral clash over the bill to restore John Lord Stourton in blood, was he much in evidence. The heirs of anyone convicted and executed for the capital offences of treason or other felony suffered legal disabilities: for example, they could not inherit property or protect their interests in the law courts. Restitution in blood restored their legal rights. Stourton's bill, which was endorsed with the queen's sign manual, rapidly passed the lords. In the lower house, however, it was debated at length before a committee added a proviso. The lords found this unacceptable and pressed for a joint conference of members from each house. Burghley, the lords' spokesman, reprimanded the lower house, in particular because 'the Bill being signed by her Majesty . . . none might presume to alter or add any thing to it without the assent of her Majesty'. The commons, however, refused to budge and at a further meeting of the joint conference the Lord Treasurer, after consultation with his fellow lords, in effect accepted the assertion of the lower house that the queen's endorsement of the bill was 'only a recommendation'. The lords, however, refused to pass the bill with the proviso attached.[32]

Burghley also had a hand in attempts by the bishops and councillors to secure the enactment of a bill requiring attendance at church and the taking of Anglican communion at least once a year. The queen had vetoed it in 1571, whilst its disappearance, during its passage through the lords in 1576 (and again in 1581), may also have been the consequence of royal action.[33] There is no doubt that, in the 1570s, Burghley was concerned about what he perceived to be increasing recusancy among the gentry. His concern was heightened when missionary priests, trained in the English seminary at Douai, began to arrive in England from 1574 onwards. Until then survivors from Mary Tudor's reign were the only priests available to minister to English Catholics. The purpose of the 'English Mission', however, was not only ministration to the existing Catholic community, but also the peaceful reconversion of England. This caused a basic change in Burghley's attitude. Previously he had acknowledged a difference between Catholics who were only religious heretics and those who were political papists and so potential traitors. However, the coming of the seminary priests, reinforced by Jesuits, the first of whom landed in 1580, led him to discard the distinction between the spiritual and political loyalties of Roman Catholics. Other councillors, especially Walsingham, took the same view. The consistent Catholic position was that the missionaries' task was spiritual, but Burghley saw them as political agents of a hostile power. Pope Gregory XIII (1572–85) instructed the Jesuits not to meddle in politics. He also advised English Catholics that they were not bound by *Regnans in Excelsis* until it could be enforced. However, such advice must have been regarded cynically by Elizabeth's government, coming as it did from a pope who, in 1579–80, had launched two military expeditions to help an Irish rebellion.

Although the queen made the policy decisions, Burghley was a major force hardening her government's attitude towards what he regarded as English political Catholicism. National security was to be achieved by bringing obstinate English Catholics to obedience and conformity or punishing them, by dealing harshly with Pope Gregory's agents, the seminaries and Jesuits, and by engaging in a print propaganda war. During the 1580s and 1590s, Privy Councillors, in particular Burghley, instituted harsh measures against recusants.[34] The new official hardline position was also signalled in 1577 by the execution of a seminary priest, Cuthbert Mayne, for bringing in a papal bull. Only two more executions occurred before 1581, probably due to Elizabeth's wish not to jeopardise marriage negotiations with Anjou. Nevertheless, there is evidence enough during these years of the council's – and especially Burghley's – willingness to take extreme measures against the missionaries. Until 1581 the council occasionally, but not regularly, authorised the interrogation, accompanied by torture, of captured priests. On 1 December 1580, however, the Privy Council directed a letter to the lieutenant of the Tower. It declared that arrested Jesuits were to be conveyed there, 'her Majestie meaninge to make some example of them by punishement, to the terrour of others'. Burghley was not present at this council meeting, but amongst those appointed by the letter to interrogate the prisoners was his client Norton.[35] During the following months (January–March 1581) parliament enacted that

> all persons whatsoever which . . . shall by any ways or means put in practice to absolve, persuade or withdraw any of the Queen's Majesty's subjects . . . from their natural obedience to her Majesty, or to withdraw them *for that intent* from the religion now by her Highness' authority established . . . to the Romish religion, or to move . . . any of them to promise any obedience to the see of Rome . . . shall be . . . adjudged to be traitors . . .

Burghley had a major hand in the wording of the measure, which reflects his deep concern with political Catholicism as a threat to the state.[36] The italicised words, *for that intent*, make it clear that the author of the text regarded withdrawal 'from their natural [political] obedience', not religious conversion, as the capital offence. The new act equipped the government with the statutory power to make an example of the seminary priests and Jesuits 'to the terrour of others'. And Burghley was active in promoting the council's attempts to hunt down and eliminate the missionaries. He was willing to approve torture and the death penalty for them, because he was, by now, convinced that there existed a grand Catholic conspiracy, encompassing English Catholics and foreign powers, against queen, state and church.

. . .

NOTES

1. J.P. Collier (ed.), *The Egerton Papers*, Camden Soc., OS, XII (1840), pp. 42–3; Levine, *Early Elizabethan Succession*, pp. 81–2, 120–1; MacCaffrey, *Elizabeth I*, pp. 106–7, 114; Wright (ed.), *Queen Elizabeth*, 11 and 21 June 1568, I, pp. 280–286.
2. Read, *Secretary Cecil*, pp. 421–30; G.D. Ramsay, 'The foreign policy of Elizabeth I', in Haigh (ed.), *Reign of Elizabeth*, p. 155.
3. Read, *Secretary Cecil*, pp. 432–5; Haynes (ed.), *State Papers*, p. 501; W. MacCaffrey, *The Shaping of the Elizabethan Regime: Elizabethan Politics, 1558–72* (London, 1969), pp. 189–95; Guy, *Tudor England*, p. 276; Read, *Burghley*, pp. 96–102.
4. Haynes (ed.), *State Papers*, pp. 579–88.
5. Read, *Secretary Cecil*, pp. 419–21; Read, *Burghley*, pp. 30–3, 51–65, 66–71, 86–91.
6. Guy, *Tudor England*, pp. 254–8.
7. See below, pp. 122–4; J. Guy (ed.), *The Reign of Elizabeth I: Court and Culture in the Last Decade* (Cambridge, 1995), pp. 38, 41–2, 47; PRO, SP, 12/12/40; ibid., 12/39/31.
8. E. Lodge (ed.), *Illustrations of British History*, 3 vols (London, 1838), I, pp. 475–6, 478–9.
9. Read, *Secretary Cecil*, pp. 431–2; *Clapham*, p. 76; Graves, *Norton*, pp. 154–5; Guy, *Tudor England*, pp. 273–4; MacCaffrey, *Elizabeth I*, pp. 118–20.
10. Read, *Secretary Cecil*, pp. 453–4; Haynes (ed.), *State Papers*, pp. 573–5, 578–93.
11. Read, *Burghley*, pp. 33–4; S. Adams, 'The patronage of the crown in Elizabethan politics: the 1590s in perspective', in Guy (ed.), *Court and Culture*, pp. 37–8, 41–2; idem, 'Faction, clientage and party: English politics, 1550–1603', *History Today*, 32 (Dec. 1982), pp. 33–9; Guy, *Tudor England*, pp. 254–8; also see below, pp. 120–2.
12. Haynes (ed.), *State Papers*, pp. 608–16, 620–1.
13. Graves, *Norton*, pp. 161–70.
14. See, for example, M.A.R. Graves, 'Managing Elizabethan parliaments', in D.M. Dean and N.L. Jones (eds), *The Parliaments*

of Elizabethan England (Oxford, 1990), pp. 37–63; idem, 'The management of the Elizabethan house of commons: the council's men of business', *Parliamentary History*, 2 (1983), pp. 11–38.

15. Graves, *Norton*, pp. 171–8; T.E. Hartley (ed.), *Proceedings in the Parliaments of Elizabeth I*, 3 vols (London, 1981–95), I, p. 257; Elton, *Parliament of England*, pp. 181–4.
16. Ibid., pp. 166, 201–2; Graves, *Norton*, pp. 291–9; Guy (ed.), *Court and Culture*, p. 146 and n. 78.
17. Beckingsale, *Burghley*, pp. 129–30; Elton, *Parliament of England*, pp. 375–7; Hartley (ed.), *Proceedings*, I, p. 317; Graves, *Norton*, pp. 186–95; idem, 'Management: council's men of business', pp. 24–9.
18. Read, *Burghley*, pp. 48–50; Sir Dudley Digges, *The Compleat Ambassador* (London, 1655), pp. 203–19; Bindoff (ed.), *House of Commons*, III, pp. 571–2; R.H. Fritze (ed.), *Historical Dictionary of Tudor England, 1485–1603* (New York, 1991), pp. 530–1.
19. Read, *Burghley*, pp. 80–2; Bindoff (ed.), *House of Commons*, III, p. 401.
20. Read, *Burghley*, pp. 82–5.
21. Ibid., p. 85; Smith, *Burghley*, pp. 17–18; W.T. MacCaffrey, *Queen Elizabeth and the Making of Policy, 1572–1588* (Princeton, NJ, 1981), p. 456.
22. Lansdowne MS, 14–18; *HMC*, Salisbury MS, 2, pp. 21–67.
23. Collinson, *Elizabethan Puritan Movement*, pp. 159–61, 194–7, 243.
24. Beckingsale, *Burghley*, p. 147; Read, *Burghley*, pp. 74–5.
25. Ibid., pp. 57–8; Graves, *Norton*, pp. 391–3; Beckingsale, *Burghley*, pp. 144–8, 151, 155; P. Clark, A.G.R. Smith and N. Tyacke (eds), *The English Commonwealth 1547–1640: Essays in Politics and Society* (Leicester, 1979), pp. 69–70.
26. Read, *Burghley*, pp. 230–4, 280–92; Williams, *Later Tudors*, pp. 299–300.
27. Read, *Burghley*, pp. 241–3; Williams, *Later Tudors*, pp. 269, 291–6.
28. Read, *Secretary Cecil*, pp. 429–30; idem, *Burghley*, p. 223; Williams, *Later Tudors*, pp. 275–6; Beckingsale, *Burghley*, pp. 148–9; MacCaffrey, *Elizabeth I*, pp. 293–4; see below, pp. 197–9.
29. Williams, *Later Tudors*, pp. 278–86; Guy, *Tudor England*, pp. 282–7.
30. See below, pp. 197–9.
31. *Calendar of State Papers, Foreign*, 23 vols (London, 1863–90), XIX, pp. 95–8.
32. Hartley (ed.), *Proceedings*, I, p. 442; Graves, *Norton*, pp. 355–6, 358–9; Elton, *Parliament of England*, pp. 306–9, 333, 335–6; W. Hakewil, *The Manner How Statutes are enacted in Parliament by Passing of Bills* (London, 1641), pp. 80–97.
33. Elton, *Parliament of England*, pp. 201–3. The measure also failed in 1581.

34. See below, pp. 171–6.
35. Graves, *Norton*, pp. 202, 248–9; *APC*, 12, 271; Read, *Burghley*, p. 238.
36. An Act to retain the Queen's Majesty's subjects in their due obedience, 23 Eliz. I, cap. 1; *Stats Realm*, 4, pp. 657–8. It was this act which also drastically increased recusancy fines.

Chapter 4

A TIME OF CONSPIRACY AND WAR, 1583–98

The *empresa* (the 'Enterprise against England'), which for so long had been phantasmagoric, acquired the quality of reality in 1583 with the discovery of the Throckmorton plot. Francis Throckmorton was not the prime mover of the Catholic conspiracy, but a minor player from whom the government extracted information about it. The grand coalition had various objectives, such as toleration for English Catholics, Mary Stuart's release, Elizabeth's deposition, the invasion of England and the restoration of Catholicism. It involved English Catholics at home and in exile, the French duke of Guise, the Spanish ambassador Mendoza (with Philip II's characteristically cautious support), Pope Gregory XIII and, of course, the potential beneficiary, Mary Stuart.[1]

The competing interests of French and Spanish participants meant little likelihood of success, even if the conspiracy had not been uncovered. Nevertheless, the plot confirmed the worst fears and strongest prejudices of Burghley and other councillors. The propaganda war did nothing to alleviate those fears. In 1584 William Allen responded in print to the Lord Treasurer's *Execution of Justice*. He upheld the papal supremacy and defended the papal expeditions to Ireland. He also demonstrated that Campion and other 'victims' were being persecuted, even killed, for their beliefs, not for treason. The insoluble problem was a total incompatibility between the convictions of the government and those of its adversaries. It was insoluble because there was no clear and accepted guideline separating papal political activists from those Catholic loyalists who simply wished to practise their religion quietly and without molestation.[2]

If the propaganda war was inconclusive, the Throckmorton plot had positive results: Mendoza, the Spanish ambassador, was expelled in 1584 because of his involvement and the council promoted the Bond of Association. It was drafted by Secretary Walsingham and revised by Burghley. The final draft of the Bond, which amounted to a form of lynch-law, was a consequence of the fear generated by the Throckmorton and other plots against Elizabeth and, in 1584, the assassination of William of Orange. In its final form it bound all signatories on oath to pursue and kill anyone trying to harm the queen. Any 'pretended successor', by or on behalf of whom an attempt was made on Elizabeth's life, was also to be put to death. The obvious target was Mary Stuart but could have been taken to include her son, James VI, as well. Copies of the Bond circulated the country late in 1584 whilst parliamentary elections were being held and thousands appended their signatures and seals. However, the Bond had no legal authority, whilst the queen disclaimed any knowledge of it until she saw signed and sealed copies. Furthermore, she disapproved of some of its terms.[3]

The ensuing parliament (November 1584–March 1585) provided the queen's councillors with the opportunity to mount a legislative counter-attack against her enemies. But, as so often happened, the complete fulfilment of their objectives was frustrated chiefly by their royal mistress. The act providing for the queen's safety (in which Burghley's hand is evident) modified the terms of the Bond of Association. In particular, the heirs of offenders were to retain their places in the succession. Nor was any provision made for the continued legitimate operation of government in the event of Elizabeth's assassination, although Burghley stressed the need for this.[4] Elizabeth did give her assent to another security measure, which enacted that all Jesuits and seminary priests were to abjure the realm within forty days, and were not to return, on pain of conviction for high treason. The language of the preamble, which declared their intentions to be the withdrawal of the queen's subjects from their allegiance and the fomenting of rebellion, accurately reflects the prevailing view of Privy Councillors such as Burghley and Walsingham.[5] So did the draft bill which sought to prevent recusants from possessing weapons and ammunition, but the queen vetoed that.[6]

During the Christmas recess the intention of Dr William Parry, a member of the house of commons, to assassinate Elizabeth was revealed to the government. It must have confirmed the urgency of the security situation. Then, in August 1586, the Babington plot was exposed. It implicated Mary Stuart in yet another plan to kill Elizabeth. The act for the surety of the queen's person had authorised a commission to bring to trial any person who claimed to be her successor and who sought 'the hurt of her Majesty's most royal person'. This enabled the government to proceed with statutory authority against Mary. Burghley, frequently afflicted with gout, was nonetheless one of the driving forces and the political manager of the move to be rid of her, once and for all. His greatest obstacle was the queen's understandable reluctance to follow the process through to the judicially justifiable conclusion of death for treason. The possibility of foreign retaliation reinforced her characteristic indecisiveness. She may have been unwilling to kill an anointed queen. She was certainly aware that she, not her advisers and ministers, would bear the ultimate responsibility and odium for Mary's execution. As she told a parliamentary deputation at Richmond, to which she had retreated during the first weeks of the session: '[I]n this late acte of Parliament you have laied an hard hand on mee that I must give direction for her death, which cannot be [to mee] but most greivous and displeasaunt and an yrksom burdon to me.' By the time Elizabeth made this speech, on 12 November 1586, she had already conceded much ground. At Fotheringhay Castle, in October, Mary had been brought to trial, during which Burghley, who was prominent in the proceedings, was accused by her of being her adversary. To this he replied 'Yea . . . I am adversary to Queen Elizabeth's adversaries.' On 15 October the commission adjourned, reassembled on the 25th and unanimously condemned her.[7]

Even before the trial, Burghley and his fellow-councillors recognised that parliamentary pressure might be necessary to coerce the queen. On 8 September he wrote to Walsingham that 'We stick upon Parliament which her Majesty mislikes to have'. But a week later she gave way and it was summoned. Elizabeth stayed away and parliament was opened by three commissioners including Burghley. The Lord Chancellor's opening address on 29 October made it clear that it was called neither for subsidies nor for new laws, but for one cause of 'great peril and dangerous consequence'. Thenceforth a concerted and intense bicameral pressure campaign was applied. In the lords Burghley played his part, speaking 'excellently and more fully' than the Lord Chancellor about Mary's treason; he was prominent in the drafting of the parliamentary petition which sought the proclamation and execution of her sentence; and he drew up the proclamation, which was issued on 4 December. He was particularly anxious that Mary should be killed by statutory authority, the 1584 act for the queen's safety, and not by the vigilante 'law' of the Bond of Association, as Elizabeth would seem to have preferred. Although, Burghley later recorded, her council constantly pressed her to authorise Mary's execution, for weeks she would not act. Finally, on 1 February she signed the death warrant, gave it into the custody of Secretary Davison and authorised it to be sealed. Even then, however, she suggested that Amias Paulet, Mary's gaoler, should have Mary murdered, thereby relieving her of the public responsibility for her death. A horrified Paulet refused. Furthermore, she did not order the warrant to be executed. According to Camden, she 'gave some Signification, but no express Command' to Davison that he should retain possession of it. Burghley now took the initiative. Acting swiftly and boldly and with the collusion of other Privy Councillors he ordered the despatch of the warrant to Fotheringhay Castle, where, on 8 February, Mary was executed.[8]

Whether the queen's rage, on receiving the news, was simulated or genuine, Mary's death produced the most serious rift in the almost fifty-year-long relationship with Burghley. There had to be scapegoats. Davison went to the Tower and the Lord Treasurer spent four months in exile from Court. When no dramatic foreign reprisals followed, especially from James VI or France, the queen later relented. Davison was released and retired on full salary and Burghley returned to Court, council and royal favour. The death of Mary Stuart had at least removed a catalyst and focus for Catholic discontent, foreign conspiracy and intervention. It was unfortunate for the government, however, that at the very time when the Spanish 'Enterprise' against England was taking shape, seminary and Jesuit missionaries were infiltrating the country and apparently making converts, and religious unity was needed, the church was becoming increasingly divided. The division had been signalled by the public launching of English Presbyterianism with the *Admonition* in 1572. Although Edmund Grindal, appointed archbishop of Casterbury in 1575, preferred reconciliation with the radicals, his disgrace and the rise of John Whitgift, as a consequence of royal favour, augured a shift towards reactionary conservatism. When, on Grindal's death in 1583, Elizabeth named him as her third archbishop of Canterbury, it was a promotion in which Burghley had no part.

Whitgift promptly launched his attack on nonconformity. The clergy were required to subscribe to three articles. When Burghley, Leicester, other councillors and many gentry and clergy objected to the article that the prayer book contained nothing contrary to the word of God, Whitgift retreated, but he did not give up. He continued to pursue nonconformist clergy through the Court of High Commission by requiring a set of questions to be answered on *ex officio* oath. Although Burghley secured Whitgift's appointment to the Privy Council in 1586 – the only episcopal councillor of Elizabeth's reign – he opposed the new interrogatories. In July 1584 he wrote to the archbishop that the Spanish Inquisition did 'use not so many questions to comprehend and to trap their prey'. Whitgift retained the queen's support and favour, but he had a divisive impact on the council: Sir Christopher Hatton supported him whilst Sir Francis Knollys, Burghley and others were opposed. Parliaments echoed such divisions. Recent episcopal appointments had tended to reflect Whitgift's position and influence and these in turn revitalised Presbyterian campaigning for abolition of the office of bishop. Both Dr Peter Turner (in 1584) and Anthony Cope (in 1586–87) introduced bills in unsuccessful attempts to replace the prayer book with a Genevan liturgy and episcopal government of the church with pastors, elders and a hierarchy of assemblies. The measure promoted by Cope and his supporters sought to restructure ecclesiastical government and end the royal governorship. Whilst Burghley sympathised with moderate puritan reforms, he could not allow such fundamental challenges to the government, structure and liturgy of the church established in 1559.[9]

Both Whitgift's disciplinarian regimen and Presbyterian responses to it evoked Burghley's hostility. However, the central and most pressing concern of his remaining years, once Mary Stuart had gone, was the imperious demand of war. MacCaffrey describes the ageing Lord Treasurer as one whose 'old crisp decisiveness and boldness were gone' and who 'remained curiously withdrawn and inactive in the years when his talents were most demanded'. Yet his initiative in securing the despatch of Mary Stuart's death warrant was the boldest stroke of his career. Thereafter he was and continued to be, more than anyone else, the co-ordinator of the Elizabethan government's war effort: as Lord Treasurer he bore the ultimate responsibility for funding it and, after Walsingham's death in 1590, he shouldered the administrative burdens of the secretaryship.[10] He was faced with the ongoing problem of how to fund, equip and supply English forces and allies, who were pitted against the gigantic resources of the Spanish empire. Furthermore, the prospects of meeting the military and financial challenges grew gloomier, as Philip II's general, the duke of Parma, steadily reconquered the rebellious Low Countries, the French Huguenot leader Henry of Navarre clamoured for assistance and Ireland remained vulnerable to rebellion and foreign intervention. Meanwhile, looming ever larger was the prospect of an attempted Spanish invasion of England.

Leicester's command of the English army in the Low Countries further complicated the situation when he accepted the Dutch offer of 'absolute government' of the rebellious provinces, contrary to Elizabeth's orders. Although Burghley acted on his promise to the earl, that he would try to placate the infuriated queen, Leicester proved to be a financially extravagant and inept commander, who also managed to antagonise her Dutch allies. In December 1587 he returned to England. Meanwhile Spain also threatened England through France, where, in 1584–85, King Henry III, the French Catholic League and Philip II joined forces against Henry of Navarre, the Huguenot heir to the throne. From then on, until the Franco-Spanish peace Treaty of Vervins in 1598, Burghley (and Walsingham, until his death in 1590) persuaded Elizabeth to provide financial and military assistance to the Huguenot leader, who, as King Henry IV from 1589, remained embattled with the forces of Catholicism. In Ireland, too, danger beckoned, because the earlier Tudor policy of consensus management had given way to one of land-dispossession, colonisation and conquest. Burghley favoured the new rigorous policies, because, like many others in English governing circles, he regarded the native Irish as savage. Such attitudes translated into violent action on the ground and, eventually, the lengthy retaliatory rebellion of Hugh, earl of Tyrone, in the 1590s.

The crucial battleground, however, was none of these, but the English Channel. The Spanish Armada, contemplated in the early 1580s, planned and organised in 1585–87, had as its objective the conquest of England. Although in 1587 Sir Francis Drake's successful raid on Cadiz, to which Burghley gave his support, delayed the Armada's departure, it sailed in the summer of the following year. By then the Lord Treasurer's long-term priority of defence over aggression had paid dividends. A decade earlier he had chosen Sir John Hawkins to manage the navy office and since then he had been active in recruitment and the provision of weaponry and naval supplies. Hawkins proved to be a skilful administrator and talented ship designer. He upgraded the queen's fighting fleet with weaponry superior to that of the Spanish navy. Defeat of the Armada resulted from tactical skill, including the use of fire-ships which scattered the Spanish fleet, when it was anchored off Calais, and the failure of Parma's invasion army to rendezvous with the Armada. Burghley's typically undramatic but energetic administrative support of Hawkins and organisation of the county levies were significant contributions to England's military preparedness in 1588. However, his practice of rigorous economy had resulted in the lack of sufficient gunpowder and ammunition. Nor was the Spanish naval threat ended in 1588. The Armada's defeat resulted in an ambitious Spanish shipbuilding programme, a more powerful fleet in the 1590s, more armadas and expeditions to Ireland.

As 'money is the sinews of war', the man who managed the state's finances had unrivalled authority in time of war. At the same time, once England embarked on open warfare against Spain and the French Catholic League, the political climate, within which Burghley operated, fundamentally changed. John Guy justifiably regards the years of war, 1585–1603, as the 'second reign' of Elizabeth I. War threatened the realm, over-extended the state's modest resources, reduced traditional forms of patronage, caused loss of life, and split the political centre over issues of military strategy and diplomacy. It all occurred at a time when the queen was ageing, her grip on government was slackening, and her Lord Treasurer was old, tired and frequently ill. The central political structure changed too as a generation of councillors, prominent politicians and royal favourites died: in rapid succession Leicester (1588), Mildmay (1589), Walsingham and Leicester's brother Warwick (1590) and Hatton (1591). Walsingham's death left Burghley burdened with the wide-ranging administrative functions of the secretaryship as well as management of the state's finances. However, although his heir Thomas had been a disappointment to him, he groomed his politically talented and ambitious younger son, Robert, for office and increasingly called upon him to share in the burdens of office. In 1591 Robert was appointed to the Privy Council, but five more years elapsed before the queen named him Secretary of State.[11]

During these transitional years Burghley, with the caution of age or a Lord Treasurer's realistic sense of economy, showed a marked preference for military defence rather than bold, aggressive strikes. The new Privy Councillors, Whitgift, Lords Buckhurst and Cobham, whose appointments he promoted in 1586, were of like mind. However, they all had to contend with the rise of the new royal favourite, Robert Devereux, earl of Essex. The young earl was a military interventionist who sought to take the war to the enemy. Although the Cecils and Essex competed for offices, which an increasingly vacillating queen left vacant for long periods, this was not, as traditionally assumed, the prime cause of conflict between them. They had fundamentally different attitudes on the conduct of the war. When, for example, Burghley secured Essex's command of the Rouen expedition to bring aid to Henry of Navarre, the earl saw France as the theatre in which Spain's bid for international supremacy had to be repulsed. Burghley, in contrast, was simply concerned to prevent Spanish control of French ports, from which an invasion of England could be launched. As Paul Hammer argues, 'The real battle was for control of the direction of the queen's policies.' In any case, Essex's battle was less with Burghley, who had been one of his guardians when he was young, than with the Lord Treasurer's son Robert, a rival of his own generation.[12]

Meanwhile the consequential problems of war continued to press on the Lord Treasurer: in Ireland the dramatic collapse of the fortunes of Sir John Perrott, Lord Deputy (1591–92) and the earl of Tyrone's rebellion (1595–1603); military and financial assistance to the Dutch rebels; and the possible dangers resulting from the Spanish capture of Calais in 1596. War requires urgent policy decisions. Unfortunately, during the 1590s Burghley was ill with increasing frequency, and often bedridden. However, if he was also, as A.G.R. Smith asserts, 'bankrupt of new ideas in a changing world' that may not have been a significant shortcoming.[13] In wartime, short-term tactical considerations tend to be more relevant, advantageous and necessary than long-range strategies and major innovations. Furthermore, despite his recurrent illnesses he remained remarkably active. He continued to produce his characteristic lengthy and detailed memoranda, *pro et contra*, on a wide variety of subjects; he was also most assiduous in his attendance at the council board and in the house of lords in his last years.[14] He was instrumental in securing increased parliamentary taxation,[15] and in his last parliament, when he was seventy-seven, the lords approved his motions cancerning absentees and the clerk's journal.[16]

There is no doubt, however, that to some extent in his final years he faded as age and ill-health overtook him. So fellow-councillors would discuss pressing matters at his bedside and his secretary, Michael Hickes, repeatedly wrote to Robert Cecil that his father was sick, in pain and 'abed'. The French envoy, Sieur de Maisse, visiting Elizabeth's Court in 1597, was dismissive of the Lord Treasurer as 'very old . . . very deaf and I had to shout quite loud'. Nor was he without his critics. Dr Thomas Wilson, a frustrated civil lawyer, accused Burghley of obstructing the rise of talented men (amongst whom he doubtless counted himself). The successful are always a target for the failed and the Lord Treasurer was no exception. He worked to the end, seeking peace with Philip II even as he organised England for war. When, in 1598, the French king signed the Treaty of Vervins, terminating war with Spain, he favoured the same course of action. Essex insisted on continued conflict, whereupon Burghley handed him the book of psalms and pointed to a passage which read, 'blood-thirsty men shall not live out half their days'. In the same way he sought peace in the church. So he deplored both the anti-puritan campaign of Whitgift, actively supported by Hatton and Buckhurst, and the anti-episcopalian *Martin Marprelate* tracts. However, Whitgift had open access to the queen, and in ecclesiastical matters Burghley was marginalised during the 1590s. Nor was there peace at Court as the queen's control of policy and politicians lessened. The Cadiz expedition of 1596, commanded by Lord Howard of Effingham and Essex, raised crucial questions about war policy, provoked furious arguments over the spoils and exacerbated tensions between the Cecils and the earl. At this point the lines of factional allegiance were clearly drawn.[17] Burghley, however, was spared the ultimate showdown in 1601, between Essex and the queen, whose policies the paranoid peer sought to control. On 4 August 1598 Burghley died.

. . .

NOTES

1. Graves, *Norton*, pp. 253–4, 265–71; Read, *Burghley*, pp. 249–50, 287–8.
2. Read, *Burghley*, pp. 254–5; Graves, *Norton*, pp. 246–7.
3. PRO, SP, 12/173/81–3; ibid., 12/174/1–18; Neale, *Eliz. I and Parls.*, II, pp. 16–17 and n. 2; Guy, *Tudor England*, pp. 331–2; A.G.R. Smith (ed.), *The Last Years of Mary Queen of Scots* (London, 1990), p. 9.
4. HLRO, Orig. Act, 27 Eliz. I no. 1; D. Dean, *Law-Making and Society in Late Elizabethan England: The Parliament of England, 1584–1601* (Cambridge, 1996), pp. 63–5; P. Collinson, 'The monarchical republic of Queen Elizabeth I', *Elizabethan Essays* (London, 1994), pp. 51–5. Burghley's draft bill or proviso for an interregnum government did not see the parliamentary light of day, presumably due to a royal prohibition. PRO, SP, 12/176/22, 28–30. Neale, *Eliz. I and Parls.*, II, pp. 45–6, 51–2; see below, p. 94.
5. Dean, *Law-Making and Society*, pp. 65–6.
6. It was not, however, initiated by either of them. Ibid., pp. 66–7.
7. Neale, *Eliz. I and Parls.*, II, pp. 105–6, 115–21; Hartley (ed.), *Proceedings*, II, p. 251; Read, *Burghley*, pp. 354–9; Smith (ed.), *Last Years of Mary*, p. 20.
8. Neale, *Eliz. I and Parls.*, II, pp. 104, 113, 114–15, 132–3; Smith (ed.), *Last Years of Mary*, pp. 20–6; A. Heisch, 'Arguments for an execution: Queen Elizabeth's "white paper" and Lord Burghley's "blue pencil"', *Albion*, 24 (1992), pp. 591–604; Sir Simonds D'Ewes, *The Journals of all the Parliaments during the reign of Queen Elizabeth* (London, 1682), p. 377; W. MacCaffrey (ed.), *The History of the most renowned and victorious Princess Elizabeth* (Chicago, 1970), p. 292.
9. Collinson, *Elizabethan Puritan Movement*, pp. 244–5, 256–9, 266–7, 271–2, 306–9; Read, *Burghley*, pp. 294–8; Dean, *Law-Making and Society*, pp. 99–102; see above, pp. 60–1.

10. MacCaffrey, *Making of Policy*, pp. 456–7.
11. Guy (ed.), *Court and Culture*, pp. 1, 4–6; Beckingsale, *Burghley*, pp. 175–7, 183–4.
12. Haigh (ed.), *Reign of Elizabeth*, pp. 67–8; P.E.J. Hammer, 'Patronage at Court, faction and the earl of Essex', in Guy (ed.), *Court and Culture*, pp. 72–5, 86.
13. A.G.R. Smith, *The Government of Elizabethan England* (London, 1967), p. 111.
14. See below, pp. 112, 145.
15. See below, p. 134.
16. See below, p. 146.
17. Smith, *Servant of the Cecils*, p. 46; G.B. Harrison and R.A. Jones (eds), *De Maisse* (London, 1931), p. 29; F.J. Fisher (ed.), 'The State of England, 1600, by Thomas Wilson', *Camden Miscellany*, 16 (London, 1936), p. 42; T. Birch (ed.), *Memoirs of the Reign of Queen Elizabeth*, 2 vols (London, 1754), I, pp. 383–4; Hammer, 'Patronage', pp. 72, 83–6.

PART TWO

AN ASSESSMENT

Chapter 5

MINISTER AND QUEEN

When Elizabeth became queen in November 1558 she and Cecil were already well-acquainted. They also had much in common: their education by Cambridge teachers, their religion and attitude to religious conformity and their political priorities of stability, security and peace. Furthermore, having already served as Edwardian Secretary of State (1550–53), he was one of the most experienced Protestant politicians and administrators. He was a natural choice for high office.[1] Between 20 November 1558 and his death on 4 August 1598 he continuously held office, first as Secretary and then from July 1572 as Lord Treasurer. He was also the queen's personal secretary (having served in the same capacity to Edward VI and the dukes of Somerset and Northumberland) and, between 1561 and 1598, Master of the Court of Wards. The secretaryship gave William Cecil broad, undefined responsibilities and consequent influence. His son Robert, also Secretary in the closing years of the reign, wrote that the office had no specific warrant or commission, 'for such is the multiplicity of occasions and the variable motions and intents of foreign princes and their daily practices, and in so many points and places', that Secretaries 'can never have any commission so large and universal' to accommodate them. Robert Beale's attempt to describe the Secretary's functions and duties simply indicated how virtually every aspect of both realm and church lay within the compass of his office. However, the extent and limits of his functions and authority were determined by the monarch. In Conyers Read's words, 'Some Tudor secretaries were little more than clerks, some little less than prime ministers.' Elizabeth's trust in him meant that he was very active in a wide range of business, from counsel on urgent and important matters of state and foreign affairs to routine administration. His prominence was reinforced by his place as her personal secretary, which gave him direct access to her, control of her household finances and possession of the stamp of the sign manual.[2]

When Cecil was appointed to the Court of Wards and later, as Lord Burghley, to the Treasury, he became both 'private treasurer and Lord Treasurer'. Although he gave up the secretaryship of state on his elevation to the Treasury, he continued to exercise many of the Secretary's functions, especially in foreign affairs. According to John Clapham, 'the choice business of the state was handled jointly' by Burghley and his brother-in-law Sir Nicholas Bacon, until the latter's death in 1579. Thereafter Burghley 'being then Treasurer of England, ordered for the most part all public affairs of state, which he despatched with such dexterity as the Queen commonly termed him *her spirit*'.[3] In addition, he was burdened with financial administration, especially in the Exchequer Court from 1572 onwards, but also in the Court of Wards. He supervised tax operations, management of crown estates, debts due and owing and customs; he authorised expenditure; and he appointed many of the Exchequer officers. He also had the right and responsibility to preside over the two courts. Although it is improbable that he regularly attended the frequent sittings of the Exchequer Court, there is evidence of his activity both there and in the Court of Wards. Contemporaries' verdicts on his judicial conduct and especially his integrity are very favourable. Clapham recorded that 'his presence was so grateful to suitors, as they desired to have their causes heard only before him'. And the anonymous biographer had personal experience of Burghley's rejection of gifts proffered by suitors and litigants:

> And I dare avow it, there was never any man living could procure him [to] take a penny in any cause depending before him in any court of justice. Here was justice without reward or respect, stopping his eyes and ears and closing his hands, neither seeing, hearing, feeling or knowing the great, rich man from the poorest soul.

Burghley's conduct, both as judge in the financial courts and as manager of the state's finances, was characterised by conscientious conservatism. His prime virtue, as manager of the crown's lean resources, was his sense of economy and careful husbanding of the queen's revenues. Clapham identified this when he wrote that 'Of the public treasure he was for the most part sparing'.[4]

In this respect Burghley was in tune with Elizabeth. Indeed, it was his relationship with her, not only financial but also political and personal, which proved to be the fulcrum of political stability during most of her reign. He was an astute politician and, by 1558, an experienced one. He was always careful not to offend her by adopting airs and graces as, for example, Leicester did. Nor, unlike Robert, earl of Essex in the 1590s, was he presumptuous or obviously seeking to monopolise the queen's counsel. Nevertheless, especially during his early years in her service, he betrayed the characteristic contemporary male prejudice about women in positions of authority. On one occasion he expressed the opinion 'that there is nothing more fulsome [i.e. offensive] than a she-fool'. And in 1560 he stated that diplomatic relations were 'too much for a woman's knowledge'. Whenever Elizabeth's obstinate, 'do-nothing' attitude prevented action on matters which, in his mind, required urgent resolution, he expressed his frustration on paper, either in memoranda or in correspondence with fellow politicians. At the end of the 1566–67 parliamentary session, in which the queen had not been persuaded to marry or name a successor, he drafted a memorandum, which was also a memorial to his failed labours. When, during the 1572 session, she procrastinated over Norfolk's execution, Burghley gave vent to his exasperation in a letter to Walsingham. He concluded with the wish that 'God's will be fulfilled and aid her Majesty to do herself good'. Her reluctance to proceed harshly against Mary Stuart caused him to put pen to paper again with complaints about her procrastination and lack of resolve. At the end of the session, when she withheld her assent to the bill against Mary and so frustrated all their endeavours, he wrote yet another anguished letter to Walsingham. He was also uncomfortably aware that the blame for failure would fall 'on some of us that are accounted inward Councillors, where indeed the fault is not'.[5]

Expressions of frustration and confidential complaint continued to figure in his correspondence with fellow councillors in the years after 1572. Sometimes he grumbled to Leicester and particularly to Walsingham about royal inaction over a wide variety of matters, including the fate of Mary Stuart and assistance to the Dutch rebels. At the same time, however, it should not be assumed that such complaints derived from and simply reflected a sense of masculine superiority. He showed respect, even admiration, for educated, cultivated women of intellect, such as the enthusiastically Protestant Catherine, duchess of Suffolk, whose friendship with him dated from the 1540s. From 1545 on Cecil himself was married to the learned Mildred Cooke, who, according to the Spanish ambassador de Silva, 'appears a much more furious heretic than he is . . . is clever and greatly influences him'. Burghley also recognised that the queen, schooled as he was by Cambridge tutors, was scholarly, cultivated and highly intelligent. During their long unequal partnership her political experience and his respect for her ability to govern grew together. Certainly he was under no illusions about the problems of service to an obstinate, volatile yet often indecisive monarch. In June 1586 he wrote to Leicester, the English military commander in the Low Countries:

> [A]lwayes I fynd two obstacles in her Majesty. One is, she is very carefull, as a good naturall prynce, although in such a case as this somewhat too scrupulous, to have her people adventured in fights. The other is, she will not have any more expended on her part, that she hath yielded unto, mislyking all extraordinary charges.[6]

Nevertheless, Burghley's anonymous biographer, who gathered together many of the late statesman's sayings, recollected that, 'He would often say he thought there was never so wise a woman born, for all respects, as Queen Elizabeth, for she spoke and understood all languages, knew all estates and dispositions of all princes, and so expert in her own as no councillor she had could tell her that she knew not.' The Lord Treasurer also described her as a ruler of 'rare gifts' who demonstrated 'wisdom and care of her country'.

The queen also displayed consummate skill in wedding together royal authority and gender power to control and even manipulate members of the male political monopoly. John Guy explains how 'the dithering, prevarication and generally dismissive behaviour which was understood to be archetypical of the conventional "mistress" provided Elizabeth with her weapons of political manipulation and manoeuvre'. Although Burghley was the professional administrator rather than the fashionable courtier, a trusted adviser and not a royal favourite like Leicester, Hatton, Raleigh and Essex, he was, like them, a Court politician. He did not, and did not have to, play the love games which the queen demanded. Nevertheless, at a decision-making level he was often just as affected as they were by her managerial skills of indecision and procrastination. Not that this appears to have affected in any fundamental way his trust, respect and loyalty. He wrote to his son Robert in 1596 that 'I am in a mixture of divinitie and polycy, preferring in polycy her Majesty afore all others on the earth, and in divynitie the King of heaven above all'. The occasion of his writing was a typical royal 'uncertainty for resolution' of a projected naval expedition against Spain. He advised Robert that whenever, now or in the future, he disagreed with the queen, 'as long as I may be allowed to give advise, I will not change my opinion by affirming the contrary, for that were to offend God, to whom I am sworn first'. However, he added that as her servant he would, having proffered his advices, then carry out her orders because, as 'God's chief minister here, it shall be God's will to have her commandments obeyed'. Whether or not he agreed with her instructions, he would in his heart wish them every success 'as I am sure she intendeth'. The principles of action, embodied in this wholesome advice from an elder statesman to his ambitious, rising, filial protégé, are largely borne out by his political record between 1558 and 1598. He emphasised the unity and harmony of service to deity and monarch in his last letter to Robert, just three and a half weeks before he died: 'Serve God by serving of the Queen, for all other service is indeed bondage to the devil.'[7]

The image of an unswervingly loyal and obedient Burghley, perpetuated by his own written protestations and the personal reminiscences of male politicians who knew him, does require modification in one significant respect. It has already been shown that he was capable of dissimulation, deception and covert politicking in what he considered to be the queen's own best interests. His thinking and actions on such occasions may have been influenced, consciously or otherwise, by an inherited belief in the superior political acumen of men. In his pursuit of what he regarded as desirable goals, such as royal marriage or at least a designated succession, and the destruction of the queen of Scots (already considered in earlier chapters), he worked within council and parliament to 'persuade' Elizabeth into necessary courses of action.[8] These would, in his perception, preserve the stability and security of the realm and guarantee her political surety and personal safety.

When, however, Burghley resorted to dissemblance and 'behind-the-scene' operations, it was usually because of royal prevarication or a difference over the preferred way to achieve mutually desired goals, rather than the pursuit of different and conflicting objectives. From the beginning of the reign queen and minister shared a common political position. They were heirs of the independent Protestant nation-state established, step-by-step, by the governments of Elizabeth's father Henry VIII and her half-brother Edward VI, and it was their first priority to preserve it. Their cautious conservatism was reinforced, if not moulded, by their experiences in the turbulent and, at times, threatening vicissitudes of mid-Tudor politics. During Mary's reign they had both respected the legitimate succession and the subject's duty to conform outwardly at least to the established religion. In brief, Elizabeth and Burghley had a common vision and priorities: internal political stability based on obedience and conformity, national security and peace.

During his forty years of service, however, he did have a number of significant differences with the queen over particular policies or courses of action. This was, as Collinson and Guy have argued, often the consequence of their contrasting perceptions of the Elizabethan polity. Whereas the queen held that conciliar advice placed no limitation on her prerogative power to make decisions and take actions, Burghley believed that it did. He also held the opinion that settlement of the succession required the assent of parliament. Yet Elizabeth persisted in the view that this was merely a prerogative concern. She also repeatedly failed to heed and act upon the advice of Burghley, his conciliar colleagues and parliament, especially in relation to Mary Stuart. When political differences occurred between queen and minister, however, they were not always the product of dissonant constitutional views. If, for example, anyone was the driving force behind English intervention in Scotland in 1559–60 it was Secretary Cecil. He steadily pressed and cajoled a reluctant but politically inexperienced monarch into the provision of financial assistance and then military and naval support for the Scottish rebels. His bold policy was a major success,[9] removing the French from Scotland and facilitating a Protestant Reformation there.

They differed too about marriage and succession. Burghley regarded royal marriage and direct heirs of the body as the most effective way of securing a settled and acceptable succession. Therefore he supported her courtships with, for example, the Austrian Habsburg archduke in the 1560s and the French Valois duke of Anjou in 1579–81. For Elizabeth, however, these were primarily useful diplomatic bargaining tools. She also enjoyed the theatre associated with Anjou's extended wooing. And it remains probable that she meant what she repeatedly said publicly, that she was not inclined to marry. The Anjou courtship, however, had, for both Burghley and Elizabeth, a value different from the earlier marriage negotiations. In the late 1570s and early 1580s he increasingly feared the threats posed by Spanish Habsburgs and French Guises. A Tudor–Valois marriage alliance might help to counter these. As for the queen, if her public enthusiasm and search for a positive conciliar response are taken at face value, the desire for emotional fulfilment may have played a more prominent part in this courtship than in the earlier matchmaking rituals and negotiations. On the other hand, she may simply have been combining, in characteristic manner, her diplomatic skills and pleasure in flirtation. Nothing eventuated, however, and after twenty years Burghley had to recognise that nothing would. During that time he had been adamantly opposed to one particular suitor for her hand, Robert Dudley. Although the mysterious death of his wife in 1560 ended the prospects of marriage, Dudley remained her favourite and the Secretary's political competitor. But also and especially after the 1560s, as Leicester and Burghley, they often worked together and confided in each other.[10]

Nor were the queen and minister of one mind so far as the church was concerned. Whereas the Elizabethan Settlement of 1559 was, for enthusiastic godly Protestants, the first instalment of reform, the queen showed scant sympathy for further change. Burghley was an Erastian, upholding the royal governorship and consistently hostile to a Presbyterian system in which it would have no place. In this, at least, he was at one with her. But, as we have seen, unlike the queen he sympathised with those who sought moderate reforms and a more effective preaching ministry; he was often critical of the bishops' failure to reform ecclesiastical abuses; and in the latter half of the reign he was openly opposed to the disciplinarian and authoritarian regime of Archbishop Whitgift. As a consequence he incurred royal criticism more than once. They also differed about the necessity for harsher penal laws against English Catholics, seminary priests and Jesuits during the 1580s and 1590s.

Furthermore, Burghley's belief in the existence of a grand Catholic conspiracy led him to seek what Elizabeth strove above all to avoid: the death of Mary Stuart, a sister-queen, albeit a deposed one. This issue, which was central to the parliament of 1584–85, brought into public focus the essentially different constitutional positions of queen and minister on the royal prerogative. It was an emergency parliament, summoned to deal with the growing threat posed by the confederacy of pope, foreign powers, missionaries, English Catholic conspirators and Mary. One of the two measures designed to provide for the queen's safety and the realm's security was the bill to give the Bond of Association statutory authority. During the parliament Burghley also drafted a scheme for an interregnum government headed by a Great Council, if Elizabeth was assassinated.[11] The Council was to exercise the monarch's powers, including the summoning of a parliament, which would then assume sovereign authority until it had chosen a successor. The scheme, which Guy describes as 'aristocratic republicanism par excellence', would have had major implications for the constitutional places of both monarchy and parliament, if it had been accepted and incorporated into statute. It was indeed devised by Burghley as a proviso to the bill for the queen's safety and its terms reflect his view of England as a mixed polity or, in Collinson's words, a 'monarchical republic'. The queen accepted neither his philosophy nor his draft proposals.[12]

The differences in temperament, gender, office, religious position and political belief suffice to explain the disagreements which occurred, between queen and minister, during their long political association. Whilst those disagreements – sometimes sharp and occasionally even dramatic – covered a broad spectrum of tactics, policies, priorities and solutions, they should be set in the context of shared objectives and unexciting and uncontroversial necessary daily management of the realm. As a trusted councillor he lived up to her expectation, voiced when she appointed him Secretary in 1558, that he would give her that counsel which he thought best. Evidence of that fulfilled trust survives in the many and often lengthy 'memorials', which he penned for her consideration. Not that, in the wisdom of hindsight, his advice always seems sound or based on accurate assessment of the political situation. This is especially so when his subject was the grand foreign Catholic conspiracy against England acting in concert with disaffected elements at home, even as early as 1569. On the other hand, when Burghley proffered possible solutions to a problem, he would weigh up the pros and cons, even in relation to a course of action which he recommended. This was not a sign of characteristic equivocation, but rather one of conscientious counsel.[13]

Burghley also proved to be the administrative hub of Elizabeth's government, not only during his term as Secretary of State, but also after his elevation to the office of Lord Treasurer. The shift in formal functional responsibility seems to have made little difference to his actual workload and range of bureaucratic activity. He was a dedicated, even obsessive worker who, according to Clapham, spent most of his time 'either in writing with his own hand or else in dictating to his secretaries, when by reason of the gout in his hand he could not write, though he would oft-times with much pain enforce himself thereto . . . God sparing that hand, it should seem, as a special instrument, whereby so much good was wrought for the public weal in his time'. Whatever he undertook – reform of the royal household, supervision of the affairs of Cambridge University, or preparations for a royal progress – he carried it through with assiduous attention to detail. He was no less attentive and dutiful when he implemented royal policies with which he was not in accord. The image which he projected to the queen, for most of the time, was that of the devoted, loyal and obedient servant – never power-seeking or manipulative. To others he could parade the virtue of passive obedience to God's anointed. When in the parliament of 1593 James Morrice, one of Burghley's subordinates in the Court of Wards, was guilty of indiscreet speech, he was placed under house arrest. Burghley instructed Morrice that, as a royal servant, it was his duty to complain to the queen privately, not publicly in parliament, if he believed that anything was 'amiss in the church or commonwealth'. And then, he added, 'to leave the matter to God and hir Majestie'.[14]

What was Morrice's real offence: that he had opposed the religious policies of Whitgift (and therefore of Elizabeth) or that he had publicly in parliament uttered his opposition?

Although Burghley was equally critical of the disciplinary campaign against nonconforming clergy, he confined his personal criticisms to the relatively confidential confines of private correspondence or the council and privy chamber. When, however, he went one step further and actively attempted to apply pressure to the queen to change her position on particular policies or coerce her into doing so, he engaged in an underhanded and risky political and managerial exercise. According to the Spanish ambassador, writing shortly after the parliamentary session of 1566–67, someone had informed Elizabeth 'that the Secretary was at the bottom of the obstinacy of the people's representatives in the matter of the succession'. When she charged him with this, in front of other councillors, he cleared himself to her satisfaction.[15] Nevertheless, as already noted, he was indeed sometimes 'at the bottom of the [commons'] obstinacy'. He and other Privy Councillors of like mind, however, were unwilling to jeopardise their career-prospects by an overt display of pressure tactics which, to Elizabeth, would have been tantamount to public disloyalty. Therefore they used 'cover men', usually their clients, to organise such parliamentary agitations and to speak out in their support. Burghley made particular use of such men in the commons, especially after his departure to the upper house in 1571.[16] Nor were such practices confined to parliaments. The secrecy and haste with which Burghley and other councillors met and authorised the despatch of Mary's execution warrant, in February 1587, was a prime example of the politics of concealment and deceit.

By focusing on Burghley, however, there is always the risk of exaggerating his importance. He was not the only nor always the most active figure in the conciliar and parliamentary lobbying of the queen. Nor did she depend on him, but also took counsel from other councillors, ministers and Court politicians, including her favourites Leicester and Hatton, until their deaths in 1588 and 1591 respectively. She took such advice individually, thereby avoiding collective pressure from the Privy Council. Sometimes she required each councillor's written opinions about such matters as the Mary–Darnley marriage and her own proposed Anjou match. Nor did she always heed Burghley's advice. On the subjects of ecclesiastical discipline and moderate puritan reforms Whitgift, Hatton and Lord Buckhurst were much closer to the queen than he was during the 1580s and 1590s.[17] Furthermore, he was not one of the courtly favourites who played gender games with an extraordinarily vain queen. Although the deaths of Leicester and Hatton left him as her unrivalled patronage manager, Natalie Mears has argued that there was no *Regnum Cecilianum* during the 1590s. It was 'a rhetorical device of criticism' devised by those who felt excluded by the Cecils and she concludes that 'it was certainly not the reality'.[18]

Nevertheless, the long-term relationship between the queen and Burghley was characterised by the steady growth of a mutual trust and confidence, reinforced by ongoing shared priorities. Confirmation of the queen's confidence occurred in 1569 when Arundel, Leicester and other nobles conspired to send him to the Tower. According to Camden, 'Cecil, through the magnanimous fortitude of his princess (who coming upon them in the very instant of time, restrained them by a beck) easily defeated the plot that was laid against him.' His security of tenure never seems to have been at risk again. His ennoblement in 1571 and elevation to the Lord Treasurership in 1572 were both royal rewards and public affirmations of Elizabeth's trust in him. Her visits to Burghley's country seats, especially Theobalds, for example in 1571, 1572, 1574, 1575, 1577, 1583, 1591 and 1594, were likewise implicit royal tributes to his stature and importance and, at the same time, prestigious and costly occasions for him. According to the anonymous biographer, her visits 'cost him £2,000 or £3,000 every time' and, although the evidence suggests that these were inflated figures, such royal descents involved considerable outlay.[19]

The queen's volatile temperament ensured that their relationship was not all sweetness and light. In 1594 and 1596 Burghley was 'well-chidden' by her for the state of Ireland; on another occasion she called him a 'froward old fool'; and in 1596 she addressed him as 'a miscreant and a coward, for that I would not assent unto her opinion' about a matter relating to the earl of Essex. One might attribute such outbursts to the acerbity of old age, when the queen was in her sixties. Yet ten years earlier, in 1586, he stayed away from the Privy Council because he was 'so wounded in the heart with the late sharp and piercing speeches of her majesty to myself'. His humiliation was all the greater because she had expressed 'the darkness of her displeasure' to him in front of Leicester and Walsingham. In self-pity he lamented that 'finding this heavy burthern of her majesty's displeasure in mine old years, so long faithfully, painfully, and dangerously spent, only for her service, to be lately rather encreased . . . I have great cause to fear that this encrease groweth more by means of some secret enemies to my self, than of any influence of her own princely nature'.[20]

On the other hand, there are many glimpses of Elizabeth's warm and caring concern for her ageing and increasingly gout-stricken minister. So in 1579 she came to his bedchamber to discuss foreign policy matters. And when, in 1591, he expressed a wish to retire to Theobalds, she responded with a witty, formal and sealed grant, discharging him from his duties: 'To the disconsolate and retyred spryte, the heremite of Tyboll . . . [w]ee upon advised consideration have commanded you, heremit, to your old cave, too good for the forsaken [i.e. abandoned], too bad for oour worthily belooved coouncillour.' She played with him in the same way, but in a more subdued manner, as she did with her courtly favourites. When, in 1597, he thanked her because she had appointed his son, Robert, to the chancellorship of the duchy of Lancaster, she sent word to him through the Lord Admiral that he was 'to her in all things and shall be Alpha and Omega'. With her penchant for nicknames she styled him *Sir Spirit* and when, in 1583, he made another appeal to resign and retire she gently chided him and concluded 'God bless you, and long may you last'. In such ways Elizabeth skilfully manipulated the men who surrounded her, not only her favourites but also Burghley and her other long-serving counsellors and administrators.

Nevertheless, there also seems to have been a dimension of genuine care and concern for the well-being of her Lord Treasurer and his family. She was godmother to his daughter Elizabeth, born in 1564. When, in 1583, the young, newly married woman followed her husband to the grave, the queen reprimanded the sorrowing father for his self-indulgence in bereavement. In the following month, she took time to visit him and his wife at Theobalds. Yet in April 1589, only a week after he had suffered the grievous loss of his wife Mildred, to whom he had been married for forty-three years, the queen ordered him back to Court for political consultations. The action in this case may have been prompted by royal insensitivity or, alternatively, by political necessity or a perception that the most effective remedy for Burghley's sorrow was work. When he was grieving over the death of his daughter Elizabeth, Walsingham had written to him that the queen thought 'if the healthe of your body may so permyt, you should do better to occupy yourself in dealing in publick causes, than by secluding yourselfe from access, to give yourself over a prey unto griefe'.[21]

Despite Elizabeth's regality and Burghley's characteristic gravity, there was a recurrent element of humour in their relationship. During one of her visits to Theobalds, for example, he persuaded her to make seven knights. Burghley arranged the order in which they should be knighted, because the first to be dubbed would be superior to the second in antiquity of title and so on. The queen learned of Burghley's disposition, passed them all by and, only at the end of the line, did she appear to remember her promise to honour them. 'With that she turned back, and knighted of the lowest first, and so upward.' One of her gentlemen of the privy chamber later told her, '"Your Majesty was too fine for my Lord Burghley". She answered, "I have but fulfilled the scripture; the first shall be last, and the last first."' In his last years the increasingly gout-stricken and bedridden Burghley exchanged penned pleasantries with Elizabeth, with his son as the go-between. In December 1593 he acknowledged that she had understood the real meaning of an allegorical letter which he had written to Robert.

> I must confesse that my cunning therein was not sufficient to hide the sense from her Majestie, although I thinke never a lady besides her . . . would have dissolved the figure to have found the sense as her Majestie hath done. And where her Majestie alloweth of me, that I made myself merry, in very truthe I did it rather to make her some sport . . .

When the wedding of Burghley's granddaughter approached in 1594, Elizabeth expressed the hope that he would dance at the nuptial celebrations. To this he replied, via Robert again, that 'I will be ready in mynd to dance with my hart, when I shall behold her favorable disposition to do such honor to her mayd, for the old man's sake'.[22]

Such pleasant (albeit occasional) exchanges with his royal mistress are in sharp contrast to his increasing irritability and impatience, especially with his inferiors, as he grew old. De Maisse described him in 1597 as 'very proud and presuming in his words'. He was variously depicted as expressing 'a kind of crossing and wayward manner', a 'tune of choler' and imprudent reflections 'in the grossest terms upon Henry IV' which 'was astonishing in a man of his age and experience'.

He was, however, more circumspect with his queen. Their longevity had a bonding effect as they both grew more conservative, cautious and, especially in Elizabeth's case, indecisive. Although their relationship contributed to political stability, it also became an obstacle to desirable changes. Burghley's long service benefited him, because he outlived other prominent Court politicians and, in consequence, he was unequalled in prestige, authority and patronage management. Even the rise of Elizabeth's new, young, paranoid favourite, Essex, and her over-indulgent attitude towards him posed no threat to the old Lord Treasurer's position. Whereas Essex was an aggressive war-hawk, queen and minister shared a preference for limited defensive war.[23]

Burghley's long service also worked against him. A variety of ailments, especially the gout which had afflicted him for so much of his life, grew progressively worse. During the 1590s he was often disabled and absent from Court, communicating with the queen through his son. Robert Cecil had performed the duties of principal Secretary for most of the last six years before 5 July 1596 when he was appointed to the office. Just a few weeks before that happened, on 26 May, his 'loving father' (as Burghley always signed himself) expressed his gratitude to the queen on receipt of Robert's 'large reports of her Majesty's allowances of my insufficiencyes as sufficient, and of her superabundant care and desyre of my amendment, as I cannot containe in the flowing of my heart'. He, whose entrenched male attitudes had demeaned her on occasions early in the reign, now prayed 'for the continuance of her happiness, wherein she exceedeth all her equalls in body and government'. Despite her fluctuating moods, the volatile queen was equally appreciative of her minister during the closing years of their partnership. When at last she made Robert Cecil Secretary in 1596, the Lord Admiral passed word to Burghley that 'Her Majesty . . . saith, wheresoever your Lordship is, your services to her giveth hourly thanks, and prayeth your Lordship to use all the rest possible you may that you may be able to serve her at the time that cometh'. In his dying days she came to his bedchamber and spoonfed him. When he died on 4 August 1598, Sir William Knollys wrote to the earl of Essex that, on receipt of the news, Elizabeth 'seemeth to take [it] very grievously, shedding of tears, and separating herself from all company'. He added, however, 'Yet doubt I not but she in her wisdom will cast this behind her, as she hath done many other before time of like nature.' Knollys' cynicism did less than justice to her trust, genuine affection and, at times, reliance on Burghley's judgement. Although she was a consummate actress and a public relations professional, her message, accompanying a cordial which she sent to Burghley during his last year, has about it a ring of sincerity: '[S]he did intreat heaven daily for his longer life – else would her people, nay, herself, stand in need of cordials too.' Furthermore, in the years after his death she shed tears at the mention of his name.[24]

Both contemporaries and historians have represented (or misrepresented) in various ways the relationship – unique, if only in its longevity – between Elizabeth and Burghley. According to de Spes, the Spanish ambassador, 'The Queen's own opinion is of little importance . . . Cecil unrestrainedly and arrogantly governs all.' But, like most foreign observers and diplomats, looking in from the outside and often dependent on biased informants, he got it wrong. The men on 'the inside' wrote (sometimes, though not always) with greater understanding and perception of the political realities. Although Robert Naunton maintained that Elizabeth 'ruled much by factions and parties', he also argued that Burghley 'was wholly intentive to the service of Hir Majesty [and] his dexterity, experience, and merit challenged a room in the Queen's favor which eclipsed the others' overseeming greatness'. Clapham, who had personal experience of service in Burghley's household, similarly defined government in terms of the queen and her minister. 'In matters of counsel, nothing for the most part was done without him, for that nothing was thought well done, whereof he was not the contriver and director. His credit with the Queen was such as his wisdom and integrity well deserved.'

Since then, until recent years at least, historians have tended to continue discussion of the Elizabethan political regime in the same narrow terms. So, in the mid-nineteenth century, J.A. Froude regarded Burghley, a male politician of sagacity, as the mastermind of a government over which a woman-ruler presided, but in which he directed policy and achieved results. Another late Victorian, Mandell Creighton, moved the other way. Although Burghley 'laboriously drew up papers which balanced the advantages and disadvantages of alternative action . . . when it came to decisive action she fell back upon her instinctive perception of what England wanted'. Almost thirty years later Lytton Strachey (1928) downgraded the Lord

Treasurer, when he described him as 'her chosen helper, a careful steward after her own heart' who often 'gave up the puzzle of his mistress's proceedings in despair'. Between the 1930s and 1950s J.E. Neale elevated her to the role of Protestant heroine, whereas Conyers Read argued that she could not get on without Burghley.[25]

Despite the assumption, erroneous as it now appears, that Court politics were faction politics and the recognition that Burghley had no monopoly of counsel, historians have tended to focus on this relationship between queen and minister. Much less attention has been given to the political establishment within which they operated. Only during the later twentieth century has the 'duet image' of top-level Elizabethan politics been significantly and realistically modified. Such works as Patrick Collinson's 'Monarchical Republic' and the recent essay collection edited by John Guy have helped to set the relationship in the broader political context of a subtle interplay between royal rule and conciliar government.[26]

. . .

NOTES

1. Beckingsale, *Burghley*, p. 67.
2. Read, *Secretary Cecil*, pp. 119–22; Starkey (ed.), *The English Court*, pp. 15, 130, 152–3, n. 26.
3. Smith, *Govt. of Eliz. England*, p. 108; Starkey (ed.), *The English Court*, p. 15; P. Wright, 'A change in direction: the ramifications of a female household, 1558–1603', ibid., pp. 152–4; *Clapham*, p. 80.
4. See above, pp. 151–9; Read, *Burghley*, p. 83; *Clapham*, pp. 81, 83; Smith (ed.), *Anon. Life*, pp. 79–80.
5. Smith, *Burghley*, pp. 9–10; PRO, SP, 12/41/36; Digges (ed.), *Compleat Ambassador*, pp. 165–6, 203, 219; Graves, 'Management: council's men of business', p. 27; Read, *Burghley*, p. 50; Graves, *Norton*, pp. 110, 195; W.P. Haugaard, *Elizabeth and the English Reformation* (Cambridge, 1970), p. 295; see above, pp. 57–8; Beckingsale, p. 68.
6. Graves, *Norton*, p. 334; Burghley to Leicester, 20 June 1586, Wright (ed.), *Queen Elizabeth*, II, pp. 299–301; Read, *Secretary Cecil*, pp. 58–9, 335–6; Smith, *Govt. of Eliz. England*, p. 7; Smith (ed.), *Anon. Life*, pp. 145–6.
7. Guy (ed.), *Court and Culture*, p. 3; Wright (ed.), *Queen Elizabeth*, II, pp. 457, 488.

8. See below, pp. 138–40.
9. Collinson, 'Monarchical republic, pp. 31–57; Guy (ed.), *Court and Culture*, p. 13; MacCaffrey, *Elizabeth I*, pp. 63–8, 359–60.
10. Ibid., pp. 99, 200–2; Graves, *Norton*, pp. 391–3; MacCaffrey, *Making of Policy*, pp. 263–4; see below, pp. 122–4.
11. PRO, SP, 12/176/22. Burghley had drawn up a similar proposal as early as 1563, presumably in response to Elizabeth's serious bout of smallpox in October 1562; ibid., 12/28/20; Neale, *Eliz. I and Parls.*, I, pp. 112–13.
12. Ibid., II, pp. 44–53; Guy (ed.), *Court and Culture*, pp. 13–15 and n. 28. See Guy's discussion of certain written objections to the interregnum scheme, PRO, SP, 12/176/32. Collinson attributes them to Burghley but Guy remains unconvinced.
13. e.g. Haynes (ed.), *State Papers*, pp. 579–93.
14. *Clapham*, p. 81; Graves, *Norton*, p. 85; P. Collinson, 'Puritans, men of business and Elizabethan parliaments', *Parliamentary History*, 7/2 (1988), pp. 194–5.
15. *Cal. SP Span., 1558–67*, p. 609; Read, *Secretary Cecil*, pp. 369–70; Elton points out that the evidence cited by Read in his account of the session indicates that Cecil did help 'to organise the pressure on her'. Elton, 'Parliament', in Haigh (ed.), *Reign of Elizabeth*, p. 99, n. 33.
16. See below, pp. 140–2.
17. Guy (ed.), *Court and Culture*, pp. 2–3; MacCaffrey, *Elizabeth I*, pp. 360–1.
18. Guy (ed.), *Court and Culture*, pp. 6–7; N. Mears, '*Regnum Cecilianum?* A Cecilian perspective of the Court', ibid., pp. 63–4.
19. See above, p. 53; Camden, *Annales*, p. 104; Beckingsale, *Burghley*, p. 279; Read, *Secretary Cecil*, pp. 352–3; Smith (ed.), *Anon. Life*, pp. 14–15; J. Nichols (ed.), *The Progresses and Public Processions of Queen Elizabeth*, 3 vols (London, 1823), I, pp. 205, 291, 308–9; II, pp. 400–4; III, pp. 241–6.
20. Birch (ed.), *Memoirs*, I, pp. 146, 169, 448; *HMC*, De L'Isle MS, 2, p. 217; J. Strype, *Annals of the Reformation*, 4 vols (Oxford, 1824), III, Pt. 2, pp. 410–11.
21. *HMC*, De L'Isle MS, p. 261; Strype, *Annals*, Vol. 3, Pt. 1, p. 241; ibid., Pt. 2, p. 125; ibid., Vol. 4, pp. 108–9; Nichols, *Progresses*, I, p. 149; ibid., II, p. 400; Beckingsale, *Burghley*, pp. 152–3; Wright (ed.), *Queen Elizabeth*, II, pp. 200–1.
22. J. Spedding, R.L. Ellis, D.D. Heath (eds), *Francis Bacon: Collected Works*, 14 vols (London, 1857–74), VII, pp. 157–8; Wright (ed.), *Queen Elizabeth*, II, pp. 428, 440.
23. Birch (ed.), *Memoirs*, I, pp. 164–5; II, pp. 328–9; Harrison and Jones (eds), *De Maisse*, p. 4; Smith, *Burghley*, p. 20; Guy (ed.), *Court and Culture*, pp. 3–9; Beckingsale, *Burghley*, p. 185.

24. Wright (ed.), *Queen Elizabeth*, II, p. 461; H. Ellis (ed.), *Original Letters Illustrative of English History*, 11 vols (London, 1824–46), 3rd ser., 4, p. 148; Birch (ed.), *Memoirs*, II, p. 390; Sir John Harington, *Nugae Antiquae*, 2 vols (London, 1804), II, p. 237.
25. *Cal. SP Span., 1568–79*, p. 265; *Naunton*, pp. 53–4; *Clapham*, p. 79; Froude, *History of England*, XII, p. 508; Read, *Secretary Cecil*, p. 454; idem, *Burghley*, p. 20.
26. See below, Ch. 6; also A.G.R. Smith's brief but useful discussion in *Burghley*, pp. 43–4.

Chapter 6

BURGHLEY: POLITICS, ADMINISTRATION, PUBLIC RELATIONS AND PATRONAGE

. . .

POLITICIAN AND ADMINISTRATOR

Any political activist or aspirant to office in Tudor England had to become a Court politician, because only at Court could he hope to secure social advancement, enjoy material benefits and influence policy. The Court provided the magnificent public context within which the monarch resided. It accommodated the Privy Council, which advised the king or queen on policy matters, executed royal policy decisions and, at times, attempted to influence or even formulate them. It was the political arena, in which political rivals competed to secure royal favour, patronage and a role in decision-making. In G.R. Elton's words, it was also a vital 'point of contact' between central government and the localities. Burghley had undergone his apprenticeship there as personal secretary to the duke of Somerset and then as principal Secretary of State. Therefore when he became Queen Elizabeth's personal and state Secretary he was already a Court politician of some experience. During the next forty years (1558–98) he was central to the political activity of both Court and council. As the queen's personal secretary he enjoyed direct access to her, whilst his friendly relations with the men and women of the privy chamber denied rivals, including Essex in the 1590s, the opportunity to build up a competing pressure group.[1]

Whilst Burghley enjoyed primacy of place, however, he did not have a monopoly of counsel or access to Elizabeth. Even when access to her was increasingly restricted in the last decade of the reign, the Cecils had to share it with Sir Walter

Raleigh, the Sackville, Knollys and Stanhope families and, until his downfall, Essex. And although, in course of time, he became the most experienced and, perhaps, realistic of her counsellors, she remained the decision-maker. Nevertheless, the queen held Burghley in high esteem and she did not take seriously his occasional pleas to resign or retire, due to age, illness, or frustrated policy proposals. The reason for his retention of high office during forty years of the reign was the consequence of two considerations: first, the queen's confidence in him and, secondly, the nature of Tudor government. As her chief minister and foremost adviser he lived up to the trust which she placed in him. He also fulfilled the dual role expected of any prominent Tudor royal servant: not only minister, proffering advice and executing royal decisions, but also civil servant, drafting memoranda, conducting an extensive correspondence with a variety of officials and local dignitaries, and engaging in multifarious administrative activities. He was neither an innovator nor a delegator. However, his relentless capacity for work, his scrupulous attention to detail and his careful paternalistic oversight of the conduct of subordinates helped to keep turning the wheels of an undermanned, ill-equipped state: as Privy Councillor (1550–53 and 1558–98) and Secretary of State (1550–53 and 1558–72) in the reigns of Edward VI and Elizabeth I; as Master of the Court of Wards (1561–98) and, from 1572 until his death, as Lord Treasurer.[2] He also served on many of the local or specialist commissions, both *ad hoc* and permanent, which supplemented the small professional bureaucracy of the Tudors.[3]

It was as Secretary Cecil, especially in Elizabeth's reign when he brought his Edwardian experience to the office, that he most clearly demonstrated his seemingly inexhaustible energy. It was the nature of the secretarial office which enabled him to engage in a wide range of business concerning church, state, defence, security and society. Nicholas Faunt, who had served Walsingham as his secretary, wrote in 1592 that 'amoungst all particuler offices and places of charge in this state, there is none of more necessarie use, nor subject to more cumber and variablenes then is the office of principall Secretarie, by reason of the varietie, and uncertaintie of his imployment, and therefore more difficultie to be prescribed by spetial methadd and order'.[4] Furthermore, as we have seen, Burghley's shift to the lord treasurership in 1571 did not mean that he relinquished all secretarial functions and responsibilities. Even when the confident, radically committed Protestant, Walsingham, became principal Secretary in 1573, Burghley's involvement in foreign affairs and security, two of the Secretary's prime concerns, continued. And, when Walsingham died in 1590, he once again assumed many of the responsibilities of his office, until his son Robert became, by degrees, *de facto* Secretary of State.

Burghley's monumental administrative endeavours rested upon a firm, but not always harmonious, bedrock of loyalties: to the state, the Tudors and, in particular, his queen. In his perception his royal mistress did not always serve the best interest of the state. As she passed beyond child-bearing age, so he had to look beyond her dynasty for the future political stability of the kingdom. For stability, which in the sixteenth century encompassed religion too, remained his constant priority. Joel Hurstfield accurately projected this. '[H]is religious policy cannot be explained by his religion but by his politics. And in politics he knew clearly and consistently what he wanted. His task was to secure 'order and government' in Church and state.' However, one of the prerequisites of order and stability was national security and, on this subject, Burghley revealed a preference (perhaps dictated by *realpolitik* and not conviction) for 'aristocratic constitutionalism' rather than 'regality'. Between Mary Stuart's arrival in England in 1568 and her execution in 1587 there was a growing fear of the threat which she posed to both monarch and kingdom. Burghley saw parliament as the immediate solution, because he perceived it to be, in some sense, the ultimate repository of constitutional authority, especially if the queen's sudden and dramatic demise left the kingdom without an appropriate royal ruler. Whilst Elizabeth reserved to herself the prerogative right to determine the succession, she had not done so.[5]

Recent history lent support to Burghley's position. This, as we have already seen, received practical expression in his interregnum bill (or proviso to the measure for the queen's safety) in 1584–85. Since the 1530s there had been a general acceptance that sovereignty resided in the king (or queen) in parliament. Burghley's legislative proposal, first mooted in 1563 and with greater urgency in 1584–85, was designed to resolve, in advance, the constitutional problems which would be created by the sudden death of the queen, who was the most important member of the parliamentary trinity. Such proposals do not belittle, throw into question or demean his acceptance of the royal role or his loyalty to the wearer of the crown. In any case his particular conception of the nature of English government acquired some political significance only when his monarch's life was placed at risk: either by disease (as in 1562) or assassination (as it seemed in the early 1580s). Nevertheless, the concept of a mixed polity was implicit in his actions at other times: when, for example, he endeavoured to use the occasion of parliaments to bend the royal will to the desires of an aristocratic élite of nobles, gentry, and a leavening of municipal dignitaries, merchants and lawyers.[6]

As a relative *nouveau* in the upper aristocratic echelons of Tudor society he also displayed a well-developed and self-conscious social awareness. The man whose first marriage, contracted in 1541, was to a woman who worked in a Cambridge wineshop, heartily disapproved, 'on the ground of social incompatibility', when, half a century later, Lord Howard of Bindon's daughter married a London merchant's son. In 1588 he was fretting about the diminished size of the peerage. By then, however, he was a baron with children married into that noble élite. In 1564 Thomas, his eldest son and sole child by his first wife, wedded the daughter of the third Lord Latimer. Seven years later, Burghley's daughter Ann, his favourite, entered into marriage with that dashing but unstable flower of the nobility Edward, seventeenth earl of Oxford. In 1582 he celebrated the nuptials of another daughter, Elizabeth, and the son of Lord Wentworth. Finally, in 1589, the marriage of Burghley's younger son Robert to a daughter of the seventh Lord Cobham, Lord Warden of the cinque ports, reinforced the Cecils' matrimonial links with the Elizabethan peerage.[7]

The social advancement and consolidation of Burghley's family was a process concurrent with his progression as a politician and administrator. However, that progression was not a smooth and continuous process, because it was affected by circumstantial and personal variables and changes. His Edwardian apprenticeship was followed by a period in the political wilderness during Mary Tudor's reign. As Elizabeth's Secretary of State between 1558 and 1572 he was both the administrative co-ordinator of her government and a forceful promoter of policy. Although he did not relinquish all of the Secretary's activities and responsibilities when he became Lord Treasurer in

1572, the shift changed his administrative role and relieved him of some of the routines and minutiae of the secretarial office. Furthermore, the gout, which plagued Burghley for most of his working life, grew worse as he grew older. During the 1570s, the 1580s and especially the 1590s his service to the queen was punctuated by periods when he was bedridden and absent from Court. When he was incapacitated he could not fulfil his administrative and judicial responsibilities, but this did not prevent him from counselling the queen. He continued to advise her and, whenever possible, to influence her on both domestic and foreign policy matters. Indeed, Elizabeth would not allow him to withdraw from the policy-making process. As she told him, 'My Lord, we make use of you not for your bad legs, but your good head.' His record confirms that his political significance did not decline. The man who could promote measures against the Jesuits, actively advocate the queen's proposed marriage to Anjou in the Privy Council and support the war in the Netherlands, secure Mary Stuart's death and successfully advance his son, Robert, as his political and administrative heir, was not a politician sidelined by illness.[8]

Burghley was, in any case, a skilful politician whose ability was steadily augmented by cumulative experience. John Clapham was guilty of exaggeration when he wrote that no government activity was regarded as effective unless he initiated it. The evidence, however, lends credence to some of his other assertions: 'Quick he was of conceit, of a ready dispatch, and of a great memory'; also that 'Such matters as he undertook, either for the good of the state or for his own private advantage, he chose to accomplish rather by patience in waiting opportunities than by open show of authority, or presumption of the Prince's favour.' Clapham divined one of the secrets of his success, because Burghley was usually a low-key politician, but always an organised one. He had his own personal secretariat, which mirrored the bureaucratic and household mix of central government. The men who served in his secretariat, such as John Clapham, Henry Maynard and Vincent Skinner, were also members of his household. Although they were few in number, considering the volume and range of business which he handled, they were essential supplements to the state's small bureaucracy. Particularly important was Michael Hickes, who, from 1580 to 1598, was Burghley's patronage secretary.[9]

Burghley was well informed on both foreign and domestic affairs, partly through Maynard, whose duties concerned international relations, but also because he received reports and advices from a wide range of sources. Much information was supplied by his own intelligence network, royal servants, or Englishmen travelling abroad, but he often received unsolicited reports too, simply out of personal loyalty to him or because he was recognised as the queen's chief minister. In addition, as Palliser points out, Tudor government especially from the 1530s onwards made a serious, albeit limited, attempt to collect statistical and other detailed data: enclosure commissions, surveys of clergy and recusants, bills of mortality and muster rolls. Burghley often acquired data on customs revenue and import–export relationships. Sometimes the information was collected for propaganda purposes, but it also enabled ministers and councillors to define the magnitude of problems with which they were faced.[10]

. . .

BURGHLEY AND THE PRIVY COUNCIL

Such data-collecting commissions and surveys were often authorised by the Privy Council and it was in the council that the responsibilities of Burghley and other advisers and administrators came together. Although the queen had a marked preference for consulting councillors individually, rather than the council as a body, the formulation of advice remained one of its chief collective functions. Another was administration: to implement the queen's policy decisions and to oversee and direct the daily operation of royal government, especially in the localities. The council was sometimes divided over policy, especially in the late 1560s (when the proposed Norfolk–Mary match and other issues provoked division), on the Anjou marriage a decade later, and over war and peace and military strategy in the 1580s and 1590s. These disputes put Burghley under considerable pressure. In 1569, as we have seen, only the queen's intervention saved him from a Court conspiracy. Between 1578 and 1581 initial support for Elizabeth's marriage to the French duke of Anjou dwindled, leaving Burghley and a small conciliar rump of isolated advocates. And during the long war with Spain his financially realistic preference for defensive military operations conflicted with the demand of the war-hawks, led by Essex, for an aggressive strategy. His problems were compounded by the carry-over of Court rivalries into the council chamber and by the queen's technique of playing off councillors against each other, in particular her favourite, Leicester, against him.[11] Nevertheless, serious disagreement was the exception rather than the rule. The social homogeneity and common political priorities of the council's membership ensured that, whilst there were divisions over particular policies and proposals, such as the Austrian archduke's proposal for marriage in the mid-1560s, harmony (though rarely unanimity) tended to prevail.

Burghley's conscientious dedication to the routine administrative business of the Privy Council, as well as his influence as counsellor to the queen, made him a force to be reckoned with in its deliberations. He had already made his mark on the Edwardian Privy Council by his assiduous attention to business and by his regular attendance in 1550–53. Between 5 September 1550 and 24 March 1552 he was present at 82 per cent of council meetings; his record for the remainder of the reign, 25 March 1552–16 June 1553, was 71 per cent. When he was reappointed as Secretary in November 1558 he was again regularly present at sittings of the Privy Council. Of course he was not the only councillor to put in a frequent appearance: in the 1560s Lord Clinton (later earl of Lincoln), Sir Francis Knollys (the queen's cousin), Lord Keeper Bacon, Robert Lord Dudley (made earl of Leicester in 1564) and others were regular participants in council business. Between 1570 and 1590 Sir James Croft, Walsingham and Hatton joined Knollys, Lincoln and Leicester amongst the most diligent councillors. During the 1590s, as an older generation died off, Robert Cecil, Thomas Sackville Lord Buckhurst, Charles Lord Howard of Effingham and Sir John Fortescue replaced them as mainstays of conciliar business.

Yet throughout four decades one man, Burghley, remained more or less regular in his attendance, despite the disabling effects of gout and the ageing process. Between 1558 and 1570 he was present at 97 per cent of Privy Council meetings. Thereafter he remained a 'regular', although he never again sustained the same high level of attendance over a lengthy period: for example, 79 per cent in 1571–75, 80 per cent in 1578–80, 70 per cent in 1581–82, and 78 per cent in 1589–90. During the 1590s an old man in his seventies, often now crippled with gout and bearing the worry and burden of funding a sustained war with the Spanish empire, still found time and energy to put in regular appearances at sittings of the Privy Council: 77 per cent of the meetings in 1590–91, 97 per cent in 1591, 88 per cent in 1592 and 80 per cent in 1592–93. However, as his physical condition deteriorated, so did his attendance record: 64 per cent of meetings in 1595–96 and 60 per cent in 1597. Yet even in his last painful year he managed to turn up to over half (52 per cent) of the sessions. His absence from one meeting, on 21 July 1598, produced a council letter to him about a dispute over cloth exports to Germany. Written just a fortnight before his death, it signals conciliar reliance on his accumulated knowledge and reputation:

> And although wee are lothe to trouble your good Lordship at this tyme, your health not servinge you so well as wee do wyshe, nevertheles this beinge a matter of very great weight, in regard of your Lordship's longe experyence and judgement wee have bene bolde to send you the demaunds of the Merchaunts Adventurers and the answere of the straingers . . . [The Privy Council sought Burghley's] advyse and opynion what course you thincke meete to be taken in this matter that maie greatlie concerne the state of the realme.

Furthermore, council letters drafted on 23 July were not despatched for three days 'by reason they were sent to the Lord Treasurer, who by reason of sickness was not able to sign the same'. Such was the Privy Council's dependence on Burghley, even to the very end.[12]

. . .

PROPAGANDA AND PUBLIC RELATIONS

Burghley was 'the most important figure after the Queen in the workings of both the Privy Council and the Court' and especially her most influential policy adviser. As such he took upon himself prime responsibility for the public justification and, when necessary, defence of the government's more controversial actions and policies. His public addresses to Justices of the Peace at the end of law terms and his parliamentary speeches when he sat in the commons (1559–66/67) provided points of contact and communication with the magisterial class. Furthermore, the advent of the printing press in the previous century had facilitated the growth of state propaganda, enabling governments to engage in public relations exercises with a wider audience. The regime of Henry VIII had been very active in this respect, especially during Thomas Cromwell's 'ministry'. So too was the government of Elizabeth, who took a personal and active interest in the drafting and publication of propagandist works. Public statements of the official position, justifying its conduct (and sometimes vilifying its opponents and enemies), appeared in a variety of forms. They included preambles to parliamentary statutes and royal proclamations, but especially pamphlets. Burghley had a hand in the drafting of justificatory preambles to subsidy bills (as in 1566 and 1588) and, especially when he was Secretary, he was the author of proclamations. He also encouraged or called upon others, such as Bishop Jewel, Dr Walter Haddon, William Charke, Thomas Norton, Robert Beale, Francis Walsingham, his younger son and political heir, Robert, and John Stubbs to defend royal policies in church and state and to reply to hostile Roman Catholic tracts.[13]

Burghley himself was particularly active in the production of pamphlets, sometimes with the queen's encouragement or at her behest. His one excursion into print, prior to Elizabeth's accession, was in 1547, early in Edward VI's reign, when he edited Catherine Parr's anti-papal and anti-Catholic *The Lamentations of a Sinner*. During Elizabeth's reign, however, he was a busy propagandist. Although no official publication appeared in praise and defence of the Elizabethan Settlement after its parliamentary enactment in 1559, Burghley had a hand in the production of a *Declaration of the proceedings of a Conference begun at Westminster*. This justified the government's action in arresting two of the staunchest papist bishops for their 'default and contempt' in the theological debate held during the Easter parliamentary recess.[14] Over the years more justificatory declarations of royal policies followed, some of them penned and published by Burghley: defending the English invasion of Normandy (1562); denying, after the northern rebellion of 1569, that the queen ever intended to persecute outwardly 'quiet and conformable' subjects for their religious beliefs; defending the despatch of military assistance to the Dutch (written in collaboration with Walsingham in 1585); and explaining why the queen had authorised the earl of Essex's expedition to Cadiz (1596). His most significant and effective piece was *The*

Execution of Justice in England, published in 1583 and reprinted six times within a year. It stated the government's consistent position in its treatment of Roman Catholics: that they were punished only for treasonable acts, not for religion. Two more of Burghley's pamphlets were directed against the forces of Catholicism and Spain. In one printed in 1588 and addressed to Bernadino Mendoza, Philip II's ambassador to France, the author masqueraded as a loyal English Catholic, who praised his queen, condemned papal policies and scorned Spanish power after the defeat of the Armada. The other, in 1594, purported to be *A True Report* of the Lopez conspiracy against the queen.[15]

As a skilled propagandist Burghley recognised the need to reach out to an international audience. So, for example, *The Execution of Justice* was also printed in Dutch, French, German and Italian, whilst the *Declaration*, justifying the Cadiz expedition, appeared in six languages, including Latin and Spanish. However, at least a dozen of his projects remained unpublished or were abandoned before completion. They included a defence of the English intervention in Scotland (1560) and of the seizure of Genoese bullion (1569), and propagandist pieces, which lauded queen and kingdom, such as *England Triumphant* (1570), *Anglia personata loquens* (1585) and *Meditation of the State of England*. Most of his pamphlets, however, whether published or not, reveal a common characteristic: that, in the words of Conyers Read, 'he had an itching hand for the pen but no marked aptitude in the use of it'. In contrast to, say, the racy and economical language and vivid imagery of Thomas Norton's productions, Burghley's prose tended to be laborious, repetitious and wearisome. It was, perhaps, just as well that many of his compositions did not go to press.[16]

. . .

BURGHLEY AS PATRON

Patronage oiled the wheels of Tudor government. Royal favours, such as honours, offices in church and state, grants of lands, economic privileges and annuities, were expressions of the strength and (falsely) the wealth of the crown and the benevolence of its wearer. They also reinforced loyalty by pandering to self-interest. Patronage not only augmented royal officials' salaries, which were not commensurate with their responsibilities and duties, but also rewarded members of the unpaid county magistracy for loyal service. Only a favoured few had direct personal access to the queen and so most supplicants and petitioners for royal favours had to secure the services of middlemen who enjoyed such access. This explains Burghley's prominence as a patron. Although he had no monopoly in the distribution of royal patronage, he was better placed than anyone else to obtain favours from the queen. She trusted his probity and valued his counsel, whilst he, as her personal secretary, had entrée to the privy chamber and so enjoyed frequent opportunities to advance suitors' causes. As a prominent officer of state he also had his own patronage to dispense. He made appointments to offices in the Court of Wards and granted the guardianship of wards and management of their estates. As Lord Treasurer he had the right of appointment, not only to positions in the central financial departments, the Exchequer and Mint, but also local customs officers, as well as unpaid escheators and paid professional feodaries, who together were the county agents of the Court of Wards.[17]

Burghley's political prominence and patronage role inevitably created a large Cecil clientele. Some, such as the members of his secretariat and James Morrice, attorney of the Court of Wards, became career-dependants. Others looked to him to intercede with the queen on their behalf for benefits which they sought. Many who approached him as suitors were men of wealth, high status, regional influence and political importance. They were not Burghley's clients, but he was on good terms with them, whilst they knew that the value of any royal grant depended on its terms and conditions, which required the Lord Treasurer's approval. At various times churchmen, including Archbishop Parker, solicited his assistance, Bishop Cox pleaded his poverty and, in 1595, the disgraced Bishop Fletcher of London sought his help to gain access to the queen. Burghley also petitioned successfully for nobles such as the earls of Bedford, Derby, Essex, Leicester, Shrewsbury and Sussex. He displayed considerable tact in his dealings with Shrewsbury, when the latter was Mary Stuart's gaoler and burdened with both cost and responsibility. Shrewsbury responded with offers of hospitality, when Burghley took the waters at Buxton in 1577. Sussex, who was assisted by him in his endeavour to buy Newhall manor from the queen, was much attached to him. When, in 1578, he learned that the Lord Treasurer had been 'ill used by lewd speeches' he wrote supportively, '[W]hosoever they are . . . I rest at your devotion, with heart and hand to stand by you as by myself, and upon all occasions to stick as near to you as your shirt is to your back.' Two years later he praised Burghley for 'the upright course which you have always taken . . . [which] have tied me to your Lordship in that knot which no worldly frailty can break; and, therefore, I will never forbear to run any fortune that may serve you . . . '. Sussex, so hostile to the earl of Leicester and so loyal to Burghley, fits neatly into the traditional scenario of ongoing faction conflict between Elizabeth's favourite and chief minister. Yet in 1566, when Leicester, seeking a major exchange of lands with the queen, had to be absent from Court, he confidently left Cecil to negotiate on his behalf. Many years later, in 1579, he expressed gratitude and hearty thanks for his willingness to persuade Elizabeth to provide some financial help to his brother, the earl of Warwick, in 'his great nede'.[18]

In his role as middleman Burghley also promoted the interests and advanced the suits of many non-noble Court politicians and prominent county gentry, such as Sir Henry and Robert Sidney, Nicholas Anthony and, at least in his early years, Francis Bacon. He was an active patron to his client and protégé Walsingham and he was on amicable terms with Sir Christopher Hatton. In Hatton's case the usual roles were reversed when, in 1581, Burghley warmly thanked him for his 'good and honorable dealing with her Majestie' in the case of his daughter Ann, unhappily married to the earl of Oxford. It was another instance of the collegiality which tended to characterise Court politics. And it extended even into the more factious political climate of the 1590s: when, for example, between 1591 and 1594, Burghley was 'very well affected' to Sir Robert Sidney in his various suits, even though Sidney was a confirmed supporter of the young earl of Essex.[19]

Burghley was acutely aware of the political value of patronage. In 1580 he advised the queen 'That you gratyfye your nobylyte and the principall persons of your realme to bynde them faste to you . . . whereby you shall have all men of value in your realme to depend only upon you'. As Lord Treasurer he exploited royal estates, but especially farming of the customs, trading privileges and grants of monopolies as sources of patronage. Meanwhile he had to cope constantly with a besieging force of patronage hunters. His anonymous biographer expressed his incredulity, when he wrote from first-hand experience of his 'pains and industry [which] were incessant' as he responded daily to a deluge of suits and petitions.

> He used also to answer the poorest soul by word of mouth . . . but, after he grew impotent and weak and could not go abroad . . . he devised a new way . . . that, by age and infirmities being forced to keep his chamber and sometimes his bed, he took order that poor suitors should send in their petitions sealed up, whereby the poorest man's bill came to him as soon as the rich. Upon every petition he caused his answer to be written . . . and subscribed it with his own name . . . [T]here was none stayed for answer, but was speedily dispatched.

The pitiless pressure of suitors continued to the end. In May 1593 Burghley wrote to Robert Cecil, that he was 'weak, and uncertayn how I shall be able to come to the Court'. But he added that 'Untill this dynner tyme I have had neither kyn nor inward friend to see me or salute me, but multitude of sutors that only come for their own causes'. Nothing had changed in November 1596 when a brief letter to Robert from 'Your loving father' informed him that 'I have not bene idle since you went, having (though not profaned this Sabbath-day) made it a full working day, such is the importunity of sutors, and now wearyed I end my scribbling'.[20]

Burghley's labours were not without their rewards. Some took the intangible form of effusive thanks and acknowledgements from grateful petitioners and those who sought his continued favour. In 1570 his 'assured friend' the earl of Bedford, who, with Burghley's help, had received some favour from the queen, assured him that 'I shall remayn a contynuall Besecher to God for her Majestie, and to you for your Gentlenes so frendely to further the same, I shall . . . be yours to the best of my Power allwayes, as you shall lyste to prove me'. Walsingham, in 1575, expressed 'most humble thankes' for his 'honorable and friendly dealing towards me, in persuading her Majesty to have some consideration or rather compassion of my poore estate'. Even in the faction-driven political climate of the mid-1590s the earl of Essex could write in order 'to crave of your Lordship that I may be continued in your good Lordship's favor, and to pray you that you will pleade for me till I returne [from the Calais expedition in 1596]'.

Burghley was the recipient of many such letters, but he was also the recipient of material benefits from both successful and aspiring suitors. Between January 1596 and 1598 he received over £3,000 in gifts from those seeking wardships. Thomas Smith made private payments of up to £2,000 in order to obtain the farm of the customs. And Burghley received gifts and gratuities from a wide range of suitors, some of them personages of social prominence or high rank. Furthermore, he made no secret of his pleasure on receipt of such presents. Rowland White wrote to Sir Robert Sidney, a frequent suitor during the 1590s, '[H]ow pleasing your present was to my Lord Treasorer, what loving speaches he used of you.' He was, of course, not alone in this practice because, in Hurstfield's words, 'The giving and taking of gifts was an inherent part of Tudor society and government. Without them officialdom would have withered and died away', because they were an essential supplement to the salaries of royal servants. Even the highest officers of state received only modest sums, which were not commensurate with their responsibilities and which did not maintain them in a lifestyle appropriate to their station. The practice was not furtive, but public knowledge. Everyone from the queen downwards knew about it and accepted it. Burghley's opportunities to advance the interests of a swarm of suitors and the consequent rewards were so considerable that Michael Hickes, a member of his secretariat, served as his patronage secretary in the 1590s. It was widely recognised that he was a valuable intermediary through whom to approach the Lord Treasurer for the advancement of suits.[21]

Although the system would be regarded as corrupt today, it was not necessarily or inherently so then. In Burghley's case, for example, it depended whether he acted to the crown's disadvantage or misused his powers as judge for the sake of personal profit. There is little evidence that such charges could be levelled against him. In particular, in contrast to Francis Bacon, who, as Lord Chancellor in the next reign, was impeached for corrupt practice, contemporaries extolled his qualities as judge and historical research has confirmed their verdict. Nevertheless, he had his share of critics, especially among disappointed suitors. He was attacked because, mistakenly, he was believed by some to enjoy a monopoly of power and patronage and so he was held culpable for their lack of success. The oft-thwarted Francis Bacon was bitter. So was the poet Spenser:

Full little knowest thou, that hast not tried,
What hell it is in suing long to bide;
. . . .
To fawn, to crouch, to wait, to ride, to run,
To spend, to give, to want, to be undone.

Burghley was also accused of securing his own position for personal gain by favouring unsuitable men and blocking the promotion of talented careerists, who might prove to be a threat. As Thomas Lake wrote in 1591, 'Old *Saturnus* is a melancholy and wayward planet, but yet predominant here . . .'. According to the frustrated, disappointed and aggrieved Spenser,

For men of learning little he esteemed
His wisedome he above their learning deemed.

Spenser saw Burghley 'now broad spreading like an aged tree', preventing men from rising 'that nigh him planted bee'. In James I's reign Francis Bacon recollected that 'in the time of the Cecils . . . able men were by design and of purpose suppressed'. *The State of England*, written in 1600 by Thomas Wilson, younger son of a country gentleman and a man of limited talent and less fortune, was similarly jaundiced. He plagiarised Spenser with his reference to the Lord Treasurer who 'like an aged tree' prevented the rise of possible rivals who 'are skillfull or studious of matters of pollicy . . . [T]he greatest politicians that rule most will not have about them other then base penn clarkes, that can do nothing but write as they are bidden, or some mecanicall dunce that cannot conceive his Master's drifts and policies . . .'.[22]

Burghley was also accused of demanding sole allegiance from his clients, and there is some justice in the charge. In 1591 Robert Sidney was advised not to look to others as well as the Lord Treasurer for advancement, 'for it is ill taken'. His correspondent, Thomas Lake, reported that 'Sir Edward Norris has fallen into the high indignation of my Lord Treasurer . . . for nourishing a dependency on others besides his Lordship, which will hardly be put up . . .'. When Thomas Wilkes, clerk of the Privy Council, promoted a suit to the queen through Walsingham instead of Burghley, he was publicly reprimanded by the Lord Treasurer. Worse still, if a recent study by Hiram Morgan of the fall, treason trial and condemnation of Sir John

Perrot is correct, Burghley must be charged with masterminding his destruction for personal reasons. Perrot, an energetic lord deputy of Ireland (1584–88), alleged bribery and corruption by Sir William Fitzwilliam, his successor. Fitzwilliam, who was Burghley's client and kin by marriage, was protected from exposure by him. According to Morgan, the Lord Treasurer had a leading hand in the proceedings which led to Perrot's conviction for treason in 1592: it was a tale of 'despicable behaviour towards a fellow privy councillor and of an irresponsible, negligent and possibly corrupt policy towards Ireland in the early 1590s'.

Whether or not Morgan's indictment of Burghley is correct – and this is not the place to debate it – most of the derogatory assessments of 'old Saturnus' relate to the 1590s. That is not surprising. He was aged, often ill and irascible, clinging to his paramountcy and working assiduously through his son Robert to ensure the future political prominence of his family. There is some justice in the charges against him. On the other hand, his oft-quoted eloquent critics – Bacon, Spenser and Wilson – were all disgruntled, disappointed and therefore biased suitors. In any case the queen, not Burghley, controlled and determined appointments to high offices. Furthermore, by the standards of his age the Lord Treasurer was not corrupt and he was certainly more scrupulous in his dealings than Secretary Robert Cecil, his son. Paul Hammer cites instances of suitors who sought 'the good lordship' not only of Burghley but also of others, including the earl of Essex. Nor, so far as we can tell, did this discredit them in his eyes.[23]

Nevertheless, though Burghley had no organised clientele network, he has often been represented as a faction leader. Robert Naunton wrote that the queen 'herself both made, upheld and weakened [factions] as her own great judgement advised'. Camden too placed faction at the centre of Court politics. For long historians, taking their lead from Naunton and Camden, wrote on the assumption that this was the dominant characteristic and organising principle of Court politics. In 1948, for example, Sir John Neale stated that 'The place of party was taken by faction', that faction rivalry focused on the ultimate concern, 'influence over the Queen and, through that influence, control of patronage with its accompanying benefits'. Furthermore, the Court, 'the Mecca of patronage', was the natural arena of faction conflict. However, as Paul Hammer and Simon Adams have pointed out, clienteles and factions were not synonymous. Client networks naturally competed for patronage, whereas 'the alleged appearance of factions meant that the contest for an office or grant had ceased to be a matter of competition between rival suitors and had become a political issue'. As Hammer points out, 'faction' was a pejorative term. If it existed at all before the 1590s it was the exception, not the norm. Ironically, it is a term which may well be applied to Edwardian politics, in which Burghley had had his apprenticeship. But it is inappropriate to describe even the 1560s as a decade of faction politics. Minister and favourite were often in disagreement: over the former's influence with the queen, the latter's possible marriage to her, policy differences and Norfolk's manœuvrings with Mary Stuart. Yet co-operation in Court politics was more common than conflict in the 1560s and certainly during the next two decades.

There was a fundamental difference between individual rivalries and competition for patronage, on the one hand, and faction on the other. Burghley summed up the essence of Court politics before the 1590s in a letter to Sir Thomas Smith in 1565:

> Agayne ther are sondry rumors that the Lordes here do not accord together, that my Lord of Leicester should not have so great favor as he had; that my Lord of Sussex and he should be in strange termes; that my Lord of Norfolk, my Lord Chamberlayn, my Lord of Hunsden, & c., should also not allow of my Lord of Leicester, that Mr Hennadg should be in very good favour with her Majestie, and so mislyked by my Lord of Leicester . . . but I trust herof no harme in dede shall follow, for all these Lords are bent towards her Majestie's service, and doo not so much vary amongst themselves, as lewd men do report.

Even in the early 1590s the hunt for patronage by suitors at Court was characterised, not by political faction but, in Hammer's words, a 'relative fluidity and pluralism'. 'Factionalism' – political conflict – emerged only with the earl of Essex's heightened challenge to the Cecils in the second half of the 1590s. He pursued not only an aggressive war policy but also a monopoly of royal patronage, as a register of his political power. And so, in the words of Simon Adams, 'a politics of patronage' developed, 'the relationship between faction and patronage was transformed' and 'factions became the norm of Court politics rather than the exception'.[24]

Any revision of the history of Court politics, faction and patronage involves a reassessment of the relationship between Burghley and Leicester. The traditional picture, reinforced by Conyers Read's lengthy two-volume biography of the former, is one of continuous and deep-seated hostility between them. Even as recently as 1993 MacCaffrey described Burghley's distrust of Leicester throughout their shared Elizabethan political life. There is no doubt that they were often competitors for royal favour, especially when they disagreed over policy. However, they did not lead contending factions against each other. Burghley was undoubtedly opposed to a possible marriage between Elizabeth and Leicester, in the interest of both political stability and personal position. The earl, in his turn, resented Burghley's considerable influence with the queen. During the 1560s they had serious differences over a variety of issues, including the projected marriages of Elizabeth and Mary Stuart, and Leicester was involved in the failed attempt to remove the Secretary in 1569. Nevertheless, there was, even in the 1560s, more drawing them together than dividing them. They had, as Adams writes, a 'similar outlook in religion and agreement on most matters of state, together with a mutual appreciation of their joint intimacy with the Queen'. Court gossip and rumour played their part in projecting and sustaining a public perception of hostility between them. As Burghley wrote to his confidant, Sir Thomas Smith, in September 1564, 'You may [by chance] heare that thynges are not sound betwixt my Lord Robert and me, but surely all is well . . . although either of us do understand well ynough, how busy many be to move the contrary. I must confess myself to be much beholden to his Lordship, and for my part I do endeavour myself in good ernestnes to merit well of hym.'[25]

Despite the ups and downs in their relationship during the 1560s, their mutual priorities enabled them to establish a *modus vivendi* and a capacity for working together. Thereafter there are many examples of their co-operation, amicable relations, confidentiality, and care for each other's interests when one of them had to be absent from Court. When, in 1575, Leicester was with the queen and Burghley was absent, the earl kept him in touch with her activities and state of health. He also thanked the Lord Treasurer for his 'friendly dealing' on his behalf and assured him that, 'when the occasion shall be offered, that I wyll deale no lesse but more ernestly than for myself . . . and what your Lordship shall imparte unto me at any time for the accomplishment hereof, you shall see how willingly and carefully I wyll deale in it'. When, in 1579, Leicester's opposition to the proposed royal match with the duke of Anjou incurred the queen's anger, it was Burghley whom he sought out to represent his 'humble dewty' to her. And, on his part, the Lord Treasurer in 1586 had sufficient trust in the earl, who was then commander-in-chief of the English forces in the Netherlands, to confide in him about the queen's limitations.[26]

Although Burghley, in stark contrast to Leicester, was for long opposed to military intervention in the Netherlands, he threw his weight behind the proposal when he recognised that, in the interest of national security, there was no alternative. Leicester was not a success, either as administrator or warrior. Nevertheless, the Lord Treasurer lent him his support and promised not to take political advantage of his absence. He was as good as his word and kept up a friendly, supportive correspondence with Elizabeth's commander-in-chief. When Leicester's acceptance of the governorship of the Netherlands incurred Elizabeth's wrath, he was supported by Burghley, who assured him that 'with good and sound reasons' he would try 'to move her majesty to alter hir hard opinion'. Later, in 1586, he also facilitated the transmission of money to the financially hard-pressed commander.[27]

None of this is to deny that the queen's favourite and minister had their differences during the 1570s and 1580s. As prominent politicians they defended their places in the regime, promoted their policies and, as an inevitable consequence, sometimes their interests collided. Their relations were estranged when, in 1584, one of Burghley's own agents, Dr William Parry, played the double-agent, deceived him and conspired to kill the queen. On one occasion, after a dispute before Elizabeth, Leicester complained that 'finding my self grieved with such cross handling . . . I told your lordship I saw your lordship very ready to cross me now a days before her majesty. That I like it so ill, that I would and could find way to anger you as well.' Yet he concluded that he desired to have Burghley 'my assured friend as any friend you have found in England'. This did not prevent him from accusing the Lord Treasurer of complaining to the queen about him when he was absent in the Netherlands. For much of the time proud Leicester was on the defensive in his dealings with Burghley. And that is understandable, because without ostentation Burghley was always careful to preserve and advance his place and fortune. So, whilst Leicester was preoccupied in the Netherlands in 1586, he secured the appointment of three of the earl's opponents, Whitgift, Buckhurst and Cobham, to the Privy Council.

All of this must be seen as no more than the competitive rivalry and interaction between prominent politicians, who, at the same time, shared some common priorities, respected and even liked each other. Leicester's penned profession of friendship, written in 1585, is a less persuasive indicator of amicable relations than his impromptu visit to Burghley's great house at Theobalds in July 1584, when the Lord Treasurer was away. The earl and his retinue were wined and dined and 'most kindly used' by his servants. He also made sport on the estate, for, as he wrote to the absent host, 'I have byn bold to make some of your stagges afrayd but kylled none.' The competitiveness of these two men, as well as their disagreements, should be integrated into a context characterised by common loyalties and priorities and also an ongoing collegiality.[28]

Between the mid-1580s and the middle years of the following decade, however, English politics underwent a radical transformation. England embarked on undeclared war with Spain. The deaths of Leicester (1588), Walsingham (1590), Hatton (1591) and other prominent politicians produced a dramatic change in the top personnel – with the exception of Burghley of course. At the same time, he groomed and promoted his younger son, Robert, as his political heir. But the concurrent rise of the new royal favourite, the young earl of Essex, presented a challenge to Cecilian aspirations. At the same time it led, as previously explained, to the emergence of factional politics, which encompassed both policy and patronage. Essex, who was Leicester's stepson, canvassed for offices for his entourage and, as the leading war-hawk, he sought naval and military commands for himself, control of military patronage for his clients and opportunities for aggressive war against Spain. In particular, he challenged Burghley's attempt to secure the office of Secretary, which had been vacant since Walsingham's death in 1590, for Robert Cecil. However, he failed because, in 1596, Elizabeth at last named Robert to the position.[29] Essex recognised that he had lost when, in 1597, he wrote to Robert

Sidney that Cecil 'at this houre is the greatest counsailor of England in all matters of dispatches, and lookes to be observed by the greatest that have occasion to use hym'.

Within the context of the factious Cecilian–Essex competition for patronage, the 'right' policy and power, the relationship between the aged Lord Treasurer and the young earl was not a simple one of rivalry, enmity or conflict. On the one hand, Burghley had been his guardian and, as late as 1597, Rowland Whyte observed in coded language that 'Here is all love and kindness between 1000 [Essex] and 900 [Burghley]'. Meanwhile the Lord Treasurer did what he could to reconcile Robert Cecil and Essex. On the other hand, he was driven to exert greater control over patronage, in the face of the young earl's challenge. So Essex unsuccessfully promoted his own men, such as Sir Henry Unton and Francis Bacon, for offices as they became vacant. And he was 'dishonoured' when, in 1597, Lord Howard of Effingham was, at Burghley's instigation, promoted to the earldom of Nottingham. If Rowland White, Sir Robert Sidney's confidential correspondent, is to be believed, that year the queen was 'grown to understand better the wrong done unto him, which she lays upon 900 [Burghley] and 200 [Robert Cecil], though they deny it'. Nevertheless, as Paul Hammer points out, the relationship between the Cecils and Essex was a 'decidedly ambivalent' one, at least until Burghley's death in August 1598. Only when the Polonius-like father-figure had been removed could the two Roberts, one a bureaucrat and the other a warrior, take the gloves off and engage in an unremitting battle for supremacy or survival – a battle which the Cecils eventually won.[30]

The question still has to be asked: did the activities of the aged Lord Treasurer and his ambitious son result in a *Regnum Cecilianum* in the 1590s? Burghley's control of wardships and his arrangement of marriages connected his family to the old nobility and solidified the Cecils' position at Court. Nevertheless, he was angry at the imputation of a *Regnum Cecilianum,* which he denied. 'They that say in a rash and malicious mockry, that England is become a *Regnum Cecilianum,* may please their own cankered humour with such a device; but if my actions be considered, if there be any cause given by me of such a nickname, there may be found out in many other juster causes to attribute other names than mine.' Disappointed suitors, military activists, courtiers jealous of his influence with the queen and an impatient younger generation: all had axes to grind and grievances to air against the ruler of a *Regnum Cecilianum.* But the simple truth is that Burghley did not head a faction or promote a Cecilian regime.[31]

It was another matter between Essex and the Lord Treasurer's son. They were abrasive competitors of a younger generation. When the near-octogenarian Burghley died in 1598, his son Robert was thirty-five years old and Essex was thirty-two. They marshalled their forces in a factional struggle for power. In contrast the Lord Treasurer had never commanded what could be termed a political faction or even an organised clientele. The tentacles of his influence, which emanated from his many roles – such as royal adviser, Treasurer, Master of the Court of Wards and elder statesman – spread throughout the political system. Nevertheless, whereas most clienteles, headed by notables such as the earls of Bedford and Leicester, expressed the patron's social status, political importance and regional influence, Burghley's network was 'business-like'. It consisted of men whose prime client-responsibility was to advance his policies and government business. They were his 'men of business', who served him in a variety of ways in and out of parliaments. Some were members of his secretariat; others were royal officials, such as Robert Beale (clerk of the Privy Council) and James Morrice (attorney of Burghley's Court of Wards), aspiring lawyers and, in particular, municipal officials such as Robert Bell, William Fleetwood, Thomas Norton and Christopher Yelverton. They were, in the Elizabethan political context, a remarkable array of men, who looked to Burghley for direction. And above all, as we shall see, they proved to be serviceable in the parliament time.[32]

. . .

NOTES

1. Smith, *Cecil*, p. 33; Pam Wright, in Starkey (ed.), *English Court*, pp. 163–5.
2. P. Williams, 'Court and polity under Elizabeth I'. *BJRL*, 65/2 (Spring 1983), pp. 270–1; Beckingsale, *Burghley*, pp. 232–4. For his record as Treasurer and in the Court of Wards, see below, pp. 151–9.
3. P. Williams, *Later Tudors*, pp. 154–5. For example, he was regularly appointed to commissions of the peace for Lincolnshire,

Northamptonshire, Middlesex and Surrey, commissions for gaol delivery, and audit of accounts of household, admiralty, Irish and other treasurers. In addition he was named to boards of enquiry on a wide range of matters: for example, to investigate 'divers' offences of merchants and customs officials; to visit universities and university colleges; to examine 'the present state of the mint'; to sell crown lands; and to survey lands close to the City of London 'and to cause them to be reduced to the same state for archers' as in 1509. *Calendar of Patent Rolls, Edward VI (1550–3) and Elizabeth I (1558–1580).*

4. Hughes (ed.), 'Nicholas Faunt's Discourse', pp. 499–500.
5. Hurstfield, *Freedom, Corruption,* p. 85; see above, p. 94.
6. See above, p. 91; D. Hoak (ed.), *Tudor Political Culture* (Cambridge, 1995), p. 302 n. 33; P. Collinson, '"De Republica Anglorum", or history with the politics put back', in *Elizabethan Essays,* pp. 19–21.
7. Palliser, *Age of Elizabeth,* p. 63; Loach, *Parl. under Tudors,* p. 24.
8. D. Lloyd, *The Statesmen and Favourites of England since the Reformation,* 2 vols (London, 1766), I, p. 360.
9. *Clapham,* pp. 79–80; A.G.R. Smith, *The Emergence of a Nation State: The Commonwealth of England, 1529–1640* (London, 1984), pp. 117, 122–3; Smith, *Servant of the Cecils,* chs. 2 and 3 *passim.*
10. Palliser, *Age of Elizabeth,* pp. 319–20.
11. Adams, 'Eliza enthroned?', in Haigh (ed.), *Reign of Elizabeth,* pp. 74–5.
12. Hoak, *King's Council,* pp. 29–31, 137–9, 153–60; Smith, *Govt. of Eliz. England,* pp. 14–15; *APC,* Vols. 3, 4, 7, 8, 11, 13, 18, 20–1, 23–8, pp. 601, 625.
13. Smith, *Burghley,* p. 33; PRO, SP, 12/41/40 and 41; BL, Lansdowne MS 58/79; C. Read, 'William Cecil and Elizabethan public relations', in S.T. Bindoff, J. Hurstfield and C.H. Williams (eds), *Elizabethan Government and Society* (London, 1961), *passim,* esp. pp. 23–6, 36–8; Graves, *Norton,* pp. 113–20, 162–70; Beckingsale, *Burghley,* pp. 225–6.
14. Read, 'Cecil and public relations', pp. 29–30; PRO, SP, 12/3/52 and 53; Jones, *Faith by Statute,* pp. 128–9.
15. Read, 'Cecil and public relations', pp. 31–2, 37–8, 40–1, 45–8, 52–3; see below, pp. 174–5; Graves, *Norton,* p. 277 and n. 122; Read, *Burghley,* pp. 498–9, 519.
16. Read, 'Cecil and public relations', pp. 30–6, 42–3, 45, 50–1, 54; Read, *Burghley,* pp. 508–12.
17. Smith, *Burghley,* pp. 20–1 and n. 28; idem, *Emergence of a Nation State,* pp. 117, 122–5; J.D. Alsop, 'Government, finance and the community of the Exchequer', in Haigh (ed.), *Reign of Elizabeth,* pp. 104–6, 116.

18. Smith, *Govt. of Eliz. England*, pp. 62–4; Adams, in Guy (ed.), *Court and Culture*, pp. 37–8; W.T. MacCaffrey, 'Place and patronage in Elizabethan politics' in Bindoff (ed.), *Elizabethan Government and Society*, pp. 109–10; H. Ellis (ed.), *Original Letters*, 11 vols (London, 1824–46), 3rd ser., Vol. 4, pp. 14–17; J. Bruce and T.T. Perrowne (eds), *Correspondence of Matthew Parker* (Cambridge, 1853), pp. 318, 324–5; J. Strype, *The Life and Acts of John Whitgift*, 3 vols (Oxford, 1822), III, pp. 315–16; Lodge, *Illustrations*, I, pp. 479, 488–9, 526–31, 542–5; II, pp. 134, 170; Wright (ed.), *Queen Elizabeth*, II, pp. 101–2; Palliser, *Age of Elizabeth*, p. 81.
19. Wright (ed.), *Queen Elizabeth*, II, p. 144; *HMC*, De L'Isle MS, 2, pp. 119, 153, 155.
20. Smith (ed.), *Anon. Life*, pp. 66–8; Wright (ed.), *Queen Elizabeth*, II, pp. 426–7, 465.
21. Haynes (ed.), *State Papers*, pp. 598–600; Wright (ed.), *Queen Elizabeth*, II, pp. 28, 462; Hurstfield, *Queen's Wards*, pp. 267–8; Smith, *Burghley*, pp. 22–3; Smith, *Servant of the Cecils*, ch. 3, *passim*; *HMC*, De L'Isle MS, 2, p. 306; Smith, *Emergence of a Nation State*, pp. 122–3.
22. Smith, *Burghley*, pp. 24–5; Smith (ed.), *Anon. Life*, pp. 79–82; *Clapham*, pp. 81–2; Smith, *Emergence of a Nation State*, p. 123; Hurstfield, *Freedom, Corruption*, pp. 228–9; Williams, 'Court and polity', p. 265; A. Fox, 'The complaint of poetry for the death of liberality: the decline of literary patronage in the 1590s', in Guy (ed.), *Court and Culture*, pp. 237–8; Smith, *Servant of the Cecils*, pp. 53–4; F.J. Fisher (ed.), 'The State of England, 1600, by Thomas Wilson', pp. v–vi, 28, 42.
23. *HMC*, De L'Isle MS, 2, pp. 122–3; Beckingsale, *Burghley*, pp. 228–9; BL, Lansdowne MS 31 no. 42; H. Morgan, 'The fall of Sir John Perrot', in Guy (ed.), *Court and Culture*, pp. 109–125; Hurstfield, *Freedom, Corruption*, pp. 152–3; Smith, *Govt. of Eliz. England*, pp. 65–6; Hammer, 'Patronage', pp. 68–9.
24. *Naunton*, p. 41; see above, pp. 101–2; Neale, 'The Elizabethan political scene', in *Age of Catherine de Medici*, p. 156; Haigh (ed.), *Reign of Elizabeth*, pp. 10–11; Hammer, 'Patronage', pp. 65–71; see also Adams, 'Patronage in Elizabethan politics', pp. 20–45; Wright (ed.), *Queen Elizabeth*, I, pp. 208–9; S. Adams 'Eliza enthroned?', in Haigh (ed.), *Reign of Elizabeth*, pp. 67–8; Guy, *Tudor England*, pp. 254–5.
25. MacCaffrey, *Elizabeth I*, pp. 73–5, 167–8; Adams, 'Eliza enthroned?', p. 63; Wright (ed.), *Queen Elizabeth*, I, p. 176.
26. PRO, SP, 12/172/37; Collinson, *Elizabethan Essays*, pp. 40–1; Adams, 'Patronage in Elizabethan politics', p. 38; Wright (ed.), *Queen Elizabeth*, II, pp. 10–13, 103–5, 300; see above, p. 90.
27. Beckingsale, *Burghley*, p. 161; Wright (ed.), *Queen Elizabeth*, II, pp. 271–3, 277–83; MacCaffrey, *Making of Policy*, pp. 357–8, 363–

4; J. Bruce (ed.), Robert Dudley, earl of Leycester, 'Correspondence during his government of the Low Countries, 1585 and 1586', *Camden Society*, 27 (1844), pp. 103–5, 196–202, 204–5.

28. Strype, *Annales*, Vol. 3, Pt. 2, pp. 386–91, 507; Adams, 'Eliza enthroned?', p. 75; PRO, SP, 12/172/37.
29. Guy, *Tudor England*, pp. 437–41; *HMC*, De L'Isle MS, 2, pp. 243–6; Read, *Burghley*, pp. 533–7.
30. *HMC*, De L'Isle MS, 2, pp. 182, 279, 284, 305; Hammer, 'Patronage', pp. 72, 78–82.
31. N. Mears, '*Regnum Cecilianum?* A Cecilian perspective of the Court', in Guy (ed.), *Court and Culture*, pp. 46–64; see above, p. 93; Strype, *Annals*, III, Pt. 2, p. 380.
32. Collinson, 'Puritans, men of business and Elizabethan parliaments, *Parl. Hist.*, 7/2 (1988), pp. 187–211; M.A.R. Graves, 'The common lawyers and the Privy Council's parliamentary men-of-business, 1584–1601', *Parl. Hist.*, 8/2 (1989), pp. 189–215; idem, 'Managing Eliz. parls.', pp. 37–63; idem, 'Elizabethan men of business reconsidered', *Parergon*, NS, 14/1 (July 1996), 111–27.

Chapter 7

BURGHLEY AND PARLIAMENTS

Parliaments in Elizabeth I's reign remained, as they always had been, meetings of a royal institution, which was summoned to assist her government and dissolved or prorogued when its work was done. Laws needed for effective governance could be made, annulled or amended only by parliament. And only the house of commons could initiate levies of taxation in order to supplement the crown's ordinary income. In addition, parliaments had the constitutional right and duty to proffer advice, whilst it was customary for them to be recognised as appropriate occasions for the presentation of grievances. Elizabeth, however, adopted a novel and narrower interpretation of parliament's legitimate role and functions, when she repeatedly placed prohibitions on the discussion of a wide variety of topics, including her marriage, the succession, religion, and administrative abuses. Such royal restrictions sometimes provoked critical and even angry responses from members of the house of commons.

This should serve to remind us that, whilst Neale's portrayal of parliaments, divided by the queen's religious conservatism and an organised reforming puritan opposition, is no longer tenable, parliaments were political occasions. Their membership was a microcosm of a socially homogenous governing class, interlaced by patron–client and other relationships, within lords and commons and between each house. This contributed to the largely co-operative nature of parliamentary sessions. Nevertheless, members of both houses lobbied for causes: they could be matters of great political importance, conscience, religious conviction, principle, grievance or simply mundane economic, local or personal self-interest. All were potentially contentious and divisive and some actually were. Parliamentary management, no matter how efficient, could not prevent or effectively stifle recurring contentious issues, which derived from royal policies, actions or inaction. Nevertheless, conciliar managers could do much to pour oil on troubled waters and satisfy the purposes for which a parliament was called. Burghley's managerial role was important in all but one of Elizabeth's parliaments.[1]

Burghley already had considerable parliamentary experience when he sat in the house of commons in 1559. Nothing is known about his activity in either the late Henrician parliament of 1542–44 or the first three sessions (1547–50) of Edward VI's first assembly. Even in the final session, in 1552, he is recorded only as bearing bills to the upper house and in receipt of one committed after its third reading. As Secretary of State in Northumberland's regime, however, he assumed a more prominent role in preparations for the parliament of March 1553.[2] During his semi-retirement in Mary Tudor's reign he was elected only once, as one of the knights for Lincolnshire in 1555, when he was active and vocal, even indiscreet.[3] Nevertheless, when he was appointed Secretary of State by Elizabeth in November 1558, he was well-versed in parliamentary proceedings and politics. After three more sessions in the lower house (1559, 1563–66/67), he was created Baron Burghley and moved to the house of lords. From there he oversaw and directed government business for all but one of the ten remaining Elizabethan parliamentary sessions.

Both as Cecil in the lower house and as Burghley in the upper his parliamentary role was a managerial one. That began before parliament met because, whilst Privy Councillors, by virtue of their prestigious position, could arrange their own election to the commons, it was incumbent upon him to secure places for clients and ensure the return of members of his secretariat, such as Michael Hickes, Henry Maynard and Vincent Skinner. He was able to influence elections and even nominate members for such boroughs as Stamford, Boston and Grantham, in his home county of Lincolnshire, but more important than this was his electoral co-operation with his friend Francis, second earl of Bedford. The earl had extensive parliamentary patronage in the western counties of Cornwall, Devon and Dorset, especially during the early parliaments of the reign. He sometimes used his influence to return men of Burghley's choice, and in both 1571 and 1572 the Privy Council delegated to him the task of supervising the elections in Cornwall and Devon.[4] The Lord Treasurer was also prepared to intervene directly in the electoral process in the interest of security and stability. In 1584, Thomas Copley, the Catholic owner of the parliamentary borough of Gatton in Surrey and sole elector of its two members, died in exile. Burghley proceeded to nominate them. When Copley's widow became involved in the Babington conspiracy, in favour of Mary Stuart, Walsingham wrote to three Surrey gentlemen that, though 'Mistress Copley hath the nomination of the two burgesses for the town of Gatton, being a parcel of her jointure, it is not thought convenient, for that she is known to be evil affected, that [she should exercise that right]'. Burghley filled in the blank return with members of his own choosing.

Nine years later, when another parliament was summoned, violence threatened to erupt in the pending county election in Nottinghamshire. This was the consequence of a bitter dispute between the earl of Shrewsbury and Sir Thomas Stanhope. It divided the county, especially when the earl contested the candidacy of Stanhope and his ally with the nomination of two of his own supporters. Two days before the election Burghley, who feared an outbreak of disorder and violence, wrote a letter of concern to the earl, particularly about his rumoured intention to attend the election with a large following. He also stressed the desirability of choosing resident county gentlemen who were of the right religious complexion.[5]

When the early Elizabethan parliaments assembled, the task of organising official business, acting as its spokesman and securing its passage through the house of commons fell chiefly, though not solely, to Secretary Cecil. It was a time-consuming activity. As Edwardian Secretary he had been involved with other councillors in drafting official legislative proposals before parliament met. Then during the session, as in March 1553 for instance, he was so preoccupied with parliamentary business that Sir Richard Morison, ambassador to Emperor Charles V, assumed he could not find time to attend to foreign affairs. As he was, in 1558, one of the most experienced administrators and house of commons men on the Privy Council, it naturally fell to him to take the leading managerial role in parliaments. It was primarily his responsibility to obtain the taxes and laws for which parliament was called, and to defuse criticisms of aspects of royal policy and administration – or admonish members for voicing them. He had to act with the awareness that the queen favoured brief sessions and so it was necessary to juggle two competing considerations: to overcome or avoid hurdles to official business in both houses and yet to allow sufficient time for the enactment of some private bills.

In characteristic fashion he was well-prepared. In a memorandum of 'Things fit to be considered of' by the law officers for the 1563 session, he noted the need 'To have the books of the subsidy put in a readiness', to choose someone 'to open unto the Lower House' why a subsidy was necessary and to signify that, as it was the queen's wish to keep the session brief, they should 'forbear to deal in unnecessary matters'. He also added a list of desirable legislative measures. Aware that this was the appropriate occasion to redress grievances, he jotted down a reminder that the assize judges were to advise on 'such griefs of the subjects . . . fit to be relieved by Parliament'. In a postscript he noted the need to arrange for the election of his protégé, Francis Walsingham, to the commons. The surviving lists of bills to be drawn, such as the 'Articles touching the Parliament' for 1566–67, which named the queen's legal counsel or judge who was to draft each law, and evidence of pre-parliamentary drafting committees in 1559 and 1576 indicate that his preparations for the 1563 session were not exceptional.[6]

Most Elizabethan parliaments were called to vote tax grants, which would supplement the crown's ordinary revenues. Only three of the twelve sessions held during Burghley's long Elizabethan career met for other purposes: establishing a Protestant church (1559) and dealing with Mary Stuart (1572 and 1586–87). And, when Mary was executed during the last of these, the Privy Council seized the opportunity to obtain a subsidy from a willing, modestly generous house of commons. Whilst Burghley sat there he was responsible for broaching and justifying the request for a subsidy, as the commons' clerk noted in 1563 and 1566–67. Later, when he was in the lords, that role was assumed by his second-in-command in the Treasury, the Chancellor of the Exchequer Sir Walter Mildmay, at least between 1576 and 1589. Professor Alsop queries whether such 'verbose and well-tuned speeches' were 'set pieces in an expected ritual'. Perhaps so, but rituals are important, often essential, and they need to be conducted with competence if not style, as Burghley and Mildmay did. Before he went to the lords, Burghley also managed the commons' subsidy committee:

so in 1566 he kept a record of its membership and attendance; when it had completed its deliberations, he it was who reported to the house.

From the upper house he continued to influence its deliberations by proxy. In 1581, for example, Mildmay proposed and Burghley's client Thomas Norton seconded the grant of supply. They dominated the proceedings of the subsidy committee. Norton drafted the terms of the grant and then was instructed to draw the subsidy bill. As Lord Treasurer, Burghley was personally responsible for financially provisioning an underfunded, archaic state. When England and Spain became locked in an undeclared war from the mid-1580s, however, the problem dramatically magnified and changed. The state's normal revenues, which were totally inadequate to meet the demands of war, had to be supplemented by parliamentary grants: the usual single subsidy in 1586–87, but an unprecedented double subsidy in 1588–89. Then, in 1593, the commons, in a smug glow of virtue, generosity and self-satisfaction, decided to repeat the grant of two subsidies. To the financially harassed Lord Treasurer this was not enough. However, as his persuasive lieutenant in the commons, Mildmay, had died in 1590, he had to operate from the lords and with the support of its members. First, he secured the support of the upper house by a speech on the threats to the kingdom and the queen's extraordinary charges in the maintenance of its security and defence. Then, as spokesman of the lords' delegation to a joint conference, he informed the commons' members that a double subsidy was unacceptable to their lordships. They would assent to nothing less than a triple subsidy. Furthermore, he sought speedier payment of subsidy instalments over a shorter period of time and a fairer assessment which imposed a greater burden on the queen's wealthier subjects. The Lord Treasurer's ultimatum resulted in a confrontation, which was defused only when the lower house 'gladly and cheerfully' resolved to grant the queen a triple subsidy on its own initiative. In Burghley's last parliament four years later, in 1597–98, the commons repeated the triple subsidy without demur. This was probably because the parliamentary issue in 1593 was not the unprecedented size of the tax grant but the fact that, under Burghley's leadership, the lords' coercive pressure impinged on the commons' sole right to initiate taxes and to determine the amount, rates and speed of payment.[7]

No matter in which house he sat, Burghley was always busily engaged in the enactment of new laws. His first priority was, of course, official business: for example, the supremacy and uniformity acts, which in 1559 established the new church on a statutory basis; the treason legislation of 1571; the law against Jesuits, missionary priests, recusants and other 'disobedient subjects' in 1581 and the severe anti-recusant bill of 1593. The various drafts of this last bill, one in his hand and others annotated or endorsed by him, signify both his involvement in the passage and his influence on the final form of a measure which he regarded as essential to national security. He was also concerned to uphold the queen's prerogative and personal interests during the legislative process, as illustrated in the case of Lord Stourton's restitution in blood in 1576. In 1584–85 he played a similar role when a government bill against secret conveyances ran into trouble in the commons. As it provided remedy in the prerogative court of Star Chamber, it was bound to be opposed by many of the common lawyers who sat there. At a joint conference Burghley sternly reprimanded the commons' delegation for redrafting a bill 'very well favoured and liked of her Majesty, yea in so much that her Highness used to call it her own Bill'. The delegates were then treated to a lecture on parliament as a tripartite body.[8]

Burghley used the parliament time to secure statutory authority for particular pet projects, especially concerning the commonweal, whilst he also lent his support to measures which he considered to be in the best public interest. His record was a mixture of success and failure. The navigation act of 1563 was not a measure initially promoted by the council, but he was responsible for the inclusion of the notorious and controversial clause making Wednesday a compulsory fish day, as well as Friday and Saturday. The ultimate purpose was not economic – to increase the market for fish – but security. Larger fishing fleets would provide a larger pool of trained seamen in time of war. The additional fish day, which became known as 'Cecil's fast', aroused some Protestant parliamentary opposition, because of its popish associations. Although the bill, with the fish day clause intact, reached the statute book in 1563, it was a law of limited duration. When it came up for renewal in 1584–85, the commons removed the offending clause and the lords finally acquiesced. Also in 1563 he was the author of an act which Elton calls 'a quirky little piece of paternalism'. The bill, which forbade clothing to be sold on credit, was, however, significantly amended by the commons during its parliamentary passage.[9]

Despite Burghley's efforts in the next session, the failure rate was high: revenue-raising measures for poor relief and to fund the renovation of Dover's decaying harbour did not proceed beyond a first reading; commonweal bills concerning apparel (which regulated the garments worn by different ranks in the social hierarchy), vagabonds and common informers all failed too. Although a major measure on informers was finally enacted in 1576, after the queen had withheld her assent from one in 1572, frustration frequently accompanied the legislative endeavours of Burghley and other councillors. In 1571, when for the first time he worked from the lords, he secured the passage through both houses of a bill to modify lawyers' fees. Elizabeth, however, having earlier commended it now vetoed it. His carefully drawn measure to encourage use of handguns, thereby increasing the nation's military capacity, lost the race against time in a short session; so did a bill designed to punish those collectors of clerical taxes who delayed payment of money in their charge into the Exchequer and instead employed it to their own financial advantage. In contrast, Burghley was successful with a similar measure to discipline the tellers of the Exchequer and other revenue officers, who often retained in their hands, for considerable periods, royal revenues including parliamentary taxes. Similarly, his work in drafting and revising a bill to regulate the export of grain was rewarded when it was enacted.[10]

One other bill, concerning usury, not only illustrated how legislation was considered in a religious context and how legislators assumed the need to reconcile man-made law with natural and divine law; it also exemplified Burghley's conservatism, tempered by a degree of pragmatism. In 1545 usury – the practice of lending money for interest – was for the first time permitted and regulated by statute at a fixed rate of 10 per cent. It was again prohibited as damnable and detestable in 1552, but the subject was raised for reconsideration. Discussion ignored the economic consequences of usury and revolved around the question whether or not it was against moral and natural law or God's word. Burghley, who had been Secretary of State and a member of parliament in 1552, was against the statutory legitimisation. Nevertheless, this conservative position was counterbalanced by realism: that it would be socially less harmful if interest-bearing loans were allowed and regulated. So he supported this in a bill which became law in 1571.

With sessional variations Burghley continued to initiate or lend support to measures which were additional to the main conciliar legislative initiatives and the reason for calling parliament. So in 1576, 1581 and 1584–85 he promoted bills to prevent smuggling and, at the same time, to facilitate trade. In 1593 he approved and amended one forbidding the building of new houses in or within three miles of the City of London. However, his legislative role was a diminishing one, especially with the elimination of Mary Stuart and the coming of war during the 1580s. Thereafter parliaments were summoned for war revenue and he was increasingly absorbed in the financial consequences of prolonged war, control of Ireland and defence of England.

War, however, aggravated what were traditional grievances about the queen's prerogative rights in financial matters, especially purveyance and wardship. They were of particular concern to Burghley as both Lord Treasurer and Master of the Court of Wards. Bills against the 'excessive takings' and corrupt practices of the queen's purveyors were put into parliaments in 1586–87 and 1589. Purveyance was the monarch's right to buy supplies and services for her household and Court at sub-market prices. The practice not only reduced vendors' profits but subjected them to the unscrupulous, extortionate and disciplinary controls of household purveyors. Burghley's solution was to replace purveyance by county compositions, which were cash payments in lieu of compulsory purchases. In the short term, however, he was in an equivocal position when the grievance of purveyance was raised in parliament, because it provoked a clash of interests: aggrieved members, such as John Hare, who served in the Court of Wards and introduced the bill against purveyors in 1589; self-interested members of the royal household; and the queen, who, in defence of her prerogative, vetoed one bill and stopped the other, promising to remedy the problem herself. Burghley must have accepted the 1587 bill, which passed the lords in two days. He effected considerable changes to that of 1589 and compiled a list of objections to it. Nevertheless, Elizabeth obliged him to deliver a waspish parliamentary message, that she was perfectly capable of managing her own household without interference.

Bills concerning the evasion of wardship obligations (1584–85) and Exchequer reforms (1589) reveal the same mixture of commons' grievances, defensive financial officers, an obdurate queen – the one consistent factor – and Burghley caught in the middle of competing interests. None of the bills became law. The Lord Treasurer's attempts to legislate against practices which defrauded the crown of its feudal dues foundered in 1584–85, when the commons rejected one and the other proceeded no further than a first reading. When, in 1589, Sir Edward Hoby introduced a bill against exactions by Exchequer officials, he later complained that, in consequence, he had been 'very sharply rebuked' by 'some great personage', probably Burghley, who had anticipated Elizabeth's predictable response. And indeed she stopped the bill in the lords. Contentious though such bills were, those with the greatest potential for extended deliberation and debate were the expiring laws continuance acts. Some statutes were 'probationers' with a limited life-span, at the end of which parliament would reconsider their effectiveness, appropriateness and desirability. They were lumped together in an official continuance bill, which renewed some and amended or repealed others. David Dean acknowledges that, as the leading conciliar manager of parliament, Burghley had an important part to play in the successful passage of these composite measures, but, as he demonstrates, the diversity of their contents could and did provoke debate on a wide range of subjects. Through the complex of competing interests and the shifting sands of parliamentary politics Burghley presents a more-or-less consistent image: a conservative yet pragmatic politician, juggling priorities, balancing interests, pursuing, sometimes successfully but other times not, what he believed to be the best interests of the commonweal, the kingdom and, above all, of the queen.[11]

To represent him simply in these terms, however, is to misrepresent his parliamentary relationship with Elizabeth. His record of service, as charted in Chapters 2–4, reveals that he was not only the loyal servant publicly advancing his royal mistress's causes. He had a dual managerial role, because her attitude to parliament, her policy priorities, and her techniques of political management differed markedly from those of her councillors. Her repeated prohibitions on discussion of a wide variety of subjects, including religion, foreign policy and other matters of state, without her explicit assent, placed serious and even stifling constraints on the national forum. When James Morrice, Burghley's subordinate in the Court of Wards, was punished for opposing Archbishop Whitgift in 1593, he lamented that, whilst petty matters could be debated without offending the queen, 'the greate thinges of the lawe and publique Justice maie not be tollerated without offence'. Elizabeth's attitude was even more inhibiting for Burghley and other vulnerable career-conscious councillors. As a consequence their parliamentary leadership tended to be publicly conformist rather than constructive and creative. So Burghley, who, like Morrice, was hostile to Whitgift's disciplinary regime in the church, meekly advised that 'Some little submission, Mr Morice, would do well'.[12]

Elizabeth used her restrictive definition of free speech in defence of her inaction on matters which, to her councillors, the governing class and its members in the two houses, were in urgent need of resolution. So, as we have seen, in order to persuade a reluctant queen into action, some of the Privy Council and Burghley in particular frequently used the occasion of parliaments, between 1563 and 1587, to mastermind intensive and concerted lobbying by the two houses in support of major causes. In the 1560s their chief objective was settlement of the succession, but this required a reluctant and evasive queen to marry or name a successor. In one of his characteristic memoranda, written in 1566 when parliament was pending, the Secretary identified the problem. 'To require the succession is hardest to be obtained, both for the difficulty to discuss the right and for the loathsomeness in the Queen's Majesty to consent thereto.' His proposed tactic, which he followed during the session, was to press for a royal marriage but, 'if it succeed not, then proceed to discussion of the right of the succession'. All to no avail. Along with other councillors and the bishops, he supported a range of proposed religious reforms in 1571. In the following year he was central to the most concerted and intensive bicameral lobbying of the reign thus far, when parliament attempted to secure the condemnation of Mary Stuart. The harvest reaped by all the parliamentary endeavours of 1563–72 was a lean one: only a law against simony and statutory confirmation of the thirty-nine articles in 1571.[13] Nevertheless, Burghley and fellow councillors risked the queen's anger and possible reprisals and her suspicions were more than once aroused.[14]

In the parliaments of 1584–85 and 1586–87 Burghley could assume a more public stance in his search for the destruction of Mary Stuart. After all, they were both summoned to deal specifically with the threats to queen and kingdom posed by the ex-Scottish queen, exemplified by her exposed complicity in the Throckmorton and Babington plots. In such circumstances Burghley could be involved openly and without jeopardy in the enactment of the statute for the queen's safety (1584–85) and in pressing Elizabeth to proceed to Mary's execution (1586–87). It is ironic that, at this point, when as so often she dampened hopes and frustrated expectations, it was a secret and extra-parliamentary action by Burghley and fellow-councillors – the despatch of Mary's death warrant to Fotheringhay – which cut the knot.[15]

Burghley and his fellow-councillors were often out-manœuvred by Elizabeth and the ultimate prize, Mary's head, eluded them until 1587. Furthermore, as her parliamentary managers and spokesmen, they were inhibited from being publicly disloyal to her. That is why they, especially Burghley, preferred to utilise the service of 'men of business' as 'front men'. Such men have already figured briefly in the text. Men of business, a historian's construct and not a contemporary description, were clients of prominent men in government, especially Privy Councillors and above all of Burghley. They were not, however, the normal kind of Tudor clients, either in their role, their relationship with their patrons or their expectations. They are not easily classified, because, whilst they included ambitious lawyers and minor office-holders in the royal administration, most of them, especially during the first half of the reign, were lesser men, especially occupants of civic or municipal offices. As such they were viewed as 'private' men, rather than as members of an official interest. Unlike the country gentry, social and political aspirants, courtier-politicians and functionaries, who formed the clienteles of great nobles and prominent royal servants, the men of business did not, as a general rule, seek out and serve patrons with an eye to patronage, promotion in royal service and social advancement.

Two of the most active, Thomas Norton and William Fleetwood, were appointed to be the Lord Mayor of London's remembrancer (secretary) and the City's recorder in 1571. In the same year their patron, William Cecil, was ennobled. Operating from the house of lords, he needed agents in the commons.

Furthermore, harmonious and close relations between the Court in Whitehall and the City were essential to effective and stable government. There is no evidence either that Norton and Fleetwood sought the offices to which they were appointed in 1571 or that thereafter Norton pestered Burghley for material or other rewards. Fleetwood, it is true, had hopes of becoming a judge in 1586. The queen, however, decided that he should remain recorder, because she feared that 'they will choose some Puritan' to succeed him. He, like Norton, continued to serve the City and the queen's government actively and loyally without further reward after 1571.

This was the essential quality of the men of business: service out of loyalty rather than calculated personal self-interest. Beyond that they cannot be categorised. They were not an organised network, just a number of individuals, varied in talent, energy and temperament. Often they did not have an exclusive single patron relationship. Norton, for example, looked also to Hatton and Walsingham – a challenge to those critics who accused Burghley of insisting on allegiance to him as sole patron. Men of business did not seek election to the commons specifically to further conciliar objectives. London's members, for example, were returned to serve the City and they constituted the most active parliamentary lobby. They were also activists, whose enthusiasms could land them in trouble with the queen, council and even patron: the lawyers Robert Bell and James Dalton, the civic officers Fleetwood and Norton and royal officials such as James Morrice and Robert Beale (clerk of the Council) all managed to do so at one time or another. But, with other men of business, they continued to serve in a variety of ways. They acted as political advisers, providing 'white papers' on all manner of subjects, ranging from Dover Harbour, fishing and London's military musters to national defence and the Catholic menace. They kept Burghley and other councillors informed about the 'state of the world' outside Whitehall. And when parliaments were summoned some were returned to the commons, where they willingly pursued conciliar ends. Norton, Fleetwood, Thomas Digges, Thomas Dannett and others of their kind shared Burghley's convictions and sense of urgency about the succession, marriage, Catholic treason and, above all, Mary Stuart. In pursuit of their goals they displayed a willingness to act as front men, provide a parliamentary lead and, in so doing, risk the queen's wrath. At the end of parliament in 1571 and 1581, Norton was amongst those whom Elizabeth rebuked (without naming them) for their promotion of the harsher anti-Catholic laws desired by the Lord Treasurer. In brief, he and his kind were publicly prepared to go where the vulnerable Burghley feared to tread: over succession in 1563–66/67, treason in 1571 and especially in the relentless pressure against Mary and Norfolk in the following year.

The parliamentary role and nature of the men of business changed during the 1580s. The 'old hands' died (most significantly Norton in 1584), or became old and inactive. The wide network of active loyalists narrowed and was largely replaced by ambitious and calculating careerist lawyers such as Thomas Egerton, Edward Coke, John Croke and John Puckering, as well as the occasional prominent and active gentleman like Sir Robert Wroth, all afforced by members of Burghley's secretariat. However, after 1586–87 there was not the same pressing need for men of business to provide vocal leadership in parliamentary pressure campaigns. Mary Stuart was dead; a royal marriage would not produce heirs; and there was a growing tacit acceptance that the Protestant king of Scotland, James VI, would succeed Elizabeth. From the mid-1580s, war, its cost and the problems which it provoked were the related central concerns of Elizabethan parliaments.[16]

The involvement of men of business in intensive lobbying of the queen was not the only way in which they assisted conciliar managers. At various times, for example, they offered advices to both councillors and commons on time-saving procedures and practices. It was a constant worry to Burghley that, whilst the queen preferred short sessions, an inefficient and often talkative lower house often experienced difficulty in handling the large number of bills submitted to it by local, personal and economic interests. In 1571 he grumbled that 'Our Parliament is dailie new with child with projects for laws, that I was never more wearie'.[17] Sometimes government measures were in competition with private bills for valuable time. Any time-saving device could help. Burghley monitored the progress of bills in the lower house. The speaker and clerk sent him lists of bills before the house and the stages which they had reached in the legislative process.[18] On the basis of such knowledge Burghley was prepared to apply pressure to the commons in order to ensure that priority was given to important official business. In 1571, when an emergency parliament was called in April, an unseasonable time of the year, to respond to a political crisis, speed was of the essence. A joint conference, requested by the lords, sent word to the lower house that 'as the season of the year waxed very hot and dangerous for sickness, so they desired that this house would spend the time in proceeding with necessary bills for the commonwealth and lay aside all private bills in the meantime'. The lords also provided a list 'of such bills as they thought meetest to be treated of'.[19]

Another mechanism through which to manage the lower house from the upper was the speakership of the commons. The speaker determined the priority of bills to be read and, to some extent, the order of debate. In theory the speaker was freely elected by commons' members, but in practice he was pre-selected by councillors who stage-managed his election. Through such amenable choices as Robert Bell (speaker in 1572) and John Puckering (1584–85 and 1586–87) Burghley was able to promote the parliamentary campaign against Mary Stuart. He had a hand in the choice of both men, personally writing in Puckering's name on the blank electoral return for Gatton in 1586. He edited, even drafted, opening and closing orations for Puckering, both as speaker and Lord Keeper, and also for Lord Chancellor Hatton. In 1593 he corrected the address of Speaker Coke, who later thanked him 'for the care and pains your lordship took for my instruction in the last Parliament'. By 'assisting' key parliamentary officers with their speeches he was able to focus attention on his political priorities: not only Mary Stuart in 1586 but, in 1593, the need for more effective funding of the war, one of the themes of Coke's address.[20]

Joint conferences provided another managerial tool. They gave the Lord Treasurer the opportunity to make direct parliamentary contact with members of the lower house. Such meetings enabled him to moderate the very severe terms of the original commons' bill against disobedient subjects in 1581, to pre-empt successfully the commons' right to determine the size of the tax grant in 1593 and, in the same parliament, to tell the commons tacitly to drop their bill against Catholic recusants, in anticipation of an official measure which would include radical Protestants too. Sometimes, however, Burghley's performance in joint conferences was counter-productive, as in the case of Stourton's restitution in 1576 and the fraudulent conveyances bill in 1584/85.[21]

Although his performance in joint conferences was not always effective, it was through these, the commons' speaker and his men of business that he was sometimes able to control the legislative initiative from his place in the lords. As David Dean points out and amply demonstrates, the large volume of surviving papers proves 'his extensive involvement in proceedings, the preparing of speeches and the drafting of bills'. His parliamentary role, however, extended beyond the fulfilment of conciliar objectives. As a consequence of prominence and influence he was the natural target of bill promoters who hoped to enlist his legislative skill and experience and his prestigious support. Individuals, institutions such as the universities and their colleges, economic lobbies, cities and towns ranging from London to Conway, Gloucester and Yarmouth (of which Burghley was high steward from 1588) sought out his assistance, many of them successfully. Throughout his career, however, he was equally willing to resist the measures of particular lobbies, such as the vintners whose bill was backed by London's governors in 1566. In Burghley's opinion the object of this bill – to repeal the licensing act of 1553 and so increase wine sales – would have had harmful economic and social effects. Despite his disapproval it reached the lords before it was rejected. In the next parliament (1571), however, he helped to draft a bill for the City. This would have authorised it to cut a canal linking it with the River Lea, east of London, in order to facilitate the movement of grain from surrounding counties.[22]

It is important to retain a sense of perspective about Burghley. His fellow Privy Councillors also patronised parliamentary lobbies and all of them were expected to play a managerial role in the royal interest. This did not mean that they constituted a united bicameral team. Serious divisions in Court and council over policies, preferred courses of action, even the faction conflict between the Cecils and Essex during the 1590s were not usually transferred to the lords and commons in the parliament time. Professor Elton, however, believed that the parliamentary move to punish Arthur Hall in 1581[23] 'reflected the politics of Council factions rather than strictly House of Commons matters'. Those councillors who took the lead in proceedings against Hall were against the queen's proposed marriage to the French duc d'Anjou, whereas Burghley favoured it. The public disgrace of Hall, who had been the Lord Treasurer's ward, would have been an embarrassment to him. Even if Elton is correct, this did not amount to a public confrontation between councillors. Likewise the Lord Treasurer was opposed by his fellow Privy Councillor, Sir Walter Mildmay, Chancellor of the Exchequer, during the joint conferences on the Stourton restitution and fraudulent conveyances bills. These were not, however, policy or personality clashes spilling over from the council chamber. They simply acted as the spokesmen of their respective houses. After the meeting on the conveyances bill, Mildmay argued that Burghley was in the wrong when he attempted to dictate conduct and procedure in the lower house.[24]

The record of Burghley's activity in the upper house is a sparse one because there are no known parliamentary diaries, whilst the journals are largely confined to information on attendance, bill readings and committee appointments. Nevertheless, regular attendance, the prerequisite of a constructive input, can be charted and his record is an impressive one: 77 per cent of sittings in 1571, 70 per cent in 1572, 91 per cent in 1576, 68 per cent in 1581, 72 per cent in 1584–85, 38 per cent in 1586–87, 90 per cent in 1589, 88 per cent in 1593, and 66 per cent in 1597–98. He attended more regularly than most members: in 1584–85, for example, only ten out of sixty-six were more frequent; in 1593 eight out of fifty-seven; and even in 1597 only fifteen out of fifty-six.[25] With the exception of 1586–87 his attendance level was high, despite recurring bouts of illness, especially gout. As early as 1566 he had been obliged to withdraw from Court and commons midway through the session. He was very ill at Easter 1572 and, in late May, he wrote that 'I am forced to be carried to the Parliament house and to her Majesty's presence'. In February 1587, after Mary's execution, he was reputedly nursing a leg injury after a fall from his horse. The injury was genuine, but it could not conceal the fact that he had been exiled from Court and parliament for his role in the Scottish queen's death.[26] He was absent from the lords from 15 February to 23 March 1587 and, although he had been one of the commissioners who presided at parliament's opening, he was pointedly omitted from the commission empowered to end it.[27]

During the 1590s Burghley's health steadily deteriorated and he was often confined to bed. There was bitter truth in his description of himself to the upper house as 'an old man, beside his years decayed in his spirits'. Yet the anonymous biographer was no less accurate in his recollection that 'when he was in never so great pain, or sickly, if he could but be carried abroad, he would go to dispatch business'. His record of attendance in the lords testifies to that.[28] So too does the frequency of his appointment to committees: for example, to eighteen out of twenty-seven in 1571, seven out of thirteen in 1584–85, and sixteen out of twenty-nine in 1597.[29] In his last parliament, the official legislative initiative was moving back to the commons, where his son and political heir was managing affairs. But even then Old Nestor could still make his mark. The lords accepted two of his motions: that the clerk's journal should be scrutinised each session by a committee to ensure a more accurate record; and that unauthorised absentees should be admonished. The earl of Essex was among the absentees. He was obliged to put in a hasty apology, pleading sickness and supplying witnesses to testify to this. So late in the day was the experienced old parliamentary politician scoring a point over the Cecils' great rival and competitor for power?[30]

. . .

NOTES

1. M.A.R. Graves, 'Patrons and clients: their role in 16th century parliamentary politicking and legislation', *Turnbull Library Record*, 18/2 (1985), pp. 82–3; idem, 'Eliz. men of business reconsidered', pp. 126–7; D. Dean, 'Revising the history of Tudor parliaments', *HJ*, 32/2 (1989), pp. 409–11; Collinson, *Elizabethan Essays*, pp. 39–40.
2. See above, p. 18; Bindoff (ed.), *House of Commons*, I, pp. 604–5.
3. See above, pp. 22–3; Bindoff (ed.), *House of Commons*, I, p. 605.
4. Hasler (ed.), *Commons*, I, pp. 59–63, 195–7, 199–200, II, pp. 310–11; III, pp. 39–40, 390–1; Graves, 'Managing Eliz. parls.', pp. 49–50; D. Dean, 'Patrons, clients and conferences: the workings of bicameralism in the 16th century English parliament', in H.W. Blom, W.P. Blockmans and H. De Shapper (eds), *Bicameralism: The Two Chamber System, Past and Present* (The Hague, 1992), pp. 219–21.
5. Hasler (ed.), *Commons*, I, p. 252; H. Ellis, *Original Letters*, 3rd ser., 4, pp. 51–2; Neale, *Eliz. Commons*, pp. 63–7; T.E. Hartley, 'The sheriff and county elections', in Dean and Jones (eds), *Parls. of Eliz. England*, p. 174.
6. PRO, SP, 12/40/68 and 90; Elton, *Parliament of England*, pp. 72–4; Graves, 'Managing Eliz. Parls.', p. 51.

7. J.D. Alsop, 'Parliament and taxation', in Dean and Jones (eds), *Parls. of Eliz. England*, pp. 104, 108, 111–12; Graves, *Norton*, pp. 233–6; Strype, *Annals*, IV, pp. 149–56; Neale, *Eliz. Parls.*, II, pp. 301–11.
8. See above, pp. 67–8; PRO, SP, 12/147/34; ibid., 12/148/5, 10; Graves, *Norton*, pp. 237–40; Hakewil, *Manner How Statutes*, pp. 80–97; Dean, *Law-Making and Society*, pp. 27–30, 67 and n. 18.
9. Ibid., pp. 262–3; Elton, *Parliament of England*, pp. 67, 259–62; Neale, *Eliz. Parls.*, I, pp. 114–16; PRO, SP, 12/27/nos. 71–2; ibid., 12/28/nos. 11–12, 17–18.
10. Elton, *Parliament of England*, pp. 70, 73–4, 170–4, 193, 243, 258, 269–73; PRO, SP, 12/78/35.
11. N. Jones, *God and the Moneylenders* (Oxford, 1989), pp. 34–42; idem, 'Religion in parliament', in *Parls. of Eliz. England*, pp. 131–4; Graves, *Norton*, pp. 366–7; Dean, *Law-Making and Society*, pp. 80–5, 94–7, 150, 256, 259–76; P. Croft, 'Parliament, purveyance and the City of London, 1589–1608', *Parl. Hist.*, 4 (1985), pp. 9–10; Loach, *Parl. under Tudors*, p. 128.
12. Guy, *Tudor England*, p. 324; Collinson, 'Puritans, men of business and Eliz. parls.', p. 207; Hasler (ed.), *Commons*, III, p. 99, see below, p. 181.
13. PRO, SP, 12/40/91; Guy, *Tudor England*, pp. 322–3; J.D. Alsop, 'Reinterpreting the Elizabethan Commons: the parliamentary session of 1566', *JBS*, 29 (1990), pp. 231–4, 238–9; Read, *Secretary Cecil*, pp. 355–7, 360, 369; Elton, *Parliament of England*, pp. 357–74; Graves, 'Patrons and clients', pp. 78–9, 81; idem, 'Managing Eliz. parls.', pp. 55–7; see above, pp. 42–5.
14. See above, p. 45.
15. See above, p. 76.
16. For Burghley and the men of business see Graves, 'Management: council's men of business', pp. 11–38; idem, 'Patrons and Clients', pp. 69–85; idem, 'Common lawyers', pp. 189–215; idem, 'Managing Eliz. parls.', pp. 37–63; idem, *Norton*, pp. 86–8 and ch. 10; idem, 'Eliz. men of business reconsidered', pp. 111–27; Collinson, 'Puritans, men of business and Eliz. parls.', pp. 191–211; D. Dean, 'Pressure groups and lobbies in the Elizabethan and early Jacobean parliaments', *Parliaments, Estates and Representation*, 11/2 (1991), pp. 139–52, esp. 143–7.
17. Digges, *Compleat Ambassador*, p. 94.
18. e.g. in 1589 Burghley and Speaker Snagge exchanged lists of bills before their respective houses, D. Dean, 'Bills and Acts, 1584–1601' (Cambridge Univ. Ph.D. thesis, 1984), pp. 161–2 n. 4; idem, *Law-Making and Society*, p. 9 and n. 8. Evidence of this monitoring activity is to be found among the many lists of bills in the Lansdowne and State Papers, e.g. PRO, SP, 12/77/54;

78/11 (1571); SP, 12/88/25–7 (1572); SP, 12/107/45–6, 58–9, 63, 77–80 (1576); BL, Lansdowne MS, 40/37 and PRO, SP, 12/175/36 (1584); Dean, 'Bills and Acts', pp. 161–2 n. 4 (1589, 1597).

19. *CJ*, I, pp. 85–6.
20. Hasler (ed.), *Commons*, I, p. 624; III, p. 257; A. Heisch, 'Lord Burghley, Speaker Puckering and the editing of HEH Ellesmere MS 1191', *HLQ*, 51 (1988), pp. 212–13, 216–26; Read, *Burghley*, p. 487; BL, Lansdowne MS, 73/1.
21. See above, pp. 67–8, 135, 143; Dean, 'Patrons, clients and conferences', pp. 212–15; idem, *Law-Making and Society*, pp. 29, 43–7, 68; Elton, *Parliament of England*, pp. 186–7, 306–9.
22. Dean, *Law-Making and Society*, pp. 9, 146–7, 150, 252–3; M.A.R. Graves, *Elizabethan Parliaments, 1559–1601* (London, 1996), pp. 81–2.
23. See above, p. 67.
24. G.R. Elton, 'Arthur Hall, Lord Burghley and the antiquity of parliament', in H. Lloyd Jones, V. Pearl and B. Worden (eds), *History and Imagination* (London, 1981), pp. 88–103; Dean, *Law-Making and Society*, p. 29; idem, 'Patrons, clients and conferences', pp. 212–14.
25. Calculated from *LJ*, I, II.
26. Hasler (ed.), *Commons*, I, p. 585; BL, Cotton MS, Vespasian, F VI, 64; Read, *Burghley*, pp. 50, 53, 370, 379; PRO, SP, 12/201/15; LJ, II, pp. 116–41.
27. PRO, SP, 12/193/37; S.E. Lehmberg, *Sir Walter Mildmay and Tudor Government* (Austin, Tex., 1964), pp. 277–8, 291; Neale, *Eliz. Parls.*, II, p. 143.
28. Read, *Burghley*, pp. 480, 485, 501, 504, 507, 514, 541–2; Smith, *Anon. Life*, p. 69.
29. Calculated from: *LJ*, I, II; D'Ewes, *Journals*; Hayward Townshend, *Historical Collections* (London, 1680); J.C. Sainty, 'Further materials from an unpublished manuscript of Lords Journals for sessions 1559 and 1597–8', *HLRO Memo*, No. 33 (1965).
30. *LJ*, II, pp. 195–6, 198.

Chapter 8

FINANCIAL MANAGEMENT AND THE ECONOMY

Elizabethan financial history is the story of an underfunded monarchy endeavouring to manage an archaic state and to govern effectively. Apart from customs revenue the crown's ordinary hereditary income derived from its medieval roles as great landowner, feudal overlord and fountain of justice: rents from royal estates; feudal dues, especially wardship and purveyance;[1] and the 'profits of justice', mainly fines and fees from the law courts. In addition, from 1559 the clergy paid first fruits and tenths to the monarch as supreme governor of the church. These consisted of one year's income on appointment of a cleric to a church living and thereafter an annual payment of 10 per cent of his income. These regular revenues were supplemented by loans or, more important, direct taxation, which required parliamentary consent. Taxes were levied on movable property (the fifteenth and tenth) and on income (the subsidy). In the past such grants had been associated with emergencies, in particular war. By the mid-sixteenth century, however, rising prices and expenditure, exacerbated by mismanagement and waste, made peacetime parliamentary assistance necessary. There were precedents in the reigns of Henry VIII and Edward VI. With only one exception between 1559 and 1586–87, Elizabeth regularly obtained peacetime grants. However, during her reign the real value of the subsidy declined due to inflation, widespread under-assessment and tax evasion. Furthermore, subsidies were collected over lengthy periods of time and they were never large enough to meet the crown's immediate or short-term requirements.[2]

A systematic campaign to clean up and render more efficient the subsidy operation, which would have yielded a greater financial return to the queen's treasury, was not attempted in Elizabeth's reign. This is one of the charges frequently made against Burghley. However, as he became Lord Treasurer only in 1572, for more than a third part of his career in the queen's service he was not formally and officially responsible for supervision of the state's revenues and expenditure. On the other hand, he was Secretary of State under Edward VI (1550–53) and for the first fourteen years of Elizabeth's reign. Robert Beale, clerk of the Privy Council from 1572 to 1601, stated that the Secretary should be acquainted with 'the matters of her Ma[jes]tie's Minte . . . remedies of her coyne . . . and of matters of exchange. Likewise w[i]th her Ma[jes]tie's revenewes . . . with the expenses . . . both ordinarie and exterordinarie, that her Highnes is at.' As the councillor often involved with drafting of the subsidy bill and with presentation of the government's need for a tax to the commons, the Secretary was inevitably involved in financial management.[3]

Cecil's record bears this out. Between 1542 and 1550 the wars of Henry VIII and Protector Somerset were funded by massive sales of crown lands, loans, which were often at high interest rates, unprecedented parliamentary taxation and debasements of the coinage. Somerset's successor, Northumberland, embarked upon a policy of retrenchment, debt-clearance and recovery. Although the marquess of Winchester became the new Lord Treasurer in 1550, he did not effectively manage the state's finances until Mary's reign. More than anyone else it was Secretary Cecil who, subject to Northumberland's approval, determined the direction of the state's financial policy in the years 1550–53. In the opening months of Elizabeth's reign he was equally active in money matters concerning the queen's foreign debts and coinage reform. By then he was well-acquainted with Lord Treasurer Winchester, Chancellor of the Exchequer Mildmay and the most skilled English financier and loan negotiator, Sir Thomas Gresham. Winchester reported to the Secretary on a range of financial matters. In 1560 Gresham advised him that, if usury was legalised in England at a 10 per cent interest rate, the queen could switch from a Continental to an English credit market, to the benefit of both the English government and economy. Although he disapproved of usury on moral grounds, he was, as we have seen, involved in the passage of the act of 1571 which legitimised it and fixed the rate at 10 per cent. From 1574, two years after Burghley became Lord

Treasurer, Elizabeth borrowed only from English merchants and financiers. Meanwhile it was Cecil who managed the crown's requests for supply in 1563 and 1566. Furthermore, as Master of the Court of Wards from 1561, he acquired skills and experience in the management of unpopular feudal payments. As feudal overlord the queen was entitled to receive from tenants-in-chief a range of feudal dues. The most significant of these was the royal custody or wardship of minors. The crown directly managed their lands or sold custodianship of wards to kin or other interested persons. There can be no doubt that, by the time Burghley succeeded Winchester as Lord Treasurer in 1572, he was well-versed in most aspects of royal finance.[4]

Prior to Elizabeth's reign and continuing throughout the 1560s, Winchester had effected a number of improvements which increased the yield from hereditary revenues. He was vigorous in debt collection; he raised rents on crown lands to keep pace with inflation; in 1558 he introduced a new book of rates which almost tripled the proceeds from customs and in 1556 he planned a recoinage, which was carried out in 1560–61. Winchester's priority was to balance income and expenditure and to this end he sought to increase the yield from existing sources of revenue and, at the same time, to achieve economies wherever possible. It was an essentially cautious and conservative policy which his successor Burghley continued. The characteristic feature of Burghley's treasurership was an absence either of adventurous experiment or novelty in fund-raising or of greater exploitation of existing resources. So, for example, the Marian revision of the book of rates dramatically increased the customs yield from £29,000 in 1556–57 to nearly £90,000 in 1558–59. At Burghley's death in 1598, however, the total was only £91,000. Whilst he steadily built up a surplus for a rainy day – £300,000 by the time England went to war with Spain – he preferred to sacrifice financial advantage in the interest of harmony between the crown and the governing class, which in turn would ensure political stability.

Penry Williams has acknowledged that the Lord Treasurer's pragmatic conservatism left 'little room for manoeuvre in a crisis' or for funding new commitments. Nevertheless, he appreciated that finance could not be divorced from 'political considerations'. So the crown assisted Henry Bourbon (Protestant claimant to the French crown), conquered Ireland, aided the Dutch and made war on Spain for eighteen years – all without incurring crippling debts. Burghley's financial management, however, has been severely criticised by recent historians. A.G.R. Smith, for example, pointed out that the limited debt of £350,000 which Elizabeth bequeathed to her successor, after a lengthy war on many fronts, should not be seen as a 'remarkable success story'. A rigorous management and overhaul of hereditary and parliamentary revenues, together with a search for new sources, could have provided James I and his Lord Treasurer, Robert Cecil, earl of Salisbury, with a much sounder financial basis for effective government.[5]

How well, then, did Burghley perform in the interest of present and future royal solvency? According to Williams, income from crown lands rose from £86,000 to £111,000 during the reign and customs revenue barely at all. Smith records that the income from wards fell during his mastership from £18,000 to £15,000 – and in real terms even more when inflation is taken into account. Such figures, however, must be treated with caution. Smith records an increase in land revenues from £78,000 to £100,000 during the reign, whereas Guy's recorded upward movement over the same period is £66,000 to £89,000. According to Guy the customs revenue ranged from £60,000 to £85,000 – markedly different from Williams' figures of £89,000 in 1558–59 and £91,000 forty years later. Furthermore, such figures are often regnal, whereas Burghley was Lord Treasurer for just twenty-six out of forty-five years.

What, then, is the true story? Despite all the numerical vagaries, there can be no doubt about Burghley's entrenched conservatism. Yet the divergent financial figures provided by historians are a commentary on the lack of precise budgetary information available either to Tudor treasurers or to Tudor historians. The regnal figures are also indicative of a general trend from 1550 onwards. Retrenchment, the fiscal priority of Tudor government during and since Northumberland's regime, was not reform but a socially and politically safer option. Burghley was not the exceptional arch-conservative but a financial manager who typified the financial conservatism of Tudor government prevalent from the 1550s. His predecessor Winchester, for example, restructured the administration of finances in 1554, but it was no more than a conservative restoration of Exchequer supremacy.[6] Nevertheless, queen and minister can be criticised for a short-sighted and even timid approach to financial management. Although their figures markedly differ, historians such as Guy, Smith and Williams agree that the revenue from royal lands increased by no more than a third or quarter at a time of rising food prices and market rentals. There was room for significant increases in royal rents without causing social discontent. 'Quickfix' cash injections into the royal treasury by land sales steadily reduced this revenue resource.

To a far greater extent, the full potential of customs duties on imports and exports was not realised. Some goods paid duties on the quantity exported and others paid *ad valorem* duties on their value. The 1558 book of rates, a government handbook which recorded official valuations of imported and exported goods, included some new items. Far more important, however, were the new upward valuations, especially on cloth, which accounted for the value of three-quarters of all exports. Thereafter nothing really changed until James I's reign. The 1562 book of rates was simply a reissue of that of 1558; the 1582 book incorporated some new items; that for 1590 just tidied up the previous edition. Meanwhile prices of most commodities rose during Elizabeth's reign, but cloth exports continued to be valued by quantity. So an opportunity to increase substantially the royal revenue was missed. To the end of Elizabeth's reign customs were still collected in accordance with Mary I's book of rates. T.S. Willan concludes that, as a consequence, she lost more than £500,000 in customs revenue.[7]

It was in his management of the Court of Wards for thirty-seven years (1561–98) that Burghley appears at his most conservative and cautious. Feudal dues, especially wardship, directly affected the landed governing class. They were unpopular and a thorough exploitation of them was liable to breed widespread discontent, as it did in the 1630s when they yielded £75,000 annually. Indeed, Burghley's introduction of two parliamentary bills, designed to prevent Elizabeth from being deprived of wardship revenue by fraudulent practices, led to extended and heated debate. Understandably he preferred political discretion and moderation, but this carried with it a financial cost. When he became Master of the Court of Wards, it was providing almost £30,000 annually, but during his long tenure that fell, despite inflation, to less than half that sum. Within five years of his death his son and successor, Robert, had increased the Court's annual income by 50 per cent.

The value of the Court of Wards, however, should not be assessed solely, or even chiefly, in terms of royal profits. It was more valuable as an instrument of royal patronage – a source of rewards to royal servants and other favoured men – whilst purchasers of wardships constituted a vested interest in support of the continuance of royal feudal rights.[8] As judge in the Court of Wards Burghley performed an important social function by protecting wards against predators, sometimes their own guardians. According to both Clapham and the anonymous biographer, he acquired a reputation for probity, which was a favourable advertisement for a prime function of monarchy, the provision of justice to all. In his administration of wardships too he had a reputation for financial integrity. In 1600 Dr Thomas Wilson wrote that the late 'Master of the Wardes gayned twice as much to him and his besides that which the Queen had', but then Wilson was a jaundiced and disappointed office-seeker. However, Clapham, one of Burghley's own household, made a similar observation. Undoubtedly Burghley accepted gifts: in a two-and-a-half-year period suitors gave him £3,000. Nevertheless, in the absence of contrary evidence, he was scrupulous in fulfilment of his duties and responsibilities.[9]

Burghley's management of the Court of Wards was characteristically conservative, but that was, in some respects, a virtue. His failure to exploit its revenue potential was financially disadvantageous to the crown. But his equitable and moderate management of feudal dues, which were unpopular and to some obnoxious, was politically beneficial to the monarch. On the other hand, he showed no inclination towards significant reform. Nicholas Bacon's ambitious proposals, submitted to Cecil in 1561, were not adopted. Apart from the 1590s, when John Hare, clerk of the Court of Wards, effected improvements in its administration, little changed. Even when, in 1585, Burghley made a move with his parliamentary bills to prevent the queen from being defrauded, a hostile commons' reception ensured their failure.[10]

Burghley was also concerned with the oversight and administration of another important, unpopular feudal right of the royal prerogative. This was purveyance, the crown's right to compel subjects to provide supplies to the royal household at discount rates. Its longstanding unpopularity was given expression, between 1563 and 1589, in parliamentary outbursts and bills. In 1589 one such bill launched the most sustained, hostile attack yet. The particular targets were the often unscrupulous and corrupt purveyors who managed the system. Elizabeth was not prepared to allow new laws on the subject and Burghley favoured the enforcement of existing laws, of which, as Hurstfield estimates, over forty had been enacted during the past three centuries. Composition was his way of ameliorating, although not solving, the problem. Negotiations between the government and individual counties replaced purveyors' direct purchase of provisions from local producers by fixed county quotas at agreed prices. By the time Burghley died, most counties were operating under this system. It had obvious limitations, because local suppliers did not receive market rates for the goods which they sold to their county authorities before re-sale to the Court. Nevertheless, it significantly reduced the local sense of grievance against the predatory operations of purveyors. Although David Dean is dismissive of 'a few gestures' made by Burghley and others in extending composition to most counties, the Lord Treasurer regarded composition as one of his greatest successes.[11]

Parliamentary taxation was a necessary supplement to the queen's ordinary revenue, both in peacetime and war. The yield from the fifteenth and tenth had been fixed as long ago as 1334, whilst the return from the subsidy steadily declined during the reign from £140,000 to £80,000. It is customary to hold Burghley culpable for the decline and, to some extent, that is true. Between 1572 and 1597 the average assessed income of nobles' lands, for tax purposes, fell from £461 to £281. Burghley set a disgraceful personal example when he assessed his own annual income at £133 from 1571 until his death, when it was, according to various estimates, actually £4,000 to £7,000. This must be seen in perspective: between 1534 and 1571 noble assessments had dropped from £921 to £461, whilst his predecessor as Lord Treasurer, Winchester, lowered his income return from £1,200 (in 1559) to £800 (in 1566). Non-noble property owners were widely under-assessed by the subsidy commissioners. It was caustically observed in one subsidy debate that, although the statutory qualification for the office of Justice of the Peace was land worth £20, few JPs were assessed at more than £8 or £10. Collection was slow and hampered by corrupt practice and slowness in making payments into the Exchequer. No attempt was made to overhaul the system and responsibility for failure to do so must, to a large extent, rest with the Lord Treasurer. But not sole responsibility, because of Elizabeth's conservatism. As Sir Thomas Heneage told the commons in

1593, in reference to the subsidy, the queen 'loved not . . . such novell invencions, but liked rather to have the auncient usages offred'.

Those who preceded or succeeded Burghley operated the existing system without seeking substantial change, although there were failed Marian attempts to obtain realistic income assessments. By 1628 the subsidy yield was only £55,000. However, in one respect Elizabeth's government deserves credit. Although, as previously noted, there were some earlier Tudor precedents, hers was the first government to request and obtain parliamentary taxation regularly in peacetime. Furthermore it was Cecil who, during the 1560s, presented its case for peacetime taxation to the commons. On occasions during the 1540s and 1550s subsidies had been justified on the grounds that the monarch needed a contribution towards defence of the kingdom and the crown. Defence, unlike war, was a normal, not extraordinary, function and responsibility of government. Royal necessity became the justification for taxation. So, among the queen's 'great charges', itemised by Cecil in his subsidy speech of 1563, were 'the costs of Berwick, Newhaven, the provision of armour and the navy'; in 1566 they again included the cost of the navy and the expedition to France in 1562, as well as the Irish rebellion of Shane O'Neill. But Cecil also treated defence as an extraordinary charge which should be paid for by extraordinary revenue, that is taxation. Elizabethan subsidy preambles, such as that amended by the Lord Treasurer in 1589, emphasised not only the costs of defence, but also the queen's necessity and her 'wise and happie Government'.

Although Burghley did not explore new sources of income or attempt major reforms, he worked with some success to increase tax revenue. His (admittedly somewhat hypocritical) concern about poor returns from previous subsidies may have strengthened his resolve to press for a triple subsidy in 1593. As he pointed out to the commons, its double subsidy of 1588–89 had contributed little more than a quarter of the queen's outlay on war. Despite the declining value of each lay subsidy, the increase from one to three between 1586–87 and 1596–97, the shorter designated periods for payment and the rising yield from clerical subsidies meant that at no time in the sixteenth century was the kingdom so highly taxed as in the 1590s.[12]

During his tenure as Lord Treasurer he also worked with his Chancellor of the Exchequer to improve procedures, tackle corruption and resolve prolonged internal disputes between conflicting vested interests in the Exchequer. Most of their efforts, however, had little effect, because as men appointed from outside to the top offices of a relatively large and undoubtedly complex department, they never acquired the same understanding and expertise as its often long-serving officers.[13] The early Elizabethan tellers, for example, were conducting official business and keeping cash surpluses in their own homes. When some of them defaulted in 1571, the crown lost £44,000. The following year Lord Treasurer Winchester died owing more than £46,000. Despite the genuine reform efforts of his successor, Burghley, and of Chancellor Mildmay, they were in most respects only partly or temporarily successful. Undoubtedly Burghley used his place to procure legitimate financial benefits for his servants and clients. But there is no evidence to show that his conduct and judgement were ever corrupted by possible profits, unlike his subordinate George Goring, receiver-general of the Court of Wards, who had embezzled about £20,000 by the time he died. Furthermore, he pursued corrupt officers, such as the defaulting teller, Richard Stonley, and Roger Manwood, Chief Baron of the Exchequer. Both Burghley and his son Robert grew rich in the queen's service from the opportunities which office afforded. Apart from his scandalously low subsidy assessment, the Lord Treasurer does not appear to have abused his position or used the more questionable practices of his son. Certainly he had his critics, such as Francis Bacon, Edmund Spenser and Thomas Wilson, who, as we have seen, accused him of greed, avarice, corruption and obstruction of the rise of able men like themselves. Contemporaries who committed their opinions to paper were, however, generally in unwitting agreement with Burghley's own words: 'I marvel, that any malicious discoverer can note me a councillor that do abuse my credit to private gain.'[14]

War from the mid-1580s created or exacerbated a variety of financial problems. Funding it was a major problem for an undernourished state. Although the policy of strict economy had built up a reserve of treasure, it was soon exhausted by the inexorable demands of war. It was in wartime that the shortsightedness of the mutually conservative queen and minister, in failing to explore possible new and additional sources of revenue, became apparent. Nevertheless, the fact that, after eighteen years of war on land and sea, the crown bequeathed a debt of only £350,000 or less was a noteworthy accomplishment.[15] This was especially so when the government's funds, afforced though they were by regular parliamentary taxation, were still very modest in relation to military and naval requirements. War, in any age, can play havoc with the finances of even the most amply funded state. Furthermore, it was war on a number of fronts: Ireland, France, the Low Countries, the English Channel, Atlantic and Caribbean. Most state-funded operations, even the critical defence against the 1588 Armada, were characterised by shortages of money, men, weapons and supplies and by frequent laments and demands for more from English commanders, Dutch rebels and the French Protestant, Henry Bourbon.[16]

The herculean labours of Burghley and other administrators cannot be denied, but much of their time was spent simply in trying to make ends meet. State activities were curtailed or the costs, in the case of poor relief, defence and military training, were passed on to local communities. Limited resources meant that naval operations sometimes depended partly on private investment. Expeditions mounted on a joint-stock basis (in which both queen and minister invested)[17] inevitably had the confused, even conflicting, objectives of victory by destruction of the enemy and profit through plunder. Burghley tended to get trapped in the middle, between the financial demands of England's warriors and allies and a queen who, in MacCaffrey's words, 'concentrated so exclusively on the trees of economy as to lose sight of the woods of war'.[18]

With much more money flowing through the state system and the inadequate supervision of both field commanders and an enlarged military bureaucracy, war created many opportunities for corrupt practices and profits. There was little that Burghley could do. Sir Thomas Shirley, treasurer at war for the Low Countries, annually diverted £30,000 to his own use. One of the means by which he did so, according to the charges against him in 1593, was that he 'infinitely bribed' the Lord Treasurer's own clerk. The basic problem with which the government had to contend, especially in wartime, was the extensive venality of a political system in which inadequate revenues and pay, economic opportunities and personal benefit were all related. With the tight economy practised during wartime the traditional sources of royal patronage were drastically reduced.

Even before the war Burghley had begun to restructure Elizabethan patronage by farming the customs, granting export concessions (which exempted specified commodities from the statutory prohibition on their export) and patents of monopoly. During the long war with Spain the number of monopolies rapidly grew. They were a useful form of patronage to a financially straitened government, because they cost the crown nothing. However, it was the community which bore the cost and suffered a variety of harmful consequences from their multiplication. Elizabeth and Burghley failed to act positively in response to the discontent expressed in the commons in 1597–98.

The Lord Treasurer died soon afterwards and so he did not have to face the uproar over monopolies in the parliament of 1601.[19] He had been a cautious Lord Treasurer, conscientiously husbanding the crown's limited resources. He had been concerned about corruption and mismanagement and tried to effect a number of improvements, by and large unsuccessfully, in the Exchequer, but more effectively with purveyance compositions. His caution was reinforced by the recognition that royal financial practice, especially in the case of wardship, could impact on political harmony and stability. Above all, he was, like his queen, conservative. In any case, he was not a free agent. Major innovations or radical changes in state funding would probably have been vetoed by her.

So far as the national economy was concerned Burghley had neither a master plan, a coherent theory, nor a grand co-ordinated strategy. To some extent that was a consequence of his conservative instincts, his pragmatism and, at times, his varying responses, often based on a rationale which was other than economic, to opportunities and problems as they occurred. To a considerable extent, however, this is less a personal criticism of someone with limited vision than a recognised consequence of the position in which all Tudor ministers found themselves. They managed a state which had neither the resources, manpower or information to organise a planned economy and impose it on economic and local interests. It had neither an annual budget nor the capacity to project a possible financial balance, surplus or deficit and plan accordingly. Burghley's economic management, if it can be termed that, consisted largely of *ad hoc* responses to changing economic circumstances and their opportunities and dangers. Furthermore, those responses were influenced, if not dictated, by the way in which he related, even subordinated, economic development to other considerations. They included the crown's sustained financial viability, internal peace and stability and national defence. These specifically non-economic concerns constituted the driving force behind what some historians have termed his 'economic nationalism'. This involved less dependence on imported commodities by resuscitating old industries and developing new ones, especially for the production of war materials such as iron and saltpetre. Burghley favoured the grant of monopolistic patents as an inducement and he was himself an investor in two metallurgical companies, the Mines Royal and Mineral and Battery Works. At the same time, far-sightedness and good intent sometimes mingled with ignorance: when, for example, he hoped that John Dee, the astrologer, would make gold and when he became involved with Leicester in a society for transmuting iron into copper.[20]

Perhaps more than any other consideration, political and social peace and stability pervaded Burghley's thinking and decisions on economic matters. He was continuously concerned with the need for full employment (reflected in the act of artificers, a council-sponsored measure in 1563) and full stomachs. Sometimes there was a conflict of priorities. In the 1580s women in London were employed in the production of starch from wheat. It was necessary for fashionable ruffs, worn by the queen among others. Burghley, however, deplored the misuse of grain 'which would staunch the hunger of many that starve in the streets for want of bread'. Nevertheless, his concern about the connection between food shortages, unemployment and social disorder was soundly based. Food shortages in the 1580s and 1590s provoked riots in the mid- and south-west counties, London and the south-east. Unemployment magnified the dreaded social problem of vagabondage. However, such non-economic concerns also influenced his approach to trade and foreign affairs. The Spanish embargo on the cloth trade with Antwerp in 1563 prompted him to worry about the queen's loss of customs revenue and 'the sudden stay at home of the people that belong to cloth-making'. Much later, in 1587 during the war with Spain, he lamented the disruption of trade, especially in cloth. Without its resumption, many of the queen's subjects 'must either perish for want, or fall into violence . . . which is the print of rebellion'.[21]

In parliament too Burghley was prepared to sponsor and assist the passage of a variety of measures, which were intended to promote public order or at least did so incidentally. Such were sumptuary laws, designating what each social rank could wear;[22] more humane and effective poor laws; and the 1576 statute 'in restraint of common promoters'. The last of these was a vexed question concerning private informers, who started actions on penal statutes in the law courts. Penal statutes punished breaches of economic or social regulation by imposing a fine or forfeiture on the offender. The private persons who brought such actions in the first place received half the forfeiture in each conviction and some of them, working in collusion with Exchequer officials, had turned the practice into a profitable profession. Their aggressiveness, inquisitorial behaviour and sharp practices made them very unpopular. Lord Chancellor Bacon and Cecil campaigned for ten years to enact appropriate legislation. In 1566 they failed. As Cecil wrote, 'the oppression of the informers not amended'. In 1571 his men of business stirred the commons to debate and action: a bill against promoters passed both houses but failed to become law, doubtless because of a royal veto. The following year Burghley became Lord Treasurer. In 1574 he launched an investigation into the promoters' practices and, two years later, he and Bacon at last obtained a statute against them: it restricted the scope of their activities and provided some protection for defendants against their malpractices.[23]

In the early years of Elizabeth's reign the new government was faced with a range of economic problems, especially inflation but also unsuccessful war and the loss of Calais as an entrepôt, dearth due to bad harvests in the mid-1550s and early/mid-1560s, plague in 1563 and unstable (even disrupted) trade with the chief English cloth market in the Low Countries. Successive debasements of coinage in the 1540s and 1550s had contributed to inflation. It was held by Sir Thomas Gresham that this could be reversed if the quality of the coinage was restored, an undertaking carried through in 1562. When it did not have the expected effect the council resorted to economic regulation of prices, wages, exports and foreign imports, apparel statutes, and controls on the breeding and export of horses.[24] Prevailing official policies and actions in the early years of the reign clearly reflected Cecil's standpoint. He was administrative, not innovative, with a preference for known and tried ways and often acting from moral premisses: as Norman Jones shows, avaricious usurers were regarded as responsible for social and economic ills and Cecil approached the problem of usury from this position in 1571.[25]

His consideration of international trade was directed and restricted by the same conservative and traditionalist parameters, tempered as always by a mixture of pragmatism and Protestantism. His motives for encouraging trade were often political, directed towards national defence and independence as well as economic growth. For example, he reputedly told the Spanish ambassador in 1561 that the pope had no right to divide the New World between Spain and Portugal. He acted on this belief when he invested in some of the voyages of Hawkins, Raleigh and others who challenged the Iberian New World economic monopoly. His mixed approach to the economy is nowhere better summed up than in his own undated notes on the 'inconveniences' of French wine imports. First, excessive wine imports contributed to an economically harmful balance of trade deficit. Secondly, by French ordinance such wines could not be paid for by exchange of goods but only by cash, which meant a drain on English gold reserves. Thus far his arguments were related to the national economy. However, he then proceeded to argue:

1. that wine imports 'enricheth France, whose power England ought not to increase';
2. that the increase of taverns, as a result of growing wine imports, would lead to drunken disorder by 'the vulgar people', who would spend their hard-earned money there;
3. that increased wine consumption would reduce the sale of ale and beer. This, in turn, would diminish the demand for those crops which were required for their production.

So Burghley's arguments concerned not only the national economy but also French power and the threat to local order and local economies. He concluded that it was not fit to increase the merchant navy in order to handle wine imports, which were already excessive. Nevertheless, conscious as he was of the navy as England's first line of defence, he added that 'all other ways should be sought to nourish mariners and to increase ships'. 'Cecil's fast day', the compulsory fish-eating Wednesday, which he successfully tacked on to the navigation act of 1563, was one of the 'other ways' in which he tried to achieve that end.[26]

England's basic trading problem was twofold: its only major export was unfinished cloth and its guaranteed market was Antwerp. However, from the mid-sixteenth century onwards, trade relations with the Spanish-controlled Low Countries became ever more precarious and insecure. In 1551, during Edward VI's reign, Cecil (in a subordinate capacity) and the Tudors' great financial expert, Gresham, were assigned the task of stabilising the commercial connection. Gresham, not Cecil, did that, but it was only a temporary reprieve. Mary's reign and her marriage to Habsburg Philip prolonged that reprieve. But, in the 1560s, growing disenchantment, abrasion and finally confrontation, between Protestant Tudor and Catholic Habsburg, blocked off the London–Antwerp 'funnel'.[27] The seizure and transference to Elizabeth of the Genoese bankers' loan to Philip II in 1568 triggered in turn a Spanish embargo on English goods and a search by English merchants for new cloth marts, especially in Germany.[28] This became just one aspect of the government's search for new markets in an attempt to reduce England's vulnerable dependence on cloth exports. Trading companies were organised to penetrate Russia, the Baltic, North Africa and the Middle East. Cecil took a personal as well as official part in such commercially expansionist ventures when, for example, he contributed to the first Russian voyage of Richard Chancellor in 1553–54 and the resultant Muscovy Company founded in 1565. It was typical of Tudor government that the personal and the national interest merged. Cecil increased his investment in the trading company in 1556 and remained actively concerned in its affairs. It was to him that the Muscovy merchants wrote in 1592, in order to secure the suppression of a book written by the ex-ambassador to Russia, Dr Giles Fletcher. It described the Russian government as 'plaine tirannycall' and contained uncomplimentary references to the Emperor and his 'intollerable exactions . . . oppression and slaverie'. The merchants complained that the book would cause offence in Russia and that, in consequence, trade would suffer.[29]

Central to Burghley's economic activity was his relationship with the City of London. It is significant that, in the same year that he was elevated to a barony and the house of lords, William Fleetwood was appointed City Recorder and Thomas Norton became first occupant of the newly created office of remembrancer to the Lord Mayor. Both men were his clients. Fleetwood frequently reported to Burghley on City affairs, whilst Norton became the vital intermediary between the Privy Council, especially the Lord Treasurer, and London's government. Although there is no direct evidence that Burghley was responsible for their appointments, the coincidence in time is so striking that it seems probable he was. As London replaced Antwerp as the government's chief money-market, due to the foresight and skilful management of Gresham, so it became even more important for the Lord Treasurer to court it.

Nevertheless, conciliar influence on English commercial activities was strictly limited. As the Antwerp market became increasingly insecure, trade links with Spain, Portugal and their islands increased, especially during the 1570s. Despite the Spanish acquisition of Portugal in 1580 and war between England and Spain from the mid-1580s, trade continued, especially in English grain, fish and other foodstuffs. These victuals provisioned the Spanish army and navy. So did English ordnance, from the 1570s and into the next century. Privy Council orders and royal proclamations had no evident effect on the illicit trade. As early as 1580 Burghley learned of the large number of cannon arriving in Spain from south and south-west England. A royal proclamation, eleven years later, implicitly acknowledged the Council's failure: 'We . . . command . . . that no person . . . within any our realms . . . do from henceforth carry . . . any kind of corn or grain, or of any ordnance . . . out of our realm into . . . any dominions of the King of Spain . . .'. Two years later, in 1593, Burghley was informed of further ordnance exports to England's enemy. At the 'higher' level, that of conflict between governments and opposed ideologies, this was inexcusable. For merchant communities, however, war interrupted mutually beneficial trading activities. Pauline Croft makes the realistic observation that merchants engaged in the Spanish trade after 1585 were not necessarily 'traitors or cryptopapists', but rather 'the representatives of a cooler and altogether more pragmatic strand of Elizabethan opinion'.[30]

Whilst Burghley was ineffective in his Canute-role, vainly endeavouring to stem the tide of economic opportunism, he did play an important part in the process of stimulating the national economy: when he encouraged the immigration of skilled foreign labour such as silk workers, linen weavers and starch makers; when he used monopolistic patents to encourage English and entice foreign manufacturers of alum, glass, paper and saltpetre (for gunpowder); and when he supported the growth of a national arms industry. For Burghley this was the continuation of a policy begun under Edward VI, and much of the credit for the diversity of manufacturing enterprises belongs to him. He promoted and personally invested in metallurgical enterprises, thereby seeking, at the same time, to advance the fortunes of the Cecil family. According to Joan Thirsk, there was a continuity between the ideals of the Edwardian Commonwealthmen and Burghley's advancement of economic projects during Elizabeth's reign. This was accompanied by his inducement of monopolistic patents to new manufacturers, especially foreigners. The first such patents of the reign were issued for white soap, saltpetre, alum and copperas (for dyeing) and furnaces and ovens. Many more monopolies followed. The economic advantages of them diminished, however, as speculators (especially courtiers) acquired them for private advantage. Monopolists had the capacity to destroy competitors, fix prices and cause intense local resentment. The patent, much favoured by Burghley as an instrument of economic growth and diversification, became instead the resource of money-grubbing courtiers and the cause of a serious parliamentary protest in 1601.[31]

Monopolistic patents, for both manufacturing and trade, were also used by Burghley as a means of economic regulation. So too were the frequent proclamations regulating prices and wages and the books of orders instructing Justices of the Peace on actions to be taken in response to plague epidemics, food shortages and failed harvests. They reflected Burghley's ongoing and deep-felt concern about law, order and stability. Similar conciliar action, through royal proclamations and orders, attempted to halt London's growth and overcrowding. How effective they all were is another matter. The language of proclamations frequently expressed a sense of failure. Some of those involved in government were very sceptical. So Sir John Mason advised Cecil in 1550 that, despite the proclamation on cheese and butter prices, 'Nature will have her course.' Cecil and his conciliar colleagues never recognised that simple truth. So they continued to issue decrees, commands, proclamations and other instructions which, for the most part, were simply ignored. There were already laws enough on economic and social management. The basic and perpetual problem was the government's inability to enforce them. High-flown ideals and grand statements of intent were one thing, but their implementation was quite another. When vital economic interests, such as London companies or the landed gentry, were in harmony with the Privy Council, its directives might be implemented, but otherwise not. Through the outflow of conciliar paperwork, however, one can discern Burghley's consistent priorities. They do not warrant the label 'economic policy', because his specific economic concerns were just part of an overall approach to government. When he sought to develop new industries, encourage immigration, achieve a balance of payments and seek out new markets, his thinking was not directed by purely economic considerations. His consistent goals were social and political stability which, in turn, guaranteed the security of the queen and her government and the independence of her Protestant English state. Burghley was not an economist but, in sixteenth-century terms, a patriot-politician.[32]

. . .

NOTES

1. See below, pp. 153–5.
2. G.R. Elton, *The Tudor Constitution* (Cambridge, 1982), pp. 39–45; Williams, *Tudor Regime*, pp. 62–80; Guy, *Tudor England*, pp. 379–85.
3. Hughes (ed.), 'Nicholas Faunt's Discourse', pp. 499–500; Read, *Walsingham*, I, p. 430.
4. Hoak, *King's Council*, pp. 203–5, 207–8, 212; Wright (ed.), *Queen Elizabeth*, I, pp. 142–5; Palliser, *Age of Elizabeth*, pp. 294–5; Guy, *Tudor England*, p. 382; Alsop, 'Parl. session of 1566', pp. 218–22; for usury see above, p. 133.
5. Guy, *Tudor England*, pp. 379–80; Palliser, *Age of Elizabeth*, pp. 16–17; T.S. Willan (ed.), *A Tudor Book of Rates* (Manchester, 1962), pp. xxvi–xxxviii; Williams, *Later Tudors*, pp. 147–8; Smith, *Burghley*, pp. 39–42.
6. Guy, *Tudor England*, pp. 379–81; Williams, *Later Tudors*, pp. 147–8; Smith, *Burghley*, pp. 40–1; Smith, *Emergence of a Nation State*, pp. 117–18.
7. Willan, *Book of Rates*, pp. xi–xv, xvii, xxiii, xxvi–xli.

8. Beckingsale, *Burghley*, pp. 234–6; J. Hurstfield, *The Queen's Wards: Wardship and Marriage under Elizabeth I* (London, 1973), pp. 262–3.
9. Wilson, 'State of England', p. 28; Hurstfield, *Queen's Wards*, pp. 264–70; Smith (ed.), *Anon. Life*, pp. 84–7; see above, p. 88.
10. K. Sharpe, *The Personal Rule of Charles I* (London, 1992), p. 129; Hurstfield, *Freedom, Corruption*, pp. 177–8, 188–9; idem, *Queen's Wards*, pp. 260 ff., esp. pp. 268–9; *Clapham*, p. 81; Smith (ed.), *Anon. Life*, pp. 79–83; Dean, *Law-Making and Society*, pp. 83–4; see above, p. 138.
11. A.G.R. Smith, 'Crown, parliament and finance', in P. Clark, A.G.R. Smith, Nicholas Tyacke (eds), *The English Commonwealth, 1547–1640* (Leicester, 1979), pp. 114–15; Guy, *Tudor England*, pp. 397–9; Hurstfield, *Freedom, Corruption*, pp. 278–80; Loach, *Parl. under Tudors*, pp. 129–31; Read, *Burghley*, p. 527; Dean, *Law-Making and Society*, p. 85; P. Croft, 'Purveyance', pp. 9–35.
12. Hartley, *Proceedings*, III, p. 108; *CJ*, I, pp. 63, 74; Guy, *Tudor England*, pp. 192–3, 381–2, 385; Elton, *Parliament of England*, pp. 154–5; Dean, *Law-Making and Society*, pp. 36–47, 49, 52 and n. 64; Smith, *Burghley*, p. 41; H. Miller, 'Subsidy assessments of the peerage in the sixteenth century', *BIHR*, 28 (1955), pp. 18, 22; R.W. Hoyle, 'Crown, parliament and taxation in sixteenth century England', *EHR*, 109 (1994), pp. 1185, 1191, 1195–6; J.D. Alsop, 'The theory and practice of Tudor taxation', *EHR*, 97 (1982), pp. 1–30; idem, 'Innovation in Tudor taxation', *EHR*, 99 (1984), pp. 83–93.
13. Alsop, 'Government, finance and the community of the Exchequer', in Haigh (ed.), *Reign of Elizabeth*, pp. 101–23; G.R. Elton, 'The Elizabethan Exchequer: war in the receipt', in Bindoff (ed.), *Government and Society*, pp. 213–48.
14. Guy, *Tudor England*, pp. 391–7; Hasler (ed.), *Commons*, III, pp. 15–17; Hurstfield, *Freedom, Corruption*, pp. 151–2; Beckingsale, *Burghley*, pp. 242–3; see above, pp. 81, 118–19.
15. Smith, *Govt. of Eliz. England*, pp. 8–9 and n. 1.
16. e.g. MacCaffrey, *Making of Policy*, pp. 364–7; Read, *Burghley*, pp. 438–9; *HMC*, De L'Isle MS, 2, esp. pp. 104, 163–74, 178, 186–98, 201, 204, 223–5, 271–2, 280–4, 292, 313, 316, 319, 326.
17. e.g. *HMC*, De L'Isle MS, 2, p. 198.
18. MacCaffrey, *Making of Policy*, p. 366.
19. See below, p. 165; Dean, *Law-Making and Society*, pp. 85–92; Adams, 'Patronage in politics', pp. 39–41.
20. Beckingsale, *Burghley*, pp. 207–9; Smith, *Burghley*, p. 39; N. Heard, *Tudor Economy and Society*, (London, 1992), p. 56; M.B. Donald, *Elizabethan Monopolies* (London, 1961), pp. 6–9, 35; Strype, *Annals*, II, Pt. 2, pp. 555–8.

21. J.A. Youings, *Sixteenth Century England* (London, 1984), p. 244; Guy, *Tudor England*, pp. 405–6; Heard, *Tudor Economy*, pp. 68, 116–17; Palliser, *Age of Elizabeth*, pp. 311–12; Wright (ed.), *Queen Elizabeth*, I, p. 175.
22. Burghley, however, also shared Bacon's belief that rigorous enforcement of existing laws was preferable to making more, if those in existence were adequate. He preferred, for example, not to sponsor new sumptuary laws, even though he was concerned that expensive, fashionable garments were wasting men's fortunes. Graves, *Norton*, p. 133.
23. Ibid., pp. 131–3; D.R. Lidington, 'Parliament and the enforcement of the penal statutes: the history of the act in restraint of common promoters, 18 Eliz. I, c. 5', *Parl. Hist.*, 8/2 (1989), pp. 309–28.
24. Jones, *Birth of Eliz. Age*, pp. 229–38; idem, 'William Cecil and the making of economic policy in the 1560s and early 1570s', in P.A. Fideler and T.F. Mayer (eds), *Political Thought and the Tudor Commonwealth: Deep Structure, Discourse and Disguise* (London, 1992), pp. 169–93; Hughes and Larkin, *Tudor Royal Proclamations*, II, nos. 493–7, 501–9, 512, 517–8, 521, 524, 527, 529–30, 532–46, 551, 559–60, 572.
25. Jones, *God and the Moneylenders*, pp. 34–42, 55; see above, pp. 136–7, 150.
26. Palliser, *Age of Elizabeth*, p. 20; PRO, SP, 12/41/58; Read, *Burghley*, pp. 371–3; SP, 12/41/58.
27. Heard, *Tudor Economy*, pp. 55, 59, 62–3; Read, *Secretary Cecil*, pp. 434–5.
28. See above, pp. 50–1.
29. Palliser, *Age of Elizabeth*, pp. 23, 294–6; Beckingsale, *Burghley*, p. 57; T.S. Willan, *The Early History of the Russia Company, 1553–1603* (Manchester, 1956), pp. 41–2; H. Ellis, *Original Letters of Eminent Literary Men*, Camden Society, 23 (1843), pp. 76–9; Graves, *Norton*, pp. 56–67, 82–3.
30. P. Croft, 'Trading with the enemy, 1585–1604', *HJ*, 32/2 (1989), pp. 281–302; Hughes and Larkin, *Tudor Royal Proclamations*, III, pp. 83–5.
31. Palliser, *Age of Elizabeth*, pp. 21–2, 323–4; Heard, *Tudor Economy*, p. 47; J. Thirsk, *Economic Policy and Projects* (Oxford, 1978), pp. 33–4, 51–61, 65, 89, 98–9.
32. Palliser, *Age of Elizabeth*, pp. 316–9, 324–5; P. Slack, 'Poverty and social regulation in Elizabethan England', in Haigh (ed.), *Reign of Elizabeth*, pp. 224, 235–6; idem, 'Books of orders: the making of English social policy, 1577–1631', *TRHS*, 5th ser., 30 (1980), pp. 3–4.

Chapter 9

BURGHLEY AND RELIGION

In common with Sir Thomas Smith, Nicholas Bacon and others of his circle, William Cecil came to Elizabeth's reign through the involved experience of the Edwardian Protestant Reformation and the detached observation of Mary I's Hispano-Catholic rule. During his forty-year-long prominence in Elizabethan government his religious position was often complicated and sometimes one of dilemma. On the one hand, he was no mere secular politician. His moderation did not signify lack of 'piety' or deep devotion. According to Clapham and the anonymous biographer, each morning and evening 'he used ordinarily to read or hear some part of Holy Writ in Latin read unto him'. The importance which he attached to preaching was given practical expression, because he 'would never miss [a] sermon if he were able' and he regularly took communion on the first of each month. Even in his last declining years, when he was sometimes too ill to leave his residence, he contrived to pray by or in his bed or have someone read to him 'so as one way or other he failed not his prayers'. In this kind of context he was a private man. However, as royal councillor and minister, he was also a focal public figure who had, indeed had to have, a religious position which was given expression in advice to the queen.[1]

In his *Short Memorial*, written in about 1569, Cecil lamented the decay of God's service and 'the syncere Profession of Christian Relligion . . . and in Place therof, partly Papacy, and partly Paganism, and Irrelligion ar crept in'. As a consequence, the 'Strength, that shuld serve the Quenes Majesty, is wasted or febled . . . [and the] Administration of the cyvill Pollycy is also weakened'. Herein is an important clue to his public stance on the state of religion, which he regarded as inseparable from political order and stability. According to the anonymous biographer, 'He would say there could be no firm nor settled course in religion without order and government . . . [and] there could be no government where there was division.' In the cause of unity he believed in uniformity and public conformity. It followed that he had a particular dislike of extreme positions. In Clapham's words, he 'dissented from the Papist and the Puritan, disliking the superstition of the one and the singularity of the other; holding the midway . . . between two extremities'. His prime concerns in religious matters, as in all things, were the establishment and preservation of security and stability. It is significant of course that Burghley and his friends had grown up and entered public life, not only in the context of a Protestant reformation but also in the political environment of Henrician and Edwardian Erastianism. Mary's reign marked the total defeat of the Protestant Erastian church. Her death in 1558, however, revived the hopes of the Edwardian opportunists, who had outwardly conformed and waited for a better day.[2]

Cecil's political priority of stability, his belief in the inseparable relationship of church and state, together with loyalty to both the new queen and the Henrician–Edwardian precedent of royal headship, dictated his approach to the first parliament of her reign. The resultant Elizabethan Settlement was, as Norman Jones in particular has convincingly demonstrated, a triumphal achievement for queen and minister. The new Protestant and Erastian creation, which also held out prospects of being a broad, moderate and unifying church, appeared to fulfil, in large measure, Cecil's priorities. However, this was not designed by Elizabeth or her Secretary as a tolerant *via media* church. The Settlement of 1559 reflected her conservative Protestantism and thereafter she was obdurately resistant to further change. Likewise Cecil, whom Professor Collinson designated, along with Nicholas Bacon and Archbishop Parker, as 'the principal devotees of the middle way', did not envisage a church characterised by a diversity of doctrine and order of worship. Only in so far as he rejected politically destabilising religious extremes was he a man of the middle way. Otherwise he was insistent on public conformity in the interest of order and stability. This, however, should not be misconstrued simply as the policy of a secular politician and loyal servant of the Supreme Governor. It also expressed the importance which he attached to 'pure religion'. That could take root and flourish only when royal leadership was not openly challenged and the church was not publicly rent by diverse opinions and loyalties.[3]

In the decades following the Elizabethan Settlement, however, the new church was faced with an array of problems and challenges. In various ways they constituted threats to Burghley's conceptual framework of an independent national state and church, bound together under the queen in inseparable union and in which political allegiance and public religious conformity were the duty of all subjects. There were two major threats, though they differed dramatically in nature and degree. One was the divisive and disruptive activity of the godly reforming Protestants within the English church; the other was the dynamic of militant international Counter-Reformation Roman Catholicism. The latter sought to recapture land and souls lost to Protestantism in the Reformation. The champions of this aggressive Catholic revival were a revitalised papacy, Philip II of Spain, and France, in particular the powerful Guise family (one of whom was Mary Stuart's mother). Although they did not constitute an active, co-ordinated international confederacy, at least during the first twenty years of Elizabeth's reign, that was Burghley's conception. To him it was a major and growing external threat to the English queen, state and church and one, moreover, which might find allies among the Catholic community in England. Time alone would demonstrate the dutiful allegiance of the great majority of English Catholics to their queen. Of course Burghley was not to know that. Furthermore, the presence of Mary Stuart in England from 1568 provided a potential focus and catalyst of anti-Protestant hostility. The northern earls raised rebellion on her behalf in the following year, whilst English Catholics' involvement in the Ridolfi (1571), Throckmorton (1582–83) and Babington (1586) plots cast the loyalty of the entire Catholic community into doubt. Such doubts and fears must have been exacerbated by the promulgation of the papal bull *Regnans in Excelsis* in 1570. Yet, in the midst of this first major crisis of the reign, Elizabeth's Secretary did not assume the existence of a treacherous Catholic stereotype. Instead he distinguished between treasonable papists and doctrinal Catholics, who could still be loyal subjects.[4]

Nevertheless, the crisis of 1568–72 contributed to a hardening of the Privy Council's and Burghley's conduct towards English Catholics. During the 1560s some Catholic gentry outwardly conformed and others apostasized. Relatively few seem to have been obstinate recusants. The government, for its part, did not pursue a consistent policy of surveillance and punishment of recusancy. The importance which Cecil attached to outward conformity, however, meant that he always regarded recusancy as a problem and potential danger. The events of 1568–72 reinforced his concern. A statement, which he drafted for public dissemination in 1570, condemned long-term recusants as guilty of 'open and willfull contempt' of the law. And, in 1571, the unsuccessful parliamentary bill to punish failure to receive communion once a year had conciliar support and, according to MacCaffrey, 'almost certainly from Burghley'.[5]

Thereafter recusants were treated with increasing severity. A more systematic surveillance led to examinations and confinements. In a memorandum of 1579 Burghley spelt out the necessary measures against recusants: 'The keeping under the bonds of law the evil contented subjects for religion . . . is the best bridle to stay them from dangers . . . to leave them without power by offices . . . or by possessing of any quantity of arms offensive.' In 1580 he and Walsingham drafted a proposal for isolating the more important and influential recusants by imprisonment. And the parliament of the following year enacted a statute which increased the penalty for non-attendance at an Anglican church from one shilling a Sunday to £20 a lunar month. The bill was promoted by Burghley's treasury subordinate, Mildmay, and his client Thomas Norton in the commons, but he redrafted it and it was this new version which passed into law. The evidence indicates that, as Elton wrote, 'the act was Burghley's and not the Queen's'. Clearly this dramatic increase in fines was not enough, for in 1583–84 Burghley drafted memoranda calling for more drastic measures. These included the disarming of recusants, their imprisonment and forfeiture of their goods and income. Early in 1587, when he feared Catholic action to save Mary Stuart, he proposed that all recusants of substance should be incarcerated. In the Armada year the Privy Council duly issued orders for all 'popish' recusants to be imprisoned or detained in reliable persons' custody.

Burghley repeatedly returned to the threat supposedly posed by the recusants even though, by the 1590s, they and indeed most Catholics had demonstrated their continuing loyalty to the kingdom and its reigning monarch. In a memorandum of 1590, for example, he again recommended further restraints, the seizure of all weapons, and fines or prison for recusant wives of English Protestants. It is not known whether he wrote the 1591 proclamation, which announced the appointment of commissioners to seek out the missionaries by enquiry and examination as to their movements, whereabouts and who had accommodated them. The recusants were, however, a natural target of suspicion, especially to Burghley, and, as he drafted many of the queen's proclamations, it is probable that this one reflected both his views and proposed remedies. He was widely regarded by Catholics as the author of the inquisitorial regime imposed by this proclamation on the recusant community.[6] Certainly in the 1593 parliament his active hand was in evidence in government measures to stiffen further the penalties against recusants: one confined their movements to within a five-mile radius of their homes; the other increased fines, which, however, could also apply to Protestant recusants. The first passed easily enough. The other, however, ran into trouble in the lower house. It was replaced by an alternative bill, dealing with Protestant recusants. This was sponsored by the Lord Treasurer and began in the lords. After extensive commons' revision it too became law. The fact that Burghley was prepared to act against both Protestants and Catholics indicates the importance which he attached to outward conformity.[7]

Burghley was not alone in his increasing focus on the recusant community as a potential threat to national security and a challenge to the established church. Other councillors, in particular Walsingham, shared his fears, which were intensified by the seminary priests' infiltration of the kingdom during the 1570s and the arrival of the first Jesuits in 1580. With Burghley in the forefront, the Privy Council took stern, even brutal, action in an effort to remove the missionaries. The statutes of 1581 and 1584–85 provided the legal muscle for a 'search and destroy' mission. Seminary priests and Jesuits were hunted down, imprisoned and, in some cases, interrogated about their political allegiance (often under torture) and executed. Burghley had no compunction and expressed no remorse for authorising torture, which eventually became a routine accompaniment to examinations, and for seeking the death of missionaries by the hideous means reserved for those convicted of treason. Like his man of business, Thomas Norton, who was often employed to interrogate those unfortunate enough to be caught, he regarded them not merely as religious heretics but as traitors and agents of an international Catholic conspiracy. In his view their offences were 'not matters of religion but merely of state'. The 'due process of law', accompanied by torture, was applied to Edmund Campion, first and most formidable of the Jesuit missionaries. He was charged with offences against Edward III's treason law, convicted and executed for sedition and conspiracy to kill the queen. Burghley was legally justified in his position by the legislation of 1581–84. His council memorandum of 1583, his *Execution of Justice in England, not for Religion but for Treason,* published in the same year, and Norton's *A discoverie of treason,* which appeared a year later, all presented that justification for proceedings against them. Ten years later he was still insisting that, though the missionaries' 'outward pretence be to be sent from the seminaries to convert people to their religion; yet without reconciling of them from their obedience to the queen, they never give them absolution'.

Burghley's ruthless treatment of political Catholicism was the exception to the otherwise essential moderation which characterised his activities as Privy Councillor and minister of state. The missionary was the spearhead of the international Catholic assault. The obdurate recusant was his potential or actual acolyte. Nor did Burghley display any real confidence and trust in the ongoing loyalty of the majority of English Catholics, despite the earlier distinction which he drew between the political papists and the merely heretical. He fretted about the unreliable religious and political loyalties of the north, in which he was seemingly justified by the rebellion of 1569. Lancashire, that hotbed of Catholic gentry, particularly troubled him. He had a map of the county specially drawn for him. It depicted the chief estates of the gentry with a + against the names of those who were devout Catholics. His tract, entitled *Copy of a letter . . . to don Bernadino Mendoza, [Spanish] ambassador in France,* might seem to contradict this general anti-Catholic image. Published late in 1588, after the defeat of the Armada, it acknowledged and focused on the proven loyalty of English Catholics to queen and country. Hurstfield believed that it 'reflected a genuine conviction on the part of Burghley that Catholic Englishmen were loyal'. It can be argued, however, that the opinions voiced in this pamphlet were rather those of the pragmatist and the experienced propagandist, which by then he certainly was. *Copy of a letter* was a public affirmation and assurance, the purpose of which may have been to reinforce the public conformity and political loyalty of faltering Catholics.[8]

Throughout forty years of change, in both internal and international religious politics, Burghley's attitude to Catholicism was consistently determined by his defence of the sovereign English nation state and Erastian church. However, whilst increasing government activity was directed against recusants, who could easily be identified by their absence from church, and against 'treasonable' seminary priests and Jesuits, there was a wider problem. English society in 1558 was conservative and the Elizabethan Settlement did not dramatically change that. There was widespread adherence to Catholicism, continued ministration by surviving Marian clergy and the persistent retention of altars and images. For a decade and often longer after 1558, as Christopher Haigh has shown, the English Protestant church retained 'many catholic churches [and] many catholic, or at least conservative, clergy'. Conservatism even affected the Court, where, in the early 1560s, the queen contemplated receiving a papal nuncio and sending a representative to the Roman Catholic Church Council, summoned by the pope at Trent in northern Italy. Cecil worked strenuously to prevent these from happening and, in fact, neither eventuated. Nevertheless, under a queen who was politically and to some extent in religion a conservative, there was no consistent and national dynamic drive for the vigorous implementation of the 1559 Settlement. As neither the state nor the church was a political monolith, enforcement depended upon a variety of often autonomous local agents and agencies. There was a variable range of enthusiasm and rigour and so enforcement was patchy.

Burghley was especially concerned to seek out and make an example of prominent men, even in the relatively crisis-free years of the 1560s. To do this, however, he needed to be informed. One lesson which he learned early as Edwardian Secretary was the need to collect information and compile records. An ignorant government was vulnerable and even weak, whereas an informed administration had a better chance of pre-empting problems before they became crises. The 1564 survey of the religious position of JPs and the later episcopal reports on recusancy, for example, were intended to alert the government to the extent of continuing Catholic affiliation, especially among members of the governing élite. That was especially important to Burghley, whose insistence on outward conformity and political loyalty, the prerequisites of security and stability, determined his policy towards conspirators, missionaries, recusants and the rest of the English Catholic community until his death.[9]

Protestant nonconformity, the other challenge to the church established in 1559, presented Burghley with a more complex personal problem and his response to it was equivocal. In one respect at least his attitude and conduct were consistent and unambiguous, because the issue was a straightforward one. The beliefs of the Anabaptists, Family of Love, Brownists (or Separatists) and other sects were all unacceptable to him on moral, theological and political grounds. They believed in religion as an essentially personal, private experience and rejected state organisation or interference. Such total rejection of outward conformity, indeed of the very existence of a state church, was anathema to Burghley, who, for example, described the Family of Love as a 'brain-sick heresy'. The Separatists, who, under their leader Robert Browne, rejected episcopal government, were also naturally regarded as subversives and became another target of state persecution. This caused difficulties for Burghley, who was related to Browne. More than once he intervened to spare his kinsman a worse fate than imprisonment. Yet, as the bishop of Norwich wrote to the Lord Treasurer in August 1581, that very same man 'late coming into my diocese, and teaching strange and dangerous doctrine, in all disordered manner, hadde greatlie troubled the whole countrie, and brought manie to great disobedience of all lawe and magistrates'. He plaintively sought Burghley's assistance, because some of the local gentry 'in winking at, if not of pollicie procuring the disordered sorte to go forwards in their evil attemptes . . . will in tyme, I feare, hazarde the overthrow of all religion . . .'. Although Browne challenged all that the queen's minister, Burghley, held so dear, kinship too counted for much.[10]

The problem of personal connection did not muddy the Lord Treasurer's hostility to the advocates of Presbyterianism, especially Wilcox and Field, the authors of the *Admonition to the Parliament* in 1572. Presbyterians, who looked to Calvin's Geneva as the model, rejected episcopacy and the Erastian church. Therefore they also repudiated governance by the Christian magistrate. Instead the church was to be governed by a hierarchical structure of elected assemblies, whilst, at the grassroots level, discipline would be provided in the local churches and their accompanying congregational courts. The Presbyterian position was unacceptable to Burghley. Furthermore, the onus of action fell upon him. Bishops, such as Scambler of Peterborough, wrote to him about 'these troubles, nowe moved and procured by . . . puritans and their fautors . . . wherefore . . . I flie unto you for advise'. Archbishop Parker lamented support for them in official quarters and warned Burghley that, whilst bishops were the first target, 'certainly yourself will shortly follow'. He played an active responsive part in 1573, when the queen issued two proclamations against the puritans and in October he addressed assembled judges and JPs in Star Chamber, at the end of the law term. They were instructed to seek out those puritan parish ministers who had encouraged their congregations 'to conceive erroneous opinions, in condemning the whole government of the Church and order ecclesiastical . . . a matter pernicious to the state of government'. Religious nonconformity also exercised his mind and occupied his time as chancellor of Cambridge University from 1559 onwards. In the 1560s, puritan activists in the University opposed the prescribed vestments and preached controversial sermons. In 1570 the Presbyterian orientation of the lectures delivered by Thomas Cartwright, the new Lady Margaret professor of divinity, raised the political temperature. Burghley had already declared his hostility to 'the leud leprosy' of nonconformist preachers and proposed action against them. Yet as late as 1595 he was the recipient of complaints about a wayward preacher, this time one full of 'divers popish errors'. As always, obedience and conformity, prerequisites of order and stability, were paramount in his thinking.[11]

Nevertheless, Burghley was faced continuously with conflicting, sometimes even incompatible, pressures and concerns. On the one hand, his desk was the natural landing place for missives from godly Protestant leaders in foreign places. From Scotland in 1561 John Knox, the dynamo of its Presbyterian church, wrote a rambling letter of lamentation, that Mary Stuart 'neyther is, neyther shalbe of our Opinion'. From Geneva Theodore Beza, Calvin's successor, sent him a gift for Cambridge University's library, as well as pleas and thanks for assistance against the duke of Savoy. In contrast, he was the object of repeated criticism and reprimand from frustrated godly reformers in England.[12] It was no new experience for him. During Edward VI's reign the redoubtable Catherine, duchess of Suffolk, chided him for his lack of zeal. In 1556, when Mary was queen, England was formally Catholic and Cecil conformed, his brother-in-law John Cheke wrote to him critically, even abrasively, from voluntary exile in Strasbourg.

Elizabeth's reign brought no reprieve. The duchess of Suffolk was scornful of the Elizabethan Settlement. Thereafter he was often the target of godly Protestants, who were not encumbered with the complicating problems of managing the state. So Thomas Sampson, a puritan divine at Oxford, reminded him 'how God hath advanced you' and advised that he should 'let not the love of that honour, which God hath given you, make you either remiss in his cause, or, for fear of the displeasure of man, slip by that which best pleaseth him'. In 1566 the militant Thomas Wood blamed him for the rigorous application of the *Advertisements* and, six years later, Edward Dering, one of the more outspoken evangelical Protestants, lamented Burghley's want of religion. Not that he always bore such crosses patiently. He penned an angry riposte to Dering's 'biting letter', after wondering 'whether I should, either for wasting of my time, or for nourishing of your humour, make you any answer'. Burghley wrote partly in self-defence: '[I]f I were so void of knowledge or godliness, as your words make me, I should be ashamed to live in the place where I do.' But he also delivered a heavy lecture to the opinionated Dering on his arrogance, professing that he himself was 'subject to sin and infirmityes; so as I may not glory of any perfection, wherein others think themselves to excel their brethren'. He concluded, '[W]ishing to myself that which you judge that I do lack; and to yourself all that which you seem to have. And what you have, for the charity I bear you, I heartily wish you more, than by your behaviour you seem to have.'[13]

If Burghley did not live up to the unrealistic hopes and high ideals of the radical godly Protestants, he was not hostile to further reformation. Admittedly the old Catholic administrative and judicial structures remained largely intact and they were duly condemned by ardent reformers. Burghley himself later acknowledged his guilt for the shortcomings of the Elizabethan Settlement and Sampson was not slow to remind him of the missed opportunity in 1559. However, as minister of state and chief royal adviser, Burghley, like prominent politicians in any age, had to temper idealism with realism, strive for what was possible and often settle for compromise. This did not mean that he was opposed to reforms which sought to improve the quality of the ministry. He was anxious to eliminate abuses such as simony and plurality of livings and, in pursuit of this objective, both he and the bishops were in favour of the so-called alphabetical bills, labelled A–F in the house of commons' journal. They were introduced too late in the 1566 session to make much headway but reappeared in the parliament of 1571. Most of them failed due to the resistance of the queen or the house of lords (which may have responded to her disapproval).[14]

Burghley also supported efforts to increase the incidence and improve the quality of preaching. Beginning in Edward VI's reign and continuing under Elizabeth, he promoted preachers whenever he had the opportunity. He sponsored Alexander Nowell, dean of St Paul's, who had drafted a brief Edwardian catechism, to produce a fuller version which was published in 1570. And he employed preachers to convey important messages at St Paul's Cross, the traditional venue for sermons in the City of London. Detectable in the Privy Council's letter to Archbishop Parker in 1569 is the opinion if not the hand of Burghley: it castigated 'an universal oversight and negligence (for less we cannot term it) of the bishops of the realm'. As a consequence, the queen's subjects, 'partly for lack of diligent teaching and information, partly for lack of correction and reformation, are entered either into dangerous errors, or into a manner of life of contempt or liberty'. There was, however, an undoubted albeit uneven general improvement in the quality and education of the clergy.

As Archbishop Parker advised Cecil, one obstacle to improvement was the queen. Lengthy episcopal vacancies, during which she received the revenues, left dioceses without effective church government and hindered the process of improvement. Later in the reign, during Whitgift's disciplinary regime, Burghley himself was the target of criticism for his failure to promote and defend 'true and peaceable' preachers. For example, he was, in effect, accused of backsliding by four such godly preachers, who were also members of Cambridge University. Therefore they were addressing not only the queen's minister but also their chancellor. Whilst the letter was couched in extravagantly courteous terms, praising him for 'the general furtherance of . . . true religion . . . and repressing the undermining malicious adversary', their praise was qualified: '[I]t might please your

Lordship, with like mindful care, to add the furthering, relieving, and comforting the true and peaceable professors of the Gospel, as your wisdom best knoweth how . . .'.[15]

Burghley was always exposed to the sometimes politically unrealistic demands of such godly preachers. For him there was always a dividing line between a preaching ministry, which sought to carry the faith to the people, and seditious preachers who questioned or rejected the structure of ecclesiastical government. In his insistence on outward conformity he was hostile also to those reforming clergy who refused to obey the queen's command that they wear the surplice and other 'comical dress' of the Catholic church. He dutifully drafted her letters on the subject and, as chancellor, he duly enforced Archbishop Parker's *Advertisements* on clerical dress at Cambridge University. His conduct in this matter was entirely consistent with his own conduct. The core of his faith was a matter of private conscience and personal devotion but, as an Erastian, he insisted on public loyalty and the state's management of the church.

It was on these particular points of principle that Burghley conflicted with both Roman Catholics and the more ardent Protestants, especially the Presbyterians. He was, therefore, placed in a position of conflicting priorities when protégés, subordinates and others, whom he respected or with whom he was on cordial terms, overstepped the mark. They were 'forward men' who, in Professor Collinson's words, 'favoured policies which were inspired by a more than formal Protestantism and were calculated to preserve the Protestant ascendancy actively rather than passively'. They could, however, be transmuted into 'froward men', preferring 'to be guided by zeal rather than by "policy"'.[16] Edward Dering, the young Cambridge evangelical who was noted for his learning and whose clash with Burghley has already been mentioned, rashly reprimanded the queen in a sermon preached before her in 1570. He then proceeded to expose what he saw as the shortcomings of Secretary Cecil and Archbishop Parker. In the process he ruined his prospects of future promotion.

Robert Beale and James Morrice, who also damaged their careers by reckless conduct, were in closer and more continuous contact with Burghley. Beale was clerk of the Privy Council from 1572 and several times deputised as Secretary of State during Walsingham's absence on diplomatic missions. He deplored Archbishop Whitgift's disciplinary regime, especially the use of the *ex officio* oath. In 1585 he was critical of Whitgift's hostile response to the commons' presentation of religious petitions. Finally, in the parliament of 1593, he caused great offence to Elizabeth by his reported opposition to the proposal for increased taxation. Exiled from Court, excluded from parliament and placed under house arrest, he wrote to Burghley questioning whether the real reason for his disfavour was a suspicion that he was 'a plotter of a new ecclesiastical government'. He denied any association with those who sought such changes and protested that he had always 'misliked such new devices'. Beale, however, then returned to his longstanding hostility to the *ex officio* oath, acknowledging that he had sent Burghley 'certain notes' against it and boldly asserting that he was not ashamed of doing so. His obstinacy was unlikely to win the Lord Treasurer's public support, mitigate the queen's anger or lessen Whitgift's hostility. He was, in effect, suspended from duty as Council clerk until 1597, although during that time Burghley sought information from him 'in sondry thyngys'. Doubtless his action in conveying Mary Stuart's death warrant to Fotheringhay in 1587 contributed to Elizabeth's disapproval – a matter on which he reflected when writing to the Lord Treasurer.[17]

The case of James Morrice, attorney of the Court of Wards and so Burghley's subordinate, who also fell foul of queen and archbishop in the 1593 parliament, has already been considered. Although he refused to join Peter Wentworth and others in raising the succession question in the commons, he attacked Whitgift's use of the *ex officio* oath and other legal proceedings against the 'godly' reformers. His speech, supported by Beale and followed by the presentation of two bills on the subject, breached the queen's frequent ban on discussion about religion. Morrice was officially rebuked and placed in a Privy Councillor's custody for two months. The queen said that 'his speaking against her in such a manner as he had done should be a bar against any preferment at her hands'. Burghley reprimanded him, but, at the same time, he endeavoured to protect and defend his departmental officer, for which Lord Keeper Puckering rebuked him.

Burghley's relationship with delinquents, such as Beale and Morrice, illustrates the contradictions inherent in his own religious position. As an Erastian and episcopalian, he did not question the ecclesiastical administration and spiritual authority of bishops. This was not, however, always reflected in his relations with particular prelates, because he was imbued with contemporary anti-clerical attitudes, especially towards the episcopate. His memoranda on church matters were often highly critical of the bishops, especially when Whitgift presided at Canterbury. In one of them he set forth proposals on how they might 'recover more Creditt by more Dilligence'. He disliked their tendency to pride and pomp. In the reigns of both Edward VI and Elizabeth I he also stated his objection to what he perceived to be clerical wealth. When he voiced this opinion in 1559, however, he was either misinformed or justifying the act of exchange, which enabled Elizabeth to exchange property with the bishops, on terms which benefited her and deprived them. At various times he also objected to the misuse of episcopal visitations for gain and expressed a preference for restraints on their authority, notably in the time of Whitgift.[18]

At a personal level, however, Burghley's anti-clericalism was tempered by the nature of his relationship with individual prelates. His correspondence with them was a mixture of the official sometimes critical voice, friendly confidentiality and support. Bishops looked to him for advice and assistance in dealing with their difficult Supreme Governor. His association with Archbishop Parker personified the apparent paradox of his relationship with members of the episcopate. Parker, who was an Edwardian moderate and, like Cecil, stayed in England during Mary Tudor's reign, was his preferred man for the position at Canterbury in 1559. The reluctant archbishop was closer than other prelates to Cecil and they kept up a frequent and confidential correspondence. The matters on which they wrote were wide-ranging: episcopal vacancies and appointments, especially in the north where the people, 'rude of their own nature', were 'offended that they be nothing cared for'; removal of offending clerics; the presence of the crucifix in the queen's chapel; and the 'precisians' hostility towards the bishops. Parker also frankly confessed to Cecil that he regarded himself as inadequate for his high office, for he was withdrawn, 'evil acquainted with strangers' and indifferent with the pen. He implored Cecil 'to help me to shadow my cowardness'.

Parker frequently lamented and, perhaps, sought reassurance in his letters about Elizabeth: her hostility to clerical marriage, her public anger at Nowell's Ash Day sermon in 1565, lack of instructions on vital matters and, above all, her unwillingness to give public sanction and support to the bishops in their attempts to carry out her commands. This was a particular problem with the campaign, commencing in 1565, to enforce uniformity of clerical dress. It was required by Elizabeth and neither Cecil nor Parker was opposed. The latter often complained, however, that neither queen nor Secretary gave public backing to enforcement of the *Advertisements* (the draft of which Cecil had corrected). He reported on the resistance not only of London ministers, of whom some 'be peevish, some froward [and some] fearful', but also of congregations. In 1566, beset with problems and lack of support, he expostulated, 'I can do no more, nor can promise any more . . . and must I do still all things alone?' Cecil listened to him sympathetically, but he was not prepared to expose himself by public support, either of Parker's complaints about the queen or his problems with the *Advertisements.* He might write to the archbishop in 1561 that if he 'were not therein very stiff, her Majesty would utterly and openly condemn and forbid' the clergy to marry, but even if we accept his words on this occasion, he rarely chanced the Supreme Governor's displeasure.[19]

Nevertheless, the correspondence between Elizabeth's minister of state and spiritual head of her church was always courteous and often warm, as they exchanged thanks for services rendered. Parker offered comfort, when 'ye profess that ye be at your wits' end', when he was ill and when, in 1573, there appeared in print an 'outrageously penned' libel against him. With most prelates, however, there was not the same shared warmth and confidentiality. More characteristic was his disapproval of the bishops' performance in office and this intensified during Whitgift's regime at Canterbury. Bishop Aylmer of London, a supporter of Whitgift, was a particular object of Burghley's unfavourable opinion. This earned him a rebuke from Aylmer, who wrote that 'to be plane with your lordship, you are the man that doth moste discorage me . . . in that by your wordes and countenances my government is hindred'. An exception to Burghley's common opinion of prelates was Edmund Grindal, archbishop of York (1570–75). Although he probably exercised considerable influence on the queen's initial choice of prelates for the new church in 1559, thereafter others, especially the earl of Leicester, were influential in episcopal appointments. When Parker died in 1575, however, Burghley was instrumental in promoting Grindal as his successor. Although it may have been difficult to persuade Elizabeth to promote someone much favoured by those Protestants anxious for reform, he succeeded after six months and Grindal duly thanked him.[20]

It is clear from their earlier correspondence in the 1560s, when Grindal was bishop of London, that they were on co-operative and friendly, even familiar terms, with a shared concern for the condition of the church, the threats posed by extreme sectaries and Catholics and the need for more preachers. If on occasion they disagreed, as in January 1572 when Grindal was unwilling to accept Burghley's nominee for a prebend, he soothed the Lord Treasurer with gentle words in order to avoid offence: '[S]urely my Lord, the Queen's Majesty only excepted, there is no creature's request upon earth can weigh more with me than yours.' Unfortunately, once Burghley's nominee was installed at Canterbury, their working association was not a long one. In 1576 the queen ordered Grindal to send instructions to the bishops for the suppression of 'prophesyings'. These were spiritual exercises at which the elergy (and sometimes members of the laity too) heard sermons, discussed the Scriptures and received religious instruction. Although he recognised that they were sometimes exploited by puritan clergy and gentry, Grindal appreciated their value, refused to comply with Elizabeth's command and informed her that he chose to offend her rather than God. He was duly suspended from the performance of his office until his death in 1583. Burghley did what he could to protect the errant archbishop. Together with Leicester he attempted to persuade Grindal to accept a compromise, whereby the laity were excluded, but to no avail. Further efforts by them to prevent a disaster were equally unsuccessful. However, as with Parker so with Grindal. Burghley did not play the part of public advocate and defender, roles which would almost certainly have incurred the queen's displeasure.[21]

To some degree John Whitgift in his earlier years was, like Grindal before him, Burghley's protégé. During Burghley's chancellorship of Cambridge University he rapidly rose to become vice-chancellor, and he also earned the admiration of the Lord Treasurer when he was bishop of Worcester (1577–83). But times were changing. Whitgift, assisted by Bishop Aylmer of London, increasingly assumed a *de facto* authoritarian and disciplinary management of the church's spiritual affairs during Grindal's suspension. In the 1581 parliament his authoritarian instinct was expressed in his censorious response to a commons' petition for reform of ecclesiastical discipline. Whitgift, the royal choice as archbishop of Canterbury in 1583, was the architect of the disciplinary regime which, through the Court of High Commission, required an unqualified subscription by clergy to three articles accepting the royal governorship, the prayer book and the thirty-nine articles of faith. Whitgift's rise, his hostility to puritans, especially the Presbyterians, and his authoritarian conduct, which enjoyed the queen's unequivocal support, all demonstrated a major change in official attitudes to politics and religion. During the 1580s the first generation of bishops, many of whom were sympathetic to moderate puritan reforms, died out. Their replacements were antagonistic to the Presbyterian threat posed by the *Admonition.* The second generation consisted of hardline anti-puritan conformists, who preached the divine right of both monarchy and episcopacy.

Burghley could not come to terms with the new position or policies, but circumstances moved against him. To some extent he was responsible for his diminished influence in religious matters. In 1586 he secured the appointment of Whitgift and Lord Buckhurst, whom he regarded as his friends, to the Privy Council. But Whitgift, who already had the support of Elizabeth's favourite, Lord Chancellor Hatton, won over Buckhurst to his religious position. When Hatton died in 1591 Sir John Puckering, another authoritarian anti-puritan, was appointed Chancellor. Meanwhile Burghley was isolated by the deaths of Privy Councillors – Leicester, Mildmay and Walsingham in 1588–90 and later Knollys (1596) – who were either puritans themselves or sympathetic to puritanism. In varying degrees they had shared with him a desire for reform and for protection of moderate reforming activists. Gradually Burghley became an ineffectual and lonely voice of dissent as he was pushed to the side by Whitgift and his supporters. In the parliament of 1584–85, for example, Lord Treasurer and archbishop together gave answer to a parliamentary petition, which sought reforms and the redress of grievances. A few days later, however, Burghley was snubbed in Whitgift's presence. The occasion was a royal audience to thank the archbishop and representatives of the clergy who, unlike the commons, had, in her words, given taxes 'voluntarily . . . whereas the laity must be entreated'. When Burghley attempted to defend the laity, he suffered an angry royal outburst. It included an attack on the lower house for meddling in religion and a threat to 'uncouncil' those Privy Councillors (probably Knollys and Mildmay) who had been involved. Thus, increasingly in the 1580s and 1590s, he was isolated and unable to prevent what he regarded as the harmful and divisive policies of an unjustifiably exalted episcopate. Yet, though he regarded the *ex officio* procedure as more appropriate to the Spanish Inquisition and continued to oppose Whitgift on this until he died, he named the archbishop as one of the overseers of his will.[22]

Simply by virtue of his position as Elizabeth's chief minister, her confidence in him and the length of his service, Burghley had considerable impact on the anti-Catholic religious policy of her government. His attitude and policy towards Roman Catholicism and to English Catholics were the consequence of his determination to defend the independent English nation-state and church and to protect the queen, on whose survival so much depended. His hunt for the death of Mary Stuart, his increasing severity towards recusants and, especially, the missionary priests, and his eventual willingness to wage war against foreign Catholic powers were all expressions of that determination.

Whereas his attitude to external Catholic threats to the Church of England was clear and consistent, his position within the church was more ambiguous. His Edwardian experience, as a prominent politician and convinced Protestant, mapped out his role as one of the architects of the Elizabethan Settlement in 1559. His role thereafter was an often uncomfortable mix of Erastianism, the priorities of security and stability, an insistence on outward conformity, support for moderate reforms (to which the queen was opposed) and a defence of episcopacy tempered by criticism of the bishops' pride and wealth. Religion should be predominant in one's private life. But in the public world political and secular considerations enjoyed priority. So the church should not be separate from the state, as the Presbyterians desired, but subordinate to it; there should be clear limitations on the authority of the clergy; and the church should be, not a divisive, but a unifying force. Unfortunately for Burghley, Elizabeth did not share all of his priorities. In the 1580s and 1590s his influence diminished as she found, in Whitgift, someone in harmony with her own authoritarian conservatism.

. . .

NOTES

1. *Clapham*, p. 80; Smith (ed.), *Anon. Life*, p. 114.
2. Haynes, *State Papers*, p. 582; Read, *Secretary Cecil*, pp. 437–8 and n. 20; Smith (ed.), *Anon. Life*, p. 113; *Clapham*, p. 80.
3. P. Collinson, *Godly People* (London, 1983), p. 137.
4. Graves, *Norton*, p. 168.
5. MacCaffrey, *Making of Policy*, p. 125; Strype, *Annals*, I, Pt. 2, pp. 371–2; see above, p. 68.
6. Graves, *Norton*, pp. 198–203, 204 and n. 14, 234–40; PRO, SP, 12/164/2; ibid., 12/198/29; Read, *Burghley*, pp. 236, 246, 421–2, 468–9; PRO, SP, 12/231/70; Hughes and Larkin, *Tudor Royal Proclamations*, III, pp. 90–3; Elton, *Parliament of England*, pp. 186–7.
7. Dean, *Law-Making and Society*, pp. 67–70; Williams, *Later Tudors*, p. 344; Neale, *Eliz. Parls.*, II, pp. 280–97.
8. See above, pp. 113–14; Graves, *Norton*, pp. 276–7; Birch, *Memoirs*, I, p. 94; J. Gillow, 'Lord Burghley's map of Lancashire, 1590', *Catholic Record Society*, 4 (1907), pp. 162–3; Read, 'Cecil and public relations', pp. 45–6; Hurstfield, *Freedom, Corruption*, pp. 96–7.
9. C. Haigh, 'The Church of England, the Catholics and the people', in idem (ed.), *Reign of Elizabeth*, pp. 196–201; Haugaard, *Elizabeth and the English Reformation*, pp. 292–302, 313; Williams, *Later Tudors*, pp. 466–7; PRO, SP, 12/16/49–51; M. Bateson (ed.), 'Collection of original letters from the bishops to the Privy Council, 1564', *Camden Society Misc.*, 9 (1893).
10. Read, *Burghley*, p. 198, n. 113; Wright (ed.), *Queen Elizabeth*, II, pp. 145–7.
11. Ibid., I, pp. 477–8; Read, *Burghley*, p. 117; Hughes and Larkin, *Tudor Royal Proclamations*, II, pp. 375–6, 379–81; Collinson, *Godly People*, pp. 198–9; for Wilcox and Field, see above, pp. 60–1.
12. Haynes (ed.), *State Papers*, pp. 372–3; Strype, *Annals*, III, Pt. 2, pp. 197–202, 250–2, 416–17.
13. Beckingsale, *Burghley*, pp. 29, 75; J. Strype, *The Life and Acts of Matthew Parker*, 3 vols (Oxford, 1821), III, pp. 316–19; Graves, *Norton*, pp. 321–2; Strype, *Annals*, II, Pt. 2, pp. 483–6; P. Collinson (ed.), 'Letters of Thomas Wood, Puritan, 1566–77', *BIHR*, special supplement no. 5 (1960), pp. xiii, 1–2; idem, *Godly People*, p. 207.
14. Loach, *Parl. under Tudors*, p. 99; see above, pp. 56–7; Graves, *Norton*, pp. 290–1, 294–5, 297.
15. Ibid., pp. 322–4; Beckingsale, *Burghley*, p. 224; Bruce and Perrowne (eds), *Matthew Parker, Correspondence*, p. 355; Palliser, *Age of Elizabeth*, pp. 331–3; J. Strype, *The Life and Acts of John Whitgift*, 3 vols (Oxford, 1822), III, pp. 265–7.
16. Collinson, *Elizabethan Puritan Movement*, pp. 71–4; idem, 'Puritans, men of business and Eliz. parls.', pp. 192–3.

17. Hasler (ed.), *Commons*, I, pp. 412–14; Collinson, 'Puritans, men of business and Eliz. parls.', pp. 197, 200–2, 204; idem, *Godly People*, pp. 304–6; Guy (ed.), *Court and Culture*, p. 137; BL, Lansdowne MS 73/2.
18. See above, pp. 95, 139; Guy (ed.), *Court and Culture*, pp. 130, 136–7; Collinson, 'Puritans, men of business and Eliz. parls.', pp. 194–5; Hasler (ed.), *Commons*, III, pp. 98–9; 'To have the church better governed', 1583, PRO, SP, 12/164/no. 2; BL, Lansdowne MS 104, no. 51; Graves, *Norton*, pp. 333–4; Jones, *Faith by Statute*, pp. 166–7.
19. Collinson, *Godly People*, p. 132; idem, *The Religion of Protestants*, Oxford, 1982, p. 55; Strype, *Parker*, pp. 49–52; Wright, II, p. 79; Bruce (ed.), *Parker*, pp. 78, 104–5, 123–4, 148, 156–8, 177–8, 182–3, 199–200, 208, 257–65, 269–72, 275–9.
20. Ibid., pp. 161, 359, 392, 444–5, 453; Collinson, *Godly People*, p. 373; W. Nicholson (ed.), *The Remains of Edmund Grindal*, Parker Society (Cambridge, 1843), pp. 375–6.
21. Ibid., pp. 253–6, 261, 265–6, 275, 280–2, 285–6, 305, 321–2, 325–6, 329–33, 345, 351–2, 356–7; Collinson, *Godly People*, pp. 373–7, 392 n. 56.
22. Guy (ed.), *Court and Culture*, pp. 127–9; Neale, *Eliz. Parls*, II, pp. 65–6, 69; MacCaffrey, *Making of Policy*, pp. 110–13.

Chapter 10

BURGHLEY, 'BRITAIN' AND EUROPE

The foreign policy of medieval and early modern European monarchical states was a royal preserve. It was chiefly concerned with dynastic glory and ambitions, rather than with the interests of subjects, even though monarchs expected them to contribute financially to the fulfilment of their foreign policy goals, especially through war. England was no exception. Elizabeth I's Tudor predecessors – Henry VIII, Edward VI and Mary I – all pursued, at various times, an aggressive, even expansionist, foreign policy, which operated both within the British Isles and in Continental Europe. British unification was one of Henry VIII's policy objectives. So he incorporated Wales into the English state, became king of Ireland and sought, ineffectually, the conquest of Scotland, a policy pursued with equal lack of success in Edward VI's reign.

Scotland was England's most serious challenge. Whilst the English monarchy was a constant threat to Scottish independence, events repeatedly demonstrated that it was unable to conquer its northern neighbour. Cecil observed this at first hand, when he accompanied the duke of Somerset's invading army in 1547. Furthermore, British politics, especially Anglo-Scottish relations, were inseparable from the politics of the European Continent. Anglo-French enmity, England's claim to the French crown and its alliance with the duchy of Burgundy were long-standing features of the European political scene. So too was the anti-English 'auld alliance' of France and Scotland. In the early sixteenth century England's foreign policy remained traditionally dynastic. Henry VIII, in alliance with the Habsburg Charles (who was Holy Roman Emperor, ruler of Spain and the Low Countries, and master of a New World empire), made war on the Valois kings of France. The 'auld alliance', however, compelled him in turn to wage war on two fronts: not only on French soil but also on the Scottish borders.

During the sixteenth century the nature and priorities of English foreign policy underwent significant change. Henry VIII's break with Rome in the 1530s was followed by the establishment of a Protestant church under Edward VI and again, after the brief Marian regime, under Elizabeth. These developments threatened to transform the Habsburgs, who emerged as the champions of European Catholicism, from allies to enemies. Indeed, the European Reformation introduced a new and powerful motive for diplomatic and military alignments. Coalitions and conflicts were now as much the consequence of religious division as of competitive dynasticism. This also affected England's relationships within the British Isles. The establishment of the Elizabethan Protestant church in Ireland in 1560 divided English from Catholic Anglo-Irish and Irish by religion as well as by ethnicity. This ended earlier Tudor attempts to secure English control of Ireland through consensus politics. Across the northern border in 1558–60, Mary Stuart's French Catholic mother, Mary of Guise, governed Scotland with French bureaucrats and soldiers. Meanwhile Mary Stuart, who lived in France, first as wife of Francis, heir to the French throne, and then in 1559 as queen consort, assumed the royal arms of England.

Therefore Elizabethan foreign policy was, from the beginning, inevitably and profoundly affected by the politics of the European Protestant Reformation and the revived militant Catholicism of the Counter-Reformation. Consensus was replaced by conflict in Ireland and might encourage foreign intervention. The claims of the Catholic queen of Scots to the English crown might be upheld by the French military presence in Scotland. The threat posed by Continental Catholic powers, not only France but also – and increasingly – Spain, was enhanced by the papal bull of 1570, which deprived Elizabeth 'of her pretended title' to the English crown and freed her subjects from 'fealty and obedience' to her.[1]

What, then, was the Elizabethan government's foreign policy, both in its response to the immediate situation in 1558/59 and in its longer-term aims? The basic principles and long-term objectives of foreign policy are always subject to modifications imposed on them. These are the consequence of changing circumstances (and the necessary *ad hoc* responses to them), as well as the need to accommodate competing, even conflicting, concerns, such as economic well-being. England was a second-rate power, governed by a monarchy with very limited resources. It could not afford a bold interventionist policy, but only, for much of the time, a limited 'holding' operation, which consisted of *ad hoc* responses to problems and challenges as they arose. Therefore, the immediate and long-term aims of both Elizabeth and Burghley were determined by necessity as well as by conviction: maintenance of the queen-regnant on her throne and defence of the independent English nation-state and church. Some of her Privy Councillors (but not Burghley) ambitiously and unrealistically cast England in the role of grand Protestant crusader. More modestly and realistically, queen and minister thought and acted in terms of national defence and security. They preferred to achieve these goals by diplomatic means and to avoid, as long as possible, the uncharted seas of war and the unfathomable costs which it involved. According to Burghley's anonymous biographer, his many aphorisms included several on military engagement, such as 'War is the curse and peace the blessing of God upon a nation' and 'A realm gaineth more by one year's peace than by ten years' war'.

Whilst foreign policy was a royal preserve and the queen alone determined general direction and specific action, it was Burghley who, as the person most responsible for its implementation, had the greater grasp of logistical needs. He sought to be informed and, to that end, he collected and studied maps, surveys, pictures, statistical data, ambassadorial reports and correspondence with colleagues, kin, friends and members of his intelligence network. He also recognised the need to project and justify the government's foreign policy, partly through his own propagandist pieces but more effectively through Bishop Jewel of Salisbury, Thomas Norton, Anthony Munday, John Stubbs, Walsingham, Robert Cecil and others. He was also aware that, although foreign policy tended to be shaped by power politics and religious hostilities, commercial interests needed to be protected and nurtured. Palliser even argues that 'English foreign policy was dictated more by the pattern of English cloth exports than by considerations of religion or the balance of power'. The expressed opinions and the actions of Elizabeth, Burghley, other councillors and politicians, however, do not give commerce first place in the list of priorities. Certainly it was one of Burghley's continuing concerns, especially as Anglo-Spanish relations deteriorated, to seek alternatives to Antwerp as England's cloth market. He sought thereby both to maintain the country's chief export and to prevent widespread unemployment and social unrest. Nevertheless, national security took primacy of place in foreign policy and that depended, first and foremost, on English control of the British Isles. This policy, which was isolationist, not interventionist, was influenced by his Edwardian experience of the Franco-Scottish connection. It also serves to explain why the loss of Calais, England's last possession, in 1558 mattered little to him. Foreign involvement had no relevance to a policy of self-containment and control within the British Isles. But preparedness did. To this end he took steps to improve the quality of the navy, England's first line of defence and springboard for attack. Nor did he neglect England's land defences. The county militia was reorganised and to some extent its equipment was updated.[2]

. . .

SCOTLAND

When Elizabeth became queen and Cecil her Secretary of State, Scotland constituted the most immediate and serious threat. It also presented the new regime with an acute political dilemma, which divided queen and minister so early in their long political relationship. Cecil wanted the French out of Scotland. Elizabeth took refuge in what time would prove to be characteristic indecision, but Cecil won. The threat from the north had to be eliminated and in 1559–60 he achieved that end.[3]

However, whilst Cecil removed the French threat he did not resolve 'the Scottish problem'. Mary Stuart continued to claim that she was not only Elizabeth's heir but the rightful ruler of England. Nor would she ratify the Treaty of Edinburgh. When she sought passage through England, en route to Scotland from France in 1561, Cecil ensured that the request was refused. Mary's brief but tempestuous rule in Scotland ended with her abdication and flight south in 1567–68. Thereafter, her presence in England became part of the tangled web of politico-religious European politics, and must be considered in that context and not merely an English one. With some justice Cecil regarded her as the focus of domestic and foreign Catholic hostility towards Elizabeth's regime, and for almost twenty years he worked to secure her destruction. The conspiracies which aimed to eliminate Elizabeth, in favour of Mary, consolidated his belief in the existence of an international Catholic league. Therefore one of his ongoing concerns was to secure and retain Scottish amity and to prevent the revival of French influence in the northern kingdom. The arrival of Esmé Stuart from France in 1579, his prominence at James VI's Court, his promotion to the duchy of Lennox and the execution of the Anglophile Morton (1581) reactivated the Franco-Scottish connection and aroused English fears. The expulsion of Lennox in 1583, however, eased English minds.

There was one other potential crisis which later concerned Burghley: the Scottish king's response to the execution of his mother. By then, however, James had signed a defensive military pact and he became Elizabeth's pensioner. He would not risk his pension or jeopardise his position as unnamed but increasingly accepted heir to the English throne. To the end of his life Burghley continued to show great interest in Anglo-Scottish affairs, which were an important component of his insular rather than European foreign policy. However, he seems to have been only occasionally involved and did not play a leading role in the often confused English manœuvres and negotiations, which nonetheless ended the danger of a renewed French threat from the north. Most of the work was done by Walsingham, and chief credit for the treaty of 1585 must go to the Secretary of State.[4]

. . .

IRELAND

In contrast to England's northern neighbour, Ireland proved to be an intractable problem. Cecil's first experience of Irish affairs was in Edward VI's reign. It was a transitional time as the consensus politics of Henry VIII's reign gave way to the politics of conflict. He should have heeded the warning signal, passed to him by the governor, Anthony St Leger, about new English settlers, that 'such handling of wild men' was having a destabilising effect. But he refused to heed it, as his Elizabethan record shows. The establishment of a Protestant church under royal governorship added religious to ethnic difference, whilst many covetous Englishmen had designs on Irish land.

Colonisation and settlement would not only provide material benefits for those who ventured there. They would strengthen England's political control and therefore its security against foreign intervention. Cecil was not short of advice on this matter. In 1565 his friend, Sir Thomas Smith, advised on the need for 'colonies, to augment our tongue, our laws, and our religion in that isle'. These were the means 'whereby the Romans conquered and kept long time a great part of the world'. This would have accorded with Cecil's sentiments, because Ireland was a potential loophole in England's British security network. As consensus was no longer a considered alternative, the options were direct control, colonisation, conquest, or a combination of these.

Cecil, however, did not at first have a clearly defined or consistent policy, because he was beset by a number of conflicting concerns. Any attempt to formulate a consistent Irish policy, especially during the early years, was jeopardised by the queen's and Privy Council's lack of interest and certainly by her reluctance to commit adequate funding for the tasks in hand. The royal obsession with financial restraint was reinforced by Cecil, who deplored the fact that a subject-kingdom of colonial status was a drain on royal revenue rather than a source of profit. He observed that 'all other princes having any dominions distant from their owne residence . . . have sufficient revenues of the same contreys to governe and defend the same, yelding some tymes a great surplus'. Whilst his continuous concern with costs tended to hamper the development and execution of a consistent Irish policy, at least he had one advantage over other contemporary politicians. His interest in cartography and use of maps, which dated from Edward VI's reign, meant that he was better informed on the political geography of Ireland than other Privy Councillors and even most English administrators in Ireland.

The events of the first Elizabethan decade served both to clarify a coherent policy and develop a willingness to adopt increasingly harsh measures. In the early 1560s the rebellion of Shane O'Neill (which lasted until his murder in 1567) was punctuated by a visit to Elizabeth's Court, where he howled his confession, prostrated himself in submission and, after a lengthy interview with Cecil, reached an agreement with the queen. It proved to be a temporary rapprochement and soon broke down; so did a treaty in 1563. Cecil was very hostile towards O'Neill.

In March 1566 he wrote to Sir Thomas Smith on the state of Ireland: 'The good subjects in all parts oppressed, the Irish bearing rule, but in all no peril, saving in Shan[e], who will (he sayth in his dronkenes) be Lord or King of Ulster; but I trust his head shall be from his shoulders before any crown can be made ready to make hym either King or Erle.'[5]

The appointment of Sir Henry Sidney as governor of Ireland in 1565, however, opened up brighter prospects for the implementation of a more co-ordinated British security policy. It is impossible to determine whether, or to what extent, Shane O'Neill's career moved Cecil towards sterner policies. He adopted a more aggressive stance, with a variety of objectives which included: an extension of colonisation (privately rather than state-funded and to which he contributed); a fortification building programme; the adoption of English common law; and a reduction in the power of both Anglo-Irish lords and Gaelic chieftains. It was an ambitious and unrealistic policy, because it underestimated the nature, size and complexity of the problems facing any English administration. And one basic problem was always lack of adequate state funding. Nevertheless, the decade after Sidney's appointment marked a radical shift in both Cecil's thinking and in government policy. The shift was motivated partly by the perceived danger of intervention by foreign Catholic powers and, more urgently, by the need to reduce the constant financial burden. As Nicholas Canny shows, 'The question facing the English Privy Council in 1565 was "whether the Queenes Majestie be . . . counselled to governe Ireland after the Irishe manner as it hath ben accustomed, or to reduce it as nere as maie be to the Englishe government".' Cecil opted for the latter and he was not alone in doing so.[6]

Thereafter, especially as Lord Treasurer Burghley, he sought, promoted and supported an aggressive, financially self-supporting Irish policy of colonisation by plantation. It was, however, a characteristically muddled Elizabethan policy. The confiscation and re-grant of Irish lands to English immigrants, in Ulster and Munster in the 1570s, was funded by private enterprise and lacked adequate financial and military support from the queen. It alienated the native Irish, led to armed conflict, bloody reprisals, suppression and, in Munster, famine. At least Burghley learned a lesson from this: that the pacification and 'civilisation' of Ireland could not depend on private enterprise, but required state funding and management. As Elizabeth's chief minister he took the lead in state intervention. So he personally devised the scheme for the plantation of Munster. His plantation schemes, however, were ill-conceived, provocative and fuelled the increasing hostility to the English administration in Dublin.

Burghley died in the midst of the earl of Tyrone's rebellion in the 1590s. His involvement in Irish affairs was one of the bleaker, if not darker, chapters in the story of his service in Elizabethan government. The queen's Irish policy was a failure and Burghley should not be exonerated from his role in it. He gave out a series of conflicting messages and signals to future generations. On the one hand, he expressed discerning sympathy for the Irish who 'naturally are impatient of oppression, though otherwise lovers of justice, and they will readily obey such governors as seem to respect them, while they are permitted to use their own customs; but being provoked by wrongs and indignities, they are hardly reclaimed'. He also acknowledged their hostility to 'the covetousness of needy officers [who were] like hungry flies'. In 1582 he wrote that the Low Countries 'had not such cause to rebel against the oppression of the Spaniards, as the Irish against the tyranny of England'. Yet his search for effective English political control of Ireland, in order to maintain stability there and to close it to foreign intervention, led him to favour increasingly oppressive measures. Conyers Read was dismissive of Burghley's Irish policy, because he lacked a specific programme for its implementation. As Lord Treasurer, however, costs were always a prime concern and, as in all aspects of Elizabethan government, he often lamented the expense and lack of adequate funding. In the end Ireland was secured by military conquest, the most brutal of all options. Whilst that was not achieved in his lifetime, his attitude towards Irish affairs revealed a common English bellicosity and ethnic arrogance towards the Irish. Furthermore, the state of religion in Ireland did not loom large in his thinking, even though it was central to considerations of order, stability, and security from foreign intervention. The English policy shift from consensus to control, plantation and colonisation, and finally conquest did much to alienate both the Gaelic Irish and the Anglo-Irish and to store up trouble for the future. It was a shift in which Burghley had a significant hand.[7]

. . .

FRANCE AND SPAIN

The reversal of traditional relationships with two great Continental powers, the Habsburgs and Valois France, could not be divorced from Scottish and Irish politics. Nor was it a simple, straightforward process. The Treaty of Edinburgh (1560) removed the French from Scotland and the Treaty of Cateau-Cambresis (1559) ended the Anglo-Spanish war against France and effectively ceded Calais, thereby removing the English from French territory. Together the treaties removed two sources of mutual hostility. The respite was only temporary, however, because in 1562–63 an English expedition assisted rebellious French Huguenots. In this venture, the regnal pattern of political stances on foreign policy was established: Robert Dudley advocated intervention, whereas Elizabeth was characteristically indecisive and also reluctant to assist rebels against their legitimate monarch. However, in contrast to the caution and preference for avoidance of Continental entanglements, which characterised his later years, Cecil was a bold interventionist in 1562, just as he had been in Scotland in 1559–60. He justified his position in July 1562, in a memorandum in which he stressed the need to act in order to forestall possible action against England by a potential Franco-Spanish alliance.

Thus far the traditional alignments remained in place: an English expeditionary force invaded France and Philip II of Spain adopted a friendly attitude towards the new Elizabethan Protestant regime. After the humiliating failure of the English intervention in France, however, a gradual change occurred. An Anglo-French rapprochement culminated, in 1572, in the mutual defensive Treaty of Blois. The limited nature of the pact revealed a division of opinion between Leicester and Walsingham, who wanted an aggressive anti-Habsburg alliance, and Elizabeth and Cecil, who wished to avoid any arrangement which might increase French power. Whilst he was concerned to balance the power of Spain and France, however, his view of the European political situation, especially potential threats to England, changed in the course of the 1560s. This was influenced by developments such as the presence of a powerful Spanish army in the Low Countries, from 1567 onwards. Anglo-Spanish relations deteriorated, with English incursions into the Spanish Caribbean, the seizure of the Genoese loan to Philip II and mutual trade embargoes.[8]

Cecil's changing views on foreign policy were reflected in his lengthy *Short Memorial* of 1569. It was a gloomy analysis of the current situation in Europe. He believed that Spain and France were motivated primarily by the desire to reassert papal authority and destroy Protestant heresy. It was simplistic, even wrong, to examine European politics and the consequent threat to England in religious terms, because, in doing so, he neglected the secular aspects of French and Spanish policy and their continuing rivalry. Nevertheless, the *Short Memorial* is significant, because it reveals that, whilst Cecil had no confidence in French amity, nor did he have any faith in the old Anglo-Spanish 'Burgundian alliance'. Although he trusted neither, the events of the 1560s and early 1570s gradually moved him further away from the Spanish Habsburgs and towards some kind of understanding with the French. This is illustrated by his attitude to Elizabeth's various matrimonial dalliances, diplomatic courtships and marriage negotiations. During the 1560s he had favoured a union with the Habsburg Archduke Charles of Austria. Between 1578 and 1581 he was the leading advocate of her marriage to François, the French duke of Anjou, even when most other Privy Councillors turned against it.[9]

Central to such developments was the prolonged rebellion against Spanish rule which began in the Low Countries in 1566. Gradually, as described in Chapter 3, England became increasingly involved and then finally committed to active participation in the Netherlands conflict. As early as 1569, in his *Short Memorial*, Burghley had favoured a policy of stirring up the internal problems of both great Catholic powers. This policy was later followed in France in the 1590s with military and financial assistance to the Huguenot Henry Bourbon. During the intervening decades, however, Spain loomed as the greater menace to English security. The expulsion of Spanish ambassadors for their part in the Ridolfi (1571) and Throckmorton (1583) conspiracies against Elizabeth exacerbated Anglo-Spanish relations. Their involvement also confirmed Burghley in his mistaken belief that the chief threat to England was a grand European Catholic alliance. Other Privy Councillors, especially Leicester and Walsingham, shared this view, but that is where the common ground ended. Leicester and Walsingham persistently pressed for a belligerent policy. The queen's more pragmatic approach, coupled with her characteristic procrastination, made her hostile to military confrontation with either of the great Catholic powers or to military intervention in their internal affairs. Somewhere in the middle was Burghley. He feared what he conceived to be the growing international Catholic threat. But he was aware of England's vulnerability to attack through Scotland and Ireland, whilst, especially as Lord Treasurer, he was acutely conscious of its military and financial incapacity to conduct a prolonged war on several fronts.

During the 1570s and early 1580s these various and conflicting views increasingly focused on rebellion against Spanish rule in the Low Countries. Debate on the subject was characteristic of Elizabethan government: a range of opinions and no likelihood of consensus. Burghley himself was the embodiment of variety: in the 1570s he wavered between isolation, minimal action and, on occasions, intervention. The pressure of events, as Spain became more aggressive and augmented its power, gradually impelled him towards direct action. The appearance of Spanish troops in southern Ireland in 1579–80 was an alarm signal. More serious was Philip II's acquisition of Portugal, its empire and ocean-going fleet in 1580. Meanwhile, in the years following the duke of Parma's appointment as Philip's governor in the Low Countries, the southern provinces voluntarily returned to Spanish rule. As Parma proceeded to conquer territory in the rebellious north, Leicester and others committed to intervention became more vocal. Burghley, however, clung to peace. He justified this stance on various grounds, such as cost and the fact that 'war is of itself unjust', though he added that 'the good cause may make it just'.

Parma's continued military advances and the assassination of the Dutch rebel leader, William of Orange, in 1584 reinforced the interventionists' lobbying. Burghley moved, albeit slowly and tentatively, in the same direction of war in a 'just cause'. He was greatly influenced by Philip II's intervention on the Catholic side in France's religious civil wars. This caused the spectre of Spanish hegemony to loom ever larger. Nevertheless, as late as October 1584, when he addressed the queen and Privy Council on the pros and cons of intervention, his argument still tended towards the cons. At last, in 1585, there was a consensus in favour of military intervention. It encompassed not only the militants but also the usually hesitant queen and the Lord Treasurer. This should not be seen as some kind of faction victory by Leicester's hawks over Cecilian doves. Walsingham openly disassociated himself from faction when writing to Burghley about their differences. The politicking and debate which led to the Treaty of Nonsuch with the Dutch in 1585 was a prolonged process of interplay between various councillors and their opinions. As Clapham observed, 'Long conversations were had about the enterprise, some of the Privy Council approving and other disliking it.' Only gradually did divergent opinions converge. Having committed himself to support of direct action, Burghley wrote confidentially to Leicester, 'I am greatly discouraged with [the queen's] lack of resolutions.' His comment was also a commentary on the characteristic royal indecision, which bonded together frustrated councillors, as they sought feasible solutions to pressing problems.[10]

It was the seizure of English vessels, as they lay in Spanish harbours, which finally resolved the queen to act. Burghley, Hatton, Leicester and Walsingham were prominent in the negotiations with the Dutch commissioners in June–August 1585. The proceedings were protracted and difficult, because of sharp differences over the size of the English expeditionary force, the financial contributions of the two allies during the war, and adequate security for Dutch repayment of the queen's expenses afterwards. On one point Elizabeth would not yield. She was prepared to be protector of the Dutch, but she would not accept their offer of sovereignty, which she regarded as rightfully belonging to Philip II. When the Dutch persisted, Burghley was peremptorily firm, advising them to be content with her help and protection, because 'We have told you over and over again that her Majesty will never think of accepting the sovereignty.' The treaty was too late to save Antwerp, which fell to Parma in August 1585, but by the end of the year the English expeditionary force had been despatched to the Low Countries. It was bedevilled by the queen's conduct: her usual procrastination and parsimony and her choice of Leicester, who was sadly deficient both as general and organiser. His acceptance from the Dutch of the title of governor-general, in disobedience to her instructions, provoked a prolonged eruption of royal anger. Eventually, in late 1587, Leicester relinquished command of a largely unsuccessful military operation.[11]

Elizabethan Dutch policy can be criticised on several grounds: that action was taken far too late; that, when it was belatedly taken, the leadership, funding and royal support were inadequate; and that it launched an under-resourced government into a state of war with Europe's mightiest power. Such criticisms must encompass not only the queen but also some of her councillors, especially her chief adviser Burghley, who, for most of the 1570s and early 1580s, opposed military intervention. Historians such as P. Geyl and C.H. Wilson have been scathing about the consequences of the many years of royal resistance to such intervention. Early action in the 1570s would, according to Wilson, have enabled the rebel leader, William of Orange, to unite the Low Countries as a sovereign independent breakaway state which was firmly allied to England. Instead, by the time queen and minister accepted the need for intervention, the southern Netherlands had returned to Spanish rule, William of Orange was dead and Parma was advancing north. However, as R.B. Wernham points out, in the 1570s England had no cause to risk war with Spain, whereas it did in the deteriorating international situation in the mid-1580s. Furthermore, to some extent foreign policy had to be tailored to the crown's meagre resources. It is to the Lord Treasurer's credit that, in the extended period of peace, his watchword was 'economy'. This enabled him to build up a considerable cash reserve, which by 1590, however, had been swallowed up by military and naval expenditure. As manager of the queen's revenues, Burghley was understandably and sensibly cautious about plunging into the seemingly bottomless financial pit of war. He was also a realist, as Conyers Read explained: 'The basic difference between Burghley's attitude and Walsingham's was that Burghley knew by long experience the reluctance of his mistress to support any aggressive policy . . . [He] knew she could not be coerced and more and more he shaped his thinking within that frame of reference. It was not what was best, but what Elizabeth could be persuaded to accept.'[12]

Wilson also criticises the unpropitious timing of England's entry into war, when Spanish naval power had grown and Parma was enjoying dramatic military success. It would now involve, he argues, an uncontrollable military and financial outlay and a prolonged war of unpredictable duration. This is a sound assessment of the problems in 1585. However, to single out Burghley as personally culpable, simply because for so long he opposed intervention, is perhaps another matter. The queen, not her minister, was the architect of foreign policy and the decision maker. There is no doubt that she valued his advice highly on both domestic and foreign matters, but there was no *Regnum Cecilianum.* She consulted many others; Walsingham, principal Secretary from 1573 to 1590, was active in foreign affairs as one of the responsibilities of his office, although he frequently conferred with the Lord Treasurer; and during the 1580s councillors such as Buckhurst, Burghley, Hatton, Sir Thomas Heneage and Leicester were often directed to work jointly on diplomatic business.[13]

With the coming of war the initiative in management and decision-making tended to pass from the queen and the bureaucratic councillors to the generals and sea-captains, whether or not they were members of the Privy Council. The martial hawks also attempted to influence policy by lobbying for offensive war, as Essex did in the 1590s. This made it difficult for the queen and her ministers to retain control of the direction and purpose of the war effort. The problem was exacerbated by lack of money. Naval expeditions were often joint stock ventures, from which investors expected a financial return. Therefore, as, for example, in the Portuguese and Cadiz expeditions of 1589 and 1596, military objectives were liable to have a lower priority than the hunt for booty. Nevertheless, Burghley's role in the war effort was an essential one, partly because, as Lord Treasurer, he had to find the money to sustain war on land and sea, but also because of his long-term attention to England's military and naval preparedness. By 1588 England was better equipped to meet the challenge of the Spanish Armada than it would have been ten or twenty years before. In the short term Burghley can be criticised for inadequate provisioning of the English defensive fleet, though he was, as usual, beset by excessive financial demands.

At the end of that year Leicester died. Although he and Burghley had often disagreed on particular points of policy, they were, as demonstrated in Chapter 6, on friendly terms, had a mutual respect and shared confidences about the queen. Burghley did what he could to protect Leicester from Elizabeth's fury, when he accepted the office of governor from the Dutch. He told him that 'I, for my own part, judge this action both honorable and profitable' and he protested to the queen that, if she continued her hostility toward the earl, 'I might be discharged of the place I held . . .'. Not long after the Armada and Leicester's death the political scenario at Court significantly changed as Robert, earl of Essex, Leicester's stepson, rose to royal favour. Essex's challenge to the Cecils, father and son, was threefold: acquisition of offices, favour with the queen and influence on war policy. The resultant factionalism, which characterised the Court in the 1590s, endangered the war effort, which became an object and symbol of the Cecils' power struggle with Essex. According to Natalie Mears, as the earl manœuvred a shift towards a more offensive policy in the mid-1590s, the Cecils 'in an uncharacteristically imprudent manner manipulated supplies and information' in order to thwart him.[14]

By then the international conflict was complicated by events in France. The Protestant Henry of Navarre was crowned in 1589 after the assassination of Henry III. But his place was contested by the French Catholic League in alliance with Philip II. Elizabeth was obliged to assist him with money and men and she did so from 1589 onwards. For the Lord Treasurer, it was another war-front for which he had to find the money; for Essex, it was 'at thys daye the theater and stage wheron the greatest actions are acted'. Meanwhile problems pressed in on Burghley from all directions. The Spanish armadas of the 1590s prompted detailed memoranda on military and naval defence preparations. Ireland was a constant financial drain, as he agonised to Robert on his bed of pain in 1594, lamenting that 'I leave no hope to amend towardes the world'. As for the Dutch, between 1594 and 1598 Burghley trod, or rather hobbled, through the maze of what he conceived to be their evasions and delays, in order to persuade them to honour their debts. It is not surprising, therefore, that an ageing queen and an ailing minister searched for peace during the 1590s. The last memorandum which he penned, during the last summer of his life, was directed to that end. And in one of his last appearances in the Privy Council he attacked Essex as a man of blood. Peace only came six years after his death.[15]

Burghley and his queen fulfilled the shared foreign policy objective of England's survival as an independent nation-state. The bastard, heretic and excommunicate queen, as the papal bull of 1570 designated her, retained her throne and the English church remained Protestant. National security was strengthened and the Spanish threat repelled. Thus far they were successful. According to Palliser, however, Burghley had a poor grasp of foreign affairs. Certainly he was in serious error when he perceived international relations primarily in religious terms. He also had little personal experience of other countries, having visited only the Low Countries (during Mary Tudor's reign) and Scotland (under Edward VI and in 1559–60). However, ignorance of the political geography, forms of government and power structures of other countries was a common feature of early modern government and Burghley was, to some extent, an exception. He was knowledgeable on matters political, economic and geographic. The information which he acquired fed into one or more of the three levels at which he operated: long-term policy objectives; their implementation by initiatives and responses to specific problems as they arose; and logistical organisation which would enable the government to react appropriately to changing circumstances. At the first level, Burghley's intentions were clear and enduring. At the third level his intelligence network and his seemingly inexhaustible capacity to seek out information, analyse it and present his conclusions helped queen and Council to make decisions which were not based on mere hearsay, fear, speculation or prejudice. It was at the second level that there were serious shortcomings. His approach to international relations was increasingly characterised by caution, a sense of economy and a preferred avoidance of what might be regarded by the great Catholic powers as provocative action. This often inhibited rapid and positive responses to European developments, such as the Low Countries' rebellion.

Nevertheless, the government muddled through, despite its frequent indecision and its inadequate resources. Furthermore, one important change should be attributed to both Elizabeth and Burghley. Foreign policy was traditionally the personal preserve of the monarch. Its prime purpose was to enhance both his or her prestige and reputation and the glory of the ruling dynasty. These considerations were not absent from Elizabeth's foreign policy, but the interests of the nation now figured far more prominently than in the past. England's dependence on the Spanish Low Countries as its staple cloth market loomed large in Burghley's thinking, as he encouraged the search for new markets and entrepôts in Europe and beyond. Henry VIII had valued the Habsburgs chiefly as a military ally against France. Burghley, in contrast, was more concerned to preserve the Anglo-Netherlands trade until, in the 1570s, that no longer seemed possible. Palliser's contention, that English foreign policy was dictated by cloth rather than by religion or balance of power, is debatable. He is certainly right insofar as Burghley was consistently concerned to ensure that the queen's foreign policy was directed not only to dynastic but also to national interests, including trade.[16]

. . .

NOTES

1. See above, pp. 50–1.
2. Smith (ed.), *Anon. Life*, p. 144; Jane Dawson, 'William Cecil and the British dimension of early Elizabethan foreign policy', *History*, 74 (1989), pp. 196–9, 203; Read, 'Cecil and public relations', pp. 26–48; Palliser, *Age of Elizabeth*, p. 278; Read, *Burghley*, pp. 411–12.
3. See above, pp. 36–7.
4. See above, pp. 63–4; Wright (ed.), *Queen Elizabeth*, I, pp. 66–7; Read, *Burghley*, pp. 290–2; Smith, *Last Years of Mary*, pp. 28–30.
5. S.G. Ellis, *Tudor Ireland* (London, 1985, pp. 230,241; N. Canny, *The Elizabethan Conquest of Ireland, 1565–1576* (Hassocks, Sussex), pp. 38–42, 43; Dawson, 'William Cecil', pp. 197–8; Wright (ed.), *Queen Elizabeth*, I, pp. 87–8, 225.
6. Canny, *Elizabethan Conquest*, pp. 46–52, 58–65, 69, 73–6, 81–7, 91, 154–7; Ellis, *Tudor Ireland*, p. 255.
7. J. Warren, *Elizabeth I: Religion and Foreign Affairs* (Sevenoaks, 1993), pp. 124–6; *Clapham*, p. 20 and n. 41; Read, *Burghley*, pp. 9–10.
8. See above, pp. 50–1.
9. Haynes (ed.), *State Papers*, pp. 579–88; Read, *Secretary Cecil*, pp. 437–9; Beckingsale, *Burghley*, pp. 120–2; MacCaffrey, *Elizabeth I*, pp. 165–9.
10. Ibid., pp. 190, 193; Beckingsale, *Burghley*, pp. 140,142–4, 149, 158–60; MacCaffrey, *Making of Policy*, pp. 59, 71–2, 291–2; Smith, *Burghley*, pp. 36–7; Hammer, 'Patronage', pp. 65–6; Read, *Burghley*, pp. 307–9, 314; Williams, *Later Tudors*, pp. 304–5; Warren, *Elizabeth I*, pp. 102–6; *Clapham*, pp. 60–1.
11. Read, *Burghley*, pp. 322–3.
12. C. Wilson, *Queen Elizabeth and the Revolt of the Netherlands* (The Hague, 1979), pp. 53–85; R.B. Wernham, *The Making of Elizabethan Foreign Policy, 1558–1603* (Berkeley, Calif., 1984), pp. 51–60; Read, *Burghley*, p. 309.
13. Wilson, *Eliz. and Revolt of the Netherlands*, pp. 84–5; Wernham, *Eliz. Foreign Policy*, pp. 8, 12, 13.

14. Williams, *Later Tudors*, pp. 330–4, 351–3; Beckingsale, *Burghley*, pp. 166–70; Bruce (ed.), *Leicester: Correspondence*, pp. 44–5, 103–5, 196–202; Mears, '*Regnum Cecilianum?*', pp. 53, 63.
15. Strype, *Annals*, IV, pp. 224–8, 309–14, 355–61; Read, *Burghley*, pp. 507, 542–5; Wright (ed.), *Queen Elizabeth*, II, pp. 428–41; Hammer, 'Patronage', p. 73 n. 38.
16. Palliser, *Age of Elizabeth*, pp. 22, 278; Warren, *Elizabeth I*, pp. 8–13, 91–3, 151–2.

Chapter 11

BURGHLEY: AN ASSESSMENT

John Clapham, who served in Burghley's household during the 1590s, described his master as a man of 'well tempered constitution of body, of stature rather comely than tall, in countenance grave but without authority; towards his equals in degree courteous and respectful, yet not neglecting the reputation of his place; of the popular sort neither a servile pleaser nor a careless condemner'. His dress was not extravagant and 'his train of attendants not very great', because he did not seek 'popular applause' and preferred to avoid the kind of public display which aroused envy. If Clapham's portrait was a respectful one, that of the anonymous biographer (clearly also in Burghley's service) was a eulogy, in which his personal qualities and political conduct were beyond reproach. History may not judge him so kindly. In one respect, however, his political record is unchallenged: the longevity of his service in the counsels and government of Queen Elizabeth I. Burghley's Elizabethan service built on the foundations of his Edwardian political apprenticeship. It was then that he acquired experience as Privy Councillor and Secretary of State. At the same time he established a wide range of valuable connections: not only Thomas Smith, Roger Ascham, Nicholas Bacon and other members of the Cambridge circle, but noble families, such as Dudleys and Seymours, and, above all, Princess Elizabeth.[1]

Although he was only occasionally employed by Queen Mary, he was, as a result of his Edwardian service, one of the more experienced ministers and councillors when Elizabeth succeeded her in 1558. It was the fate of all politicians, who rose from lesser stock to prominence, power and noble rank, to be branded as upstarts, *arrivistes* or *nouveaux* and Burghley was no exception. He did not, however, rise from lowly social status, but came from respectable lesser gentry stock. His rise to become a knight, part of the political establishment and eventually a baron was a story of transformation from respectability to nobility. Although his critics accused him of hostility towards the 'ancient nobility', the charge is unjustified. He was, however, an inveterate enemy of nobles who were wedded to the papal cause and they included such old noble lines as the Nevilles and Percies. Excluding such traitors, he displayed a constant concern to uphold the nobility, old and new, as a mainstay of the queen's government, order and political stability. In the latter part of Elizabeth's reign he attempted, unsuccessfully, to persuade his niggardly queen to make some new creations in order to counter its diminishing size. In 1597 Rowland White, servant to Sir Robert Sidney, observed that she had likewise displayed meanness in conferring a mere barony on her most prominent counsellor.[2]

There is no doubt that he was convinced of the especial importance of the nobility in a hierarchical social structure, in which 'some must rule, some obey'. Nevertheless, his fascination with the nobility, his genealogical search to establish his royal ancestry and the marriage of his surviving sons and daughters into noble families all smack of *nouveau* endeavour and mentality. So did the superior air with which he dismissed 'gentility' as 'nothing else but ancient riches'. He embraced the norms of the noble lifestyle by his provision of generous hospitality, especially for the queen. Because he recognised that 'the foundation of aristocratic wealth, power, and honour rested on the land', he exploited the moneymaking opportunities which government service provided to acquire extensive landed estates. He also displayed his success to the world by the erection of magnificent residences, especially Cecil House, between London and Westminster, and two country mansions, Burghley House in Lincolnshire and Theobalds in Hertfordshire. Theobalds, with its series of courtyards, elaborate interiors, statuary and ornate gardens was the most extravagant and pretentious of his creations. It was designed for the entertainment of the queen and her Court, especially during her summer progresses, and she visited him there a dozen times. Apart from such lavish displays of loyal generosity, as Clapham recalled, 'His own household he governed with great moderation, his ordinary expenses being without excess but not without decency.' Clapham went on to observe that '[T]o his kindred Cecil was not altogether so liberal as many times they expected' and that in his later years he was 'as some have thought, too much inclined to parsimony'. Although he was willing to spend, in order to proclaim to the world his risen status, the record of his management of both personal and state finances indicates that, in common with the queen, he had a cautious, sparing attitude to expenditure.[3]

If Burghley sometimes conveys the impression of a risen man self-consciously parading the emblems of newly acquired noble status, there can be no doubt about the genuineness of his love of learning. The 'cultivated man' was not a pose. In his second marriage he took as his partner Mildred, one of the learned daughters of Sir Anthony Cooke. He read in Latin, Greek, French, Italian and Spanish and 'he was able . . . to discourse of matters concerning the best and most learned professions'. He was the patron of prominent writers, especially historians and chroniclers, such as William Camden, Richard Grafton and Raphael Holinshed. Burghley encouraged Camden to write the *History of the famous Empresse Elizabeth* and the author later recalled this with effusive thanks in his introductory address to the readers. Burghley was also the recipient of books from authors and editors who knew of his love of scholarship. So Archbishop Parker gave him a copy of his newly edited Asser's life of King Alfred, whilst Richard Hooker, 'presuming to offer to your Lordship's view my poor and slender labours', sent him the manuscript of his *Laws of Ecclesiastical Polity*. He did so out of gratitude for Burghley's 'painful care to uphold al laws, and especially the ecclesiastical'.[4] Burghley valued learning, partly for its practical value to those who governed the realm, but also for its own sake. His library, a wide-ranging collection, numbered over one thousand volumes, which he had been amassing ever since Edward VI's reign. From the Continent friends and colleagues sent him additional works: for example, Dr Nicholas Wotton from Poissy in 1553, his father-in-law from Strasbourg in 1558 and Thomas Smith in France in 1563. Closer to home his fellow bibliophile, Archbishop Parker, who shared with him the joys of the library, sent him William Lambarde's unpublished *Perambulation of Kent* for 'your correction and amendment when your leisure can serve you' as well as Gervase of Tilbury and his own *Antiquitates Britannicae Ecclesiae*.[5]

Burghley attached great importance to education, especially for the future governors of the realm. His occupancy of the office of Master of the Court of Wards enabled him to place minors of high social rank, such as the earl of Oxford, in his custody. Noble and gentle wards and other young aristocrats were educated in his household by some of the most distinguished scholars of the day. John Clapham later expressed gratitude for his schooling there and, although some noble wards did not respond well to the rigours of education, the young earl of Essex wrote to Burghley from Cambridge in 1577, thanking him for his 'great care of placing me here in the University'. Doubtless the educational process which he sought for those in his care was a pleasurable as well as fruitful experience. Roger Ascham, who taught both Edward VI and Elizabeth, recounted an after-dinner conversation at Windsor Castle in 1563, when some of the Privy Councillors present argued that 'the rod only was the sword that must keep the . . . scholar in good order'. They were resisted by Secretary Cecil and Ascham, who maintained that 'young children were sooner allured by love than driven by beating to attain good learning'. Ascham was a great admirer of Cecil. In 1570, after his death, his widow dedicated his manual, *The Scholemaster*, to the Secretary of State, 'remembering how much all good learning oweth unto you for defense thereof'. Cecil reputedly carried Cicero's *Offices* with him, wherever he went. It is an image which captures him as the lover of learning.[6]

The cultivated man was also the informed man. He was, for example, an assiduous collector of instructive histories, whilst depiction of the arms of English noble and gentle families on the walls of the Green Gallery at Theobalds was not only decorative but also informative. Burghley's attachment both to scholarship and to the utilitarian value of learning for those engaged in government was given an opportunity for practical expression in his capacity as chancellor of Cambridge University. It proved at times to be a burdensome addition to his multifarious responsibilities. Much of his business as chancellor was concerned with university government and politics, in particular the introduction of new university statutes (1570), which aroused some objections and opposition, the queen's patronage activity, and, of course, religious nonconformity. During his long tenure of office as chancellor he also had to adjudicate on disputes between 'Town and Gown', the Cambridge printing press and the London stationers' company and the perceived threat to the university posed by the newly founded and London-based Gresham lectures. Most time-consuming were the many disputes and 'disorders' in Benet, Christ's, Corpus Christi, Gonville, Queen's, St John's, Trinity and other colleges, usually between the master and fellows. Complaints about bear-baiting and play acting also occupied his attention. It is therefore no surprise that, in 1581, Burghley lamented the calls on his time 'for every such trifling cause . . . being otherwise greatlie charged with matters of much more moment'.[7]

Burdened as he was by both matters of great moment and trifling causes, he did not neglect kinship and family, to which he attached great emotional, social and political importance. Kinship loyalty caused him to help Thomas Copley, a Catholic exile and kin to Lady Burghley, the separatist Robert Browne and his wayward son-in-law, the earl of Oxford. His children extended those kinship connections by marriages which consolidated the Cecils' social status. In 1595 his granddaughter's wedding to the earl of Derby provided another link with a great noble family. The fate of Burghley's daughters, however, brought him much grief. Elizabeth's marriage, celebrated in 1582, was short-lived. Her husband succumbed to the plague in the following November and she died a few months later. The union of his eldest daughter, Ann, with his ex-ward endured for a longer period, 1571–87, but it was an unhappy marriage fraught with problems. Oxford was wayward, spendthrift and unfaithful. He was also given to violence, brawling with Sir Philip Sidney and feuding with Thomas Knyvet. The distressed Lord Treasurer even wrote to the queen in 1576 about Oxford's unkindness to Ann. Yet the unstable nature of his ex-ward must have been known to him. Perhaps he considered it less important than the prospect of a marriage alliance with 'ancient nobility'.[8]

Ann's death was a grievous loss to Burghley. Nevertheless, the sons were more important in dynastic and social terms, because they would perpetuate the dynasty and also the social status and prestige which Burghley had given it. At the same time, however, his attitude to his two sons was an inversion of the usual parental priorities. He showed scant respect and affection for his eldest son and heir, Thomas. Nor did he seek to advance him. Thomas did not obtain his first important office, the presidency of the Council of the North, until the year after his father's death. Perhaps Burghley's relations with his sons reflected his attitude to the different status of their mothers. Or it may have been a consequence of their very different records of public conduct and performance. Although Burghley wrote a set of precepts for each of his sons, they were quite different in tone and purpose. Thomas's was weighed down with a rigorous programme of prayer, Bible reading, self-examination and attendance at sermons, as though this spiritual diet might help to restrain a natural waywardness. Yet Burghley may have perceived that he was at least partly responsible for Thomas's lack of promise, when he wrote, 'I never showed any fatherly fancy to him but in teaching and correcting.' In contrast, Robert was showered with practical advice – and not only in the precepts – which would further his career and the reputation of the Cecil dynasty: how to manage his patron, avoid popularity, practise moderate hospitality, spurn 'parasites and sycophants' but welcome 'thy kindred and allies', and so on. He was tactless when he advised his short, slightly hunchbacked son to 'make not choice of a dwarf as wife'. But he spoke with the voice of both political astuteness and conscious conviction when he wrote, 'never oppose the Queen's will and pleasure'.

Burghley's tenacious schooling and promotion of Robert to high office was eventually successful although, in the process, it contributed to the rise of faction conflict in the 1590s. During the last years of his life he steadily shed responsibilities onto Robert, whom, during his bedridden illnesses, he also used as his Court correspondent. The letters which the son received from 'your languishing' or 'loving sick' father reveal a bond of affection. Although the bulk of Burghley's estate passed to his natural heir, Thomas Cecil, he ensured that his political heir, Robert, would not go penniless. The younger son received the palatial Theobalds and other lands with an income of about £1,800, to which of course he was to add substantially in the years ahead, from the rewards of high office.[9]

Burghley's death brought to a close a record of service to Elizabeth which spanned four decades. During and after that time his public reputation was recorded, affected, even moulded, by both the ignorant and knowledgeable, by political insiders and foreign observers, and by those whose opinions were formed by his impact, real or imagined, on their fortunes. Glowing tributes are to be expected from admirers in his own secretariat and household. They also overstated his role and influence. According to Clapham, only policies which were devised and recommended by him and duly acted upon by the queen were effective and beneficial to the kingdom. The anonymous biographer waxed lyrical about Burghley's virtues and he proclaimed that 'next to God's goodness, his skilful guiding the helm as a perfect pilot and his painful, careful service as a wise councillor have been a principal . . . cause of . . . so long time of peace and plenty as hath seldom been seen or never enjoyed'. In contrast, there were, in John Guy's words, 'courtiers who picked up their pens in defeat or out of office'. Numbered among them were Francis Bacon, Sir Walter Raleigh and Edmund Spenser, who repeatedly sniped at Burghley 'the fox'. 'Old Saturnus', his nickname in some quarters, was not flattering. Nor was the opinion of de Maisse, French ambassador to Elizabeth's Court in 1597. One might expect a detached observation from a foreign observer, but de Maisse was soon sucked into Court politics,[10] acquiring a qualified preference for Essex and a positive dislike of Burghley. There was no contemporary consensus about the strengths and weaknesses, virtues and vices of Elizabeth's long-serving minister.

An assessment of Burghley must rest on his own performance record rather than on the opinions of others. However, that assessment should not be unduly influenced by the simple fact of his extraordinary length of service. He was Elizabeth's chief adviser and principal minister for forty years. But the queen's retention of his services for so long is no endorsement of his ability. Early modern monarchs tended to employ trusty ministers overlong. Lord Treasurer Winchester, Burghley's predecessor, died in office aged between eighty-five and ninety. Charles Howard, earl of Nottingham, Elizabeth's Lord Admiral, finally sold his office in 1619 when he was about eighty-three. We may admire the monarchs' loyalty to long-serving ministers, but what was its effect on the efficiency of government? Burghley died in harness when he was seventy-eight. Not only was he aged but also crippled with illness. Gout afflicted him from the 1550s, when he was only in his thirties. The condition steadily worsened. He was in agony during the parliament-time in 1566–67 and 1572. There is hardly a year thereafter which lacks record or report of pain and incapacity. During the 1590s he was often litter-bound or bedridden, causing prolonged delays in a variety of official activities, such as ambassadorial meetings, policy discussions and decisions. It was wartime, when decisions needed to be taken promptly. However, prompt decisions were unlikely when a vacillating monarch and a cautious, ailing and often incapacitated minister were so important in the process of formulating plans of action.

Even when Burghley was old and ill he displayed a remarkable will and tenacity. So he was assiduous both in his attendance at Council, parliaments and the Court of Wards and in his attention to routine government business. During prolonged illness in his last years he sought leave to retire, but that was denied by the queen. Efficiency and activity inevitably declined. During the 1590s his secretaries, Michael Hickes and Henry Maynard, sometimes advised Robert Cecil that Burghley was 'unfit to hear suits' or was simply 'too ill to get out of bed'.[11] To adopt, in modified form, Oliver Cromwell's words, it might be argued that he had sat in his place too long for the good that he did. Nevertheless, his long 'partnership' with Elizabeth had accomplished their main aims. They had successfully defended England's independent nation-state and Protestant church against foreign Catholic threats. The longevity of the queen–minister relationship provided continuity at the centre and internal political stability in the kingdom. Together, and with other councillors and a generally supportive governing class, they were able to deflect, defuse and even defeat both domestic and external threats. In retrospect, Burghley must take full credit for his prominent role in the preservation of the national state and church created by Thomas Cromwell. One also has to admire his extraordinary capacity to cope both with the unrelenting pressure of major government decisions and the variegated minutiae of daily routine government business. At the same time, he must bear a share of the responsibility for unresolved and bequeathed problems. When he died, the state was still financially archaic, unreformed and ill-equipped; the Church of England was not at peace; and society in Ireland was at war with itself. Burghley's long political career was transitional. During it he helped to consolidate the achievements of earlier Cromwellian reforms. But in his last decade his promotion of Robert Cecil contributed to the emergence of serious, competitive factional alignments. They threatened political destabilisation in the years immediately following his death and they were to become a common feature of early Stuart government.

. . .

NOTES

1. *Clapham*, pp. 79, 83; Smith (ed.), *Anon. Life*, pp. 36–9.
2. Palliser, *Age of Elizabeth*, p. 85; Beckingsale, *Burghley*, p. 270; *HMC*, De L'Isle MS, 2, p. 298.
3. Palliser, *Age of Elizabeth*, pp. 70, 102; Read, *Burghley*, pp. 121–4; *Clapham*, pp. 82–4.
4. Ibid., p. 82; Beckingsale, *Burghley*, pp. 249–53; Bruce (ed.), *Parker: Correspondence*, p. 468; Strype, *Whitgift*, III, pp. 299–300.
5. Haynes (ed.), *State Papers*, pp. 152, 205; Wright (ed.), *Queen Elizabeth*, I, p. 150; Bruce (ed.), *Parker: Correspondence*, pp. 253–4, 424–6.
6. *Clapham*, p. 71; Wright (ed.), *Queen Elizabeth*, II, p. 55; R. Ascham, *The Scholemaster* (London, 1570; Orbis Terrarum Ltd., Amsterdam, 1968), pp. 3–7; Read, *Burghley*, pp. 124–6.
7. Dawson, 'William Cecil', pp. 197–8; Collinson, *Elizabethan Essays*, pp. 197–8, 205; Bruce (ed.), *Parker: Correspondence*, pp. 67, 238–9, 248–53, 343–5, 393–4, 436–40; *APC*, 18, pp. 427–8; 24, pp. 427–9; Strype, *Parker*, III, pp. 128–34, 219–25; Strype, *Whitgift*, III, pp. 8–10, 16–17, 24–31, 37–40, 209–11; Strype, *Annals*, II, Pt. 2, pp. 537–8, 629–31; III, Pt. 2, pp. 273–4, 439–40, 445–7, 496–8, 606–8; IV, pp. 30–1, 103–5, 319–22, 324–6, 376, 434–6; J.P. Collier (ed.), *The Egerton Papers*, Camden Soc., OS, XII (1840), pp. 127–30.
8. Beckingsale, *Burghley*, p. 283; Read, *Burghley*, pp. 271–7; Strype, *Annals*, II, Pt. 2, pp. 602–4; R.M. Warnicke, 'Family and kinship relations at the Henrician court', in Hoak (ed.), *Tudor Political Culture*, p. 34.
9. *HMC*, De L'Isle MS, Vol. 2, p. 441; Strype, *Annals*, IV, p. 480; L.B. Wright (ed.), *Advice to a Son: Precepts of Lord Burghley, Sir Walter Raleigh, and Francis Osborne* (Ithaca, NY, 1962), pp. 3–13; Wright (ed.), *Queen Elizabeth*, II, pp. 428–32, 437, 439–41, 444, 453–4, 464–5, 474; L. Stone, *Family and Fortune* (Oxford, 1973), pp. 3–4; Read, *Secretary Cecil*, p. 212.
10. *Clapham*, p. 79; Smith (ed.), *Anon. Life.*, pp. 37–8; Guy, *Tudor England*, pp. 409–10; Harrison and Jones (eds), *De Maisse*, pp. 4–12; see above, pp. 81, 99.
11. *Clapham*, p. 77; Smith (ed.), *Anon. Life.*, pp. 15–16, 65–70, 103.

BIBLIOGRAPHICAL ESSAY

Burghley's surviving correspondence, memoranda, official documents and the great miscellany of papers with which he was constantly bombarded are a monument both to his industry and his publicly perceived importance. Many of these manuscripts are to be found in the British Library, Lansdowne MSS and the Public Record Office, State Papers. There is additional material in the Historical Manuscripts Commission Reports, especially the early volumes of the *Salisbury Manuscripts* and the *De L'Isle and Dudley Manuscripts.* Other relevant printed collections include: Thomas Birch, *Memoirs of the reign of Queen Elizabeth, 1581–1603* (selected from the Bacon MSS); J.P. Collier (ed.), *The Egerton Papers,* Camden Soc., XII (1840); H. Ellis (ed.), *Original Letters illustrative of English History,* 11 vols (1824–46); H. Ellis (ed.), *Original Letters of Eminent Literary Men,* Camden Soc., XXIII (1843); S. Haynes and W. Murdin (eds), *Collection of State Papers left by William Cecil Lord Burghley* (1740–59); E. Lodge (ed.), *Illustrations of British History,* 3 vols (London, 1838); T. Wright (ed.), *Queen Elizabeth and her Times,* 2 vols (1838). Most of the relevant material in these was printed from the British Library or Salisbury collections.

As Burghley was such an important politician for all but five years of Queen Elizabeth's reign, he figured prominently in the historical works such as Holinshed's *Chronicles* and Camden's *Annales,* which were produced during or soon after his lifetime. It was Burghley who encouraged his client, William Camden, to write the *Annales.* He portrayed Elizabeth's reign as an age of greatness and this, of course, reflected favourably on the minister who played such an important part in her government's achievements. Particularly valuable are E.P. and C. Read (eds), John Clapham, *Elizabeth of England* (University of Pennsylvania Press, 1951), and A.G.R. Smith (ed.), *The Anonymous Life of William Cecil, Lord Burghley* (Edwin Mellen Press, 1990). Clapham and the anonymous biographer were both members of Burghley's household. A.G.R. Smith has demonstrated that the anonymous writer was probably one of the Lord Treasurer's secretaries, Michael Hickes. Whilst Clapham and especially 'Hickes' were devoted admirers, the latter was also concerned to protect the Lord Treasurer's reputation, justify his conduct and refute the charges levelled against him by his critics and enemies.

Major biographies and other works, in which historians from J.A. Froude (1856–70) to A.G.R. Smith (1991) have offered assessments of Burghley, have been considered in Chapter 1 (pp. 6–11) above. Biographers of the queen are also compelled to evaluate the minister's performance, because to demean the role of one is often to enhance the role of the other. J.E. Neale, *Queen Elizabeth* (Cape, 1934) regarded her, not Burghley, as the architect of national success. More recent studies, such as C. Haigh (ed.), *The Reign of Elizabeth I* (Macmillan, 1984), W.T. MacCaffrey, *Elizabeth I* (Routledge, 1993), and especially C. Haigh, *Elizabeth I* (Longman, 1988, Second Edition 1998), are more equivocal, indeed critical, of her role. A number of other works, varying in scope from the sixteenth century to parts or aspects of Elizabeth's reign, are also useful on Burghley's policies, conduct and impact: J. Guy, *Tudor England* (Oxford University Press, 1988), N.L. Jones, *The Birth of the Elizabethan Age* (Blackwell, 1993), D.M. Palliser, *The Age of Elizabeth: England under the later Tudors 1547–1603* (Longman, 1983), A.G.R. Smith, *The Government of Elizabethan England* (Arnold, 1967), A.G.R. Smith, *The Emergence of a Nation State, 1529–1660* (Longman, 1984), P. Williams, *The Later Tudors: England 1547–1603* (Clarendon Press, 1995).

Ministers had to operate in the context of Court politics, a subject on which little had been written until the last fifteen years. During that time, however, our knowledge and understanding of the Court have been considerably advanced by: P. Williams, 'Court and polity under Elizabeth I', *Bulletin of the John Rylands Library*, 65, No. 2 (1983), D. Starkey, *The English Court* (Longman, 1987), S.L. Adams, 'Eliza enthroned? The Court and its politics', in Haigh (ed.), *Reign of Elizabeth*. It was for long accepted that politics in the Court and Privy Council were characterised by faction conflict. This was, however, overstated, as in C. Read, 'Walsingham and Burghley in Queen Elizabeth's Privy Council', *English Historical Review*, 28 (1913). S. Adams, 'Eliza enthroned?' (see above), S. Adams, 'Faction, clientage and party: English politics, 1550–1603', *History Today* (1982), and especially essays by J. Guy (the 1590s), S. Adams (patronage), N. Mears (*'Regnum Cecilianum*? A Cecilian perspective of the Court') and P.E.J. Hammer ('Patronage at Court, faction and the earl of Essex') in J. Guy (ed.), *The Reign of Elizabeth I: Court and Culture in the Last Decade* (Cambridge University Press, 1995) have identified considerable political harmony, with faction as a phenomenon largely limited to the later 1560s and the 1590s. The succession, a major political issue in the 1560s, is discussed in M. Levine, *The Early Elizabethan Succession Question 1558–1568* (Stanford University Press, 1966) and M. Levine, *Tudor Dynastic Problems 1460–1571* (Allen & Unwin, 1973). W.T. MacCaffrey, *The Shaping of the Elizabethan Regime 1558–72* (Cape, 1969), and W.T. MacCaffrey, *Queen Elizabeth and the Making of Policy 1572–1588* (1981)are clear, chronologically structured accounts of the succession and other Elizabethan political developments. W.T. MacCaffrey *Elizabeth I* (Routledge, 1993), is useful for the key political relationship of queen and Burghley. P. Collinson, 'The monarchical republic of Queen Elizabeth I', in *Elizabethan Essays* (Hambledon Press, 1994), is important for an understanding of their political differences. For Burghley's relations with other prominent politicians there are HMC Reports 1925–36 *De L'Isle and Dudley MS* (on Leicester); C. Read, *Mr Secretary Walsingham*, 3 vols (Clarendon Press, 1925), P. Collinson, 'Sir Nicholas Bacon and the Elizabethan via media', *Historical Journal*, 23 (1980), R. Tittler *Nicholas Bacon: The Making of a Tudor Statesman* (Cape, 1976).

Apart from a brief sketch, J. Hurstfield, 'Burghley, minister to Elizabeth I', *History Today* (1956), there is little published work specifically concerned with his ministerial record. However, D. Hoak, *The King's Council in the Reign of Edward VI* (Cambridge University Press, 1976) is important for his early career as Privy Councillor and Secretary. The record of much conciliar business, J. Dasent (ed.), *Acts of the Privy Council* (1890–1907), is an invaluable source for both his Edwardian and Elizabethan service. In common with other royal servants, William Cecil as Secretary and Burghley as Lord Treasurer employed private secretaries, who were crucial to the discharge of his responsibilities: A.G.R. Smith, 'The secretariat of the Cecils', *English Historical Review,* 83 (1968), A.G.R. Smith, *Servant of the Cecils: The Life of Sir Michael Hickes* (Cape, 1977). An enduring scholarly study of the Chancellor of the Exchequer, S.E. Lehmberg, *Sir Walter Mildmay and Tudor Government* (University of Texas Press, 1964), includes much on his departmental superior, although Lehmberg's political assessment of Burghley is somewhat outdated. G.R. Elton, 'The Elizabethan Exchequer: war in the receipt', in S.T. Bindoff *et al.* (eds), *Elizabethan Government and Society* (Athlone Press, 1961) reconstructs Burghley's attempt to prevent the reversal of earlier Tudor administrative innovations. In two major studies – H.E. Bell, *Introduction to the History and Records of the Court of Wards and Liveries* (Cambridge University Press, 1953), J. Hurstfield, *The Queen's Wards: Wardship and Marriage under Elizabeth I* (Frank Cass, 1973) – Burghley naturally looms large as Master of the Court, 1561–98. *The Queen's Wards* and J. Hurstfield, 'Political corruption in modern England', in *Freedom, Corruption and Government in Elizabethan England* (Cape, 1973) are both revealing and thought-provoking about Burghley's integrity and his personal profits and patronage. On patronage see also P. Williams, *The Tudor Regime* (Clarendon Press, 1979), ch. 3 and A.G.R. Smith, *The Emergence of a Nation State, 1529–1660* (Longman, 1984), ch. 14.

The resources available for Elizabethan parliamentary studies are considerable but unevenly distributed. The *Journals of the House of Commons and House of Lords* and A. Luders *et al.* (eds), *Statutes of the Realm* provide a basic record of parliamentary business and output. For the sessions of 1584–98 Simonds D'Ewes, *The Journals of all the Parliaments during the Reign of Queen Elizabeth* (London, 1682), is necessary because the original commons' journals are missing for those sessions. P.W. Hasler, *The House of Commons, 1558–1603* (Her Majesty's Stationery Office, 1981) provides biographical information on commons' members. T.E. Hartley (ed.), *Proceedings in the Parliaments of Elizabeth I,* 3 vols (Leicester University Press, 1981, 1995), is a rich collection of texts, especially parliamentary diaries.

Most of this material pertains to the lower house; for the lords there is little apart from its relatively uninformative journal. Nevertheless, historiographical developments have rendered much of the source material on the commons very relevant to an understanding of Burghley's parliamentary role. Until the

1980s Sir John Neale's interpretation of events enjoyed general acceptance. In J.E. Neale, *Elizabeth I and her Parliaments*, 2 vols (Cape, 1953–57) he described growing disagreement, even conflict, between a hard-pressed government and an aggressive commons, especially an organised puritan opposition. At the same time, he lauded Elizabeth's managerial skills, which so often secured what she wanted and thwarted the opposition.

In recent years revisionist historians have replaced the Nealean thesis with an image of parliaments which were productive and largely co-operative: for example, G.R. Elton, *The Parliament of England, 1559–1581* (Cambridge University Press, 1986), D. Dean, *Law-Making and Society in Late Elizabethan England, 1584–1601* (Cambridge University Press, 1996), M.A.R. Graves, *The Tudor Parliaments, 1485–1603* (Longman, 1985), M.A.R. Graves, *Elizabethan Parliaments 1559–1601* (Longman, 1996). Much of the revisionists' credit for this parliamentary success has gone to Burghley. The significance of his role in the succession agitation of 1566, when he sat in the commons, has been questioned in J.D. Alsop, 'Re-interpreting the Elizabethan Commons: the Parliamentary session of 1566', *Journal of British Studies*, 29 (1990). From his seat in the lords from 1571, however, he operated a managerial network of clients and men of business in the commons, not only to secure the queen's needs, but also to coerce her into action on important matters: M.A.R. Graves, 'The management of the Elizabethan House of Commons: the Council's men of business', *Parliamentary History*, 2 (1982), M.A.R. Graves, 'The common lawyers and the Privy Council's parliamentary men of business, 1584–1601', *Parliamentary History*, 8/2 (1989), M.A.R. Graves, 'Managing Elizabethan parliaments', in D. Dean and N.L. Jones (eds), *The Parliaments of Elizabethan England* (Blackwell, 1990), M.A.R. Graves, *Thomas Norton: The Parliament Man* (Blackwell, 1994), M.A.R. Graves, 'Elizabethan men of business reconsidered', *Parergon*, NS, 14/1 (1996).

P. Collinson, 'Puritans, men of business and Elizabethan parliaments', *Parliamentary History*, 7 (1988) is an important critical assessment of revisionism. David Dean too has emphasised the need for revisionists 'to put the politics back into parliament': in particular to recognise that there existed a prominent puritan 'opposition', albeit not a rampant one, in some sessions: D. Dean, 'Revising the history of Tudor parliaments', *Historical*

Journal, 32/2 (1989), D. Dean, 'Pressure groups and lobbies in the Elizabethan and early Jacobean parliaments', *Parliaments, Estates and Representation*, 11/2 (1991).

In religion Burghley stood somewhere between the queen and the more radical godly Protestants. Neale described the Elizabethan Settlement (1559) as the product of a parliamentary struggle between royal conservatism and commons-based puritanism. That thesis has been displaced by N.L. Jones, *Faith by Statute* (Royal Historical Society, 1982), which identified Roman Catholics in the lords as the focus of parliamentary opposition, despite which Elizabeth and Cecil got the settlement they sought. The search by the godly for further reformation is charted in the classic account of P. Collinson, *The Elizabethan Puritan Movement* (Cape, 1967). This also illuminates Burghley's sometimes uncomfortable middle position, as does P. Collinson, 'The downfall of Archbishop Grindal and its place in Elizabethan political and ecclesiastical history', in P. Clark, A.G.R. Smith and N. Tyacke (eds), *The English Commonwealth, 1547–1640* (Barnes and Noble, 1979).

Foreign policy is a particular concern of MacCaffrey's works (already cited); also R.B. Wernham, *Before the Armada: The Growth of English Foreign Policy, 1485–1588* (Cape, 1966), R.B. Wernham, *The Making of Elizabethan Foreign Policy, 1558–1603* (University of California Press, 1980), R.B. Wernham, *After the Armada, 1588–1595* (Clarendon Press, 1984), C. Wilson, *Queen Elizabeth and the Revolt of the Netherlands* (Macmillan, 1970). All of these histories give due attention to Burghley's role in foreign policy, but one of them, by Wilson, is very critical of queen and minister for their delayed intervention in the Netherlands. J.E.A. Dawson, 'William Cecil and the British dimension of early Elizabethan foreign policy', *History*, 74 (1989) is not only a clear assessment of policy objectives but also a reminder of two of Burghley's strengths: the desire to be well informed and the recognition of propaganda as an important weapon. The latter theme is the subject of C. Read, 'William Cecil and Elizabethan public relations', in S.T. Bindoff *et al.* (eds), *Elizabethan Government and Society* (Athlone Press, 1961). His skill in managing the queen, moulding public opinion in preparation for Mary Stuart's death and afterwards justifying it are revealed in A.G.R. Smith, *The Last Years of Mary Queen of Scots* (Roxburghe Club, 1990), and especially A. Heisch, 'Arguments for an execution:

Queen Elizabeth's "white paper" and Lord Burghley's "blue pencil"', *Albion*, 24 (1992). It was Burghley's long-term conviction that Mary was the focus of an international Catholic conspiracy against Elizabeth. That conviction is examined in M.R. Thorp, 'Catholic conspiracy in early Elizabethan foreign policy', *The Sixteenth Century Journal*, 15/4 (1984).

The rewards of office and long devoted service can be glimpsed in C. Read, 'Lord Burghley's household accounts', *Economic History Review*, 2nd ser., 9 (1956). He left two heirs, one to his title and the other to his political position. The precepts which he wrote for them are in L.B. Wright (ed.), *Advice to a Son* (Folger, 1962). They reflect a very human mixture of discriminating sentiment, indifferent towards the disappointing Thomas but warmly supportive, with practical advice, to Robert, on whom he placed his dynastic hopes.

CHRONOLOGY

1520/21	Birth of William Cecil
1529	Appointed a page of the robes
1535	Cecil admitted to Cambridge University
1541	Cecil marries Mary Cheke; he leaves Cambridge and enters Gray's Inn
1542	His son, Thomas, born; Cecil sat in parliament
1544	His first wife dies
1545	Cecil marries Mildred Cooke
1547	He enters duke of Somerset's service, present at battle of Pinkie; elected to King Edward VI's 1st parliament (1547–52)
1548	Cecil becomes Somerset's personal secretary
1549	Somerset falls from power, Cecil sent to the Tower (1549–50)
1550/1	Cecil appointed Privy Councillor, Secretary of state, personal secretary to the king and duke of Northumberland and surveyor of Princess Elizabeth's estates
1551	Involved in Eucharist discussions
1553	Death of his father; sits in 2nd Edwardian parliament; death of Edward VI and fall of Northumberland; Cecil pardoned by Queen Mary I

1554	Escorts Cardinal Pole to England
1555	Involved in unsuccessful peace negotiations between Charles V and France; examined by councillors for his parliamentary conduct
1558	Death of Queen Mary I; accession of Queen Elizabeth I; Cecil appointed Privy Councillor and Secretary of state
1559	Cecil helps to achieve enactment of Elizabethan religious settlement; he secures English intervention in Scotland
1560	Architect of the Treaty of Edinburgh
1560/62	Plays a part in the issue of a new coinage
1561	Queen Mary Stuart returns to Scotland; Catherine Grey and earl of Hertford sent to the Tower; Cecil appointed Master of the Court of Wards
1562/3	English expedition to Normandy
1563 and 1566/7	Cecil seeks settlement of succession in parliament; his 'fish day' clause in the Navigation Act.
1564	Thomas Cecil marries Lord Latimer's daughter
1565	Mary Stuart marries Henry Lord Darnley; birth of Cecil's son Robert
1567	Mary Stuart abdicates
1568	Mary Stuart flees to England; Cecil's role in seizure of Genoese loan to king of Spain
1569	Court conspiracy against Cecil fails; northern rebellion
1570	Papal bull *Regnans in Excelsis*; Cecil becomes responsible for stamping queen's letters
1571	Cecil raised to peerage as Lord Burghley; secures treason laws in parliament; favours ABC bills; Burghley's daughter Ann marries earl of Oxford; Ridolfi Plot
1572	Burghley appointed Lord Treasurer; Treaty of Blois with France; duke of Norfolk condemned and

executed for treason; Burghley manages parliament in unsuccessful attempt to secure Mary Stuart's death or exclusion from the succession; presbyterian *Admonition to the Parliament*

1573 Walsingham appointed Secretary of state

1575 Death of Archbishop Parker of Canterbury; Burghley secures Grindal's appointment as Parker's successor

1576 Burghley reprimands commons' delegation in joint conference on Stourton's restitution bill

1578 He secures John Hawkins' appointment as Treasurer of the Navy

1578–81 Burghley supports Queen Elizabeth's proposed marriage to Anjou

1581 Burghley secures a severe statute against recusants and missionaries

1582 Burghley's daughter Elizabeth marries Lord Wentworth's son; Throckmorton Plot (1582–3)

1583 Burghley's pamphlet, *The Execution of Justice in England*; Whitgift appointed archbishop of Canterbury; death of Burghley's daughter Elizabeth

1584 The Bond of Association; Burghley secures an act for the queen's safety but not one to provide an interrgnum government; his wardship bills fail

1585 Burghley supports intervention in Netherlands; Treaty of Nonsuch

1586 Babington Plot exposed; Mary Stuart condemned to death

1587 Burghley secures Mary Stuart's execution; he is exiled from Court; death of his daughter Ann

1588 Spanish Armada; death of Leicester

1589 Death of Burghley's wife; Robert Cecil marries Lord Cobham's daughter; expedition to Portugal and intervention in Normandy

1590	Deaths of Secretary Walsingham and Sir Walter Mildmay
1591	Burghley's son, Robert, appointed Privy Councillor; earl of Essex's intervention in Normandy
1593	Burghley obtains triple subsidy and anti-recusant statute; Essex becomes Privy Councillor
1596	Robert Cecil appointed Secretary of state; Howard and Essex lead expedition to Cadiz
1598	Death of Burghley

MAPS

Map 1 Elizabethan England

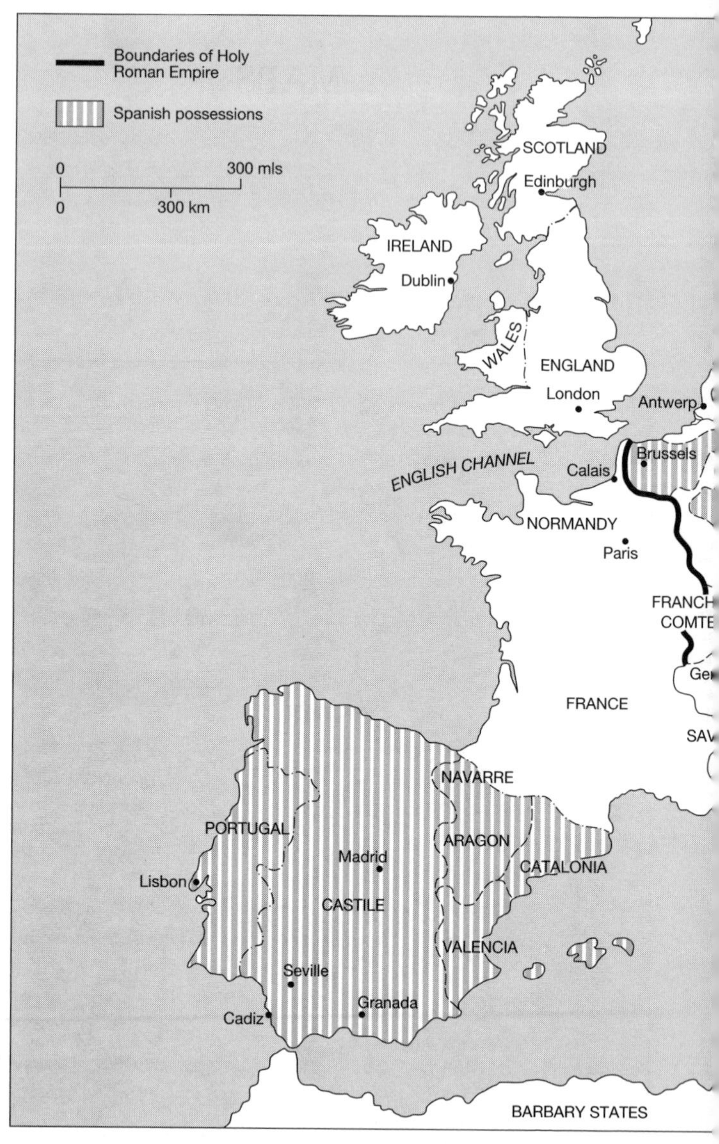

Map 2 Europe in the late 16th century

S W E D E N
NORWAY
DENMARK
BALTIC SEA
MUSCOVY
(RUSSIA)
Rebel Dutch
Provinces
POLAND
HOLY
ROMAN
EMPIRE
Prague
BOHEMIA
Vienna
AUSTRIA
FEDERATION
KINGDOM OF HUNGARY
OTTOMAN
EMPIRE
VENICE
PARMA
TUSCANY
FLORENCE
PAPAL
STATES
DALMATIA
(Venice)
Rome
KINGDOM
OF
NAPLES
Naples
SICILY

INDEX